Questions and Answers:

Strategies for Using the
Electronic Reference Collection

Papers presented at the 1987 Clinic on Library Applications
of Data Processing, April 5-7, 1987

Clinic on Library Applications
of Data Processing: 1987

Questions and Answers:

Strategies for Using the Electronic Reference Collection

Edited by
Linda C. Smith

Graduate School of Library and Information Science
University of Illinois at Urbana-Champaign

ISBN 0-87845-077-7   ISSN 0069-4789

CONTENTS

Introduction 1
  Linda C. Smith

Beyond Technical Issues:
The Impact of Automation on Library Organizations 4
  Sheila D. Creth

Extending the Access and Reference Service Capabilities
of the Online Public Access Catalog 14
  Charles R. Hildreth

Extending the Online Catalog 34
  Dana L. Roth

Reference Services and the Networks:
Some Reflections on Integration 38
  Betsy Baker

Online Ready Reference in Academic Libraries:
Current Practices and a Review of Planning Issues 55
  Virgil Diodato

Online Ready Reference in the Public Library 71
  Charles R. Anderson

Full-Text Databases: Implications for Libraries 85
  Dianne Rothenberg
  Mima Spencer

Optical Publishing: Effects on Reference Services 94
  Terry Noreault

Online Searching as a Problem-Solving Process 103
  Stephen P. Harter

Tailoring System Design to Users 121
  Charles T. Meadow

**Strategies for Providing Public Service with an
Online Catalog** 132
  Beth S. Woodard

The Online Catalog: Beyond a Local Reference Tool 144
  Sharon Clark

**University of Illinois Library Catalog on CD-ROM:
Impact on Resource Sharing and Reference Work** 153
  Paula D. Watson

**The New CD-ROM Technology: Shaping the Future of
Reference and Information Research** 177
  Barton M. Clark
  Karen Havill Bingham

**An End User Search Service with Customized
Interface Software** 188
  William H. Mischo
  Melvin G. DeSart

Index 205

Introduction

The twenty-fourth annual Clinic on Library Applications of Data Processing was held April 5-7, 1987, at the University of Illinois at Urbana-Champaign. The clinic theme, "Questions and Answers: Strategies for Using the Electronic Reference Collection," addressed the impact of automation on public services in libraries. Reference work in libraries of all types is being transformed by the availability of sources in electronic form which supplement printed sources and paper files. These new sources offer an opportunity to enhance reference and information services if librarians can learn how to use them effectively.

The articles in this volume are drawn from the three components of the clinic. Nine papers were prepared in response to invitations to discuss particular aspects of the clinic theme. One short paper (by Roth) was part of the poster session in which clinic participants had an opportunity to make presentations on topics related to the theme. The last five articles, authored by librarians from the University of Illinois at Urbana-Champaign, formed a preconference session highlighting the impact of automation on reference and information services in a major university library.

Sheila D. Creth's keynote article describes how automation in the library workplace is creating new roles, relationships, and communication patterns in libraries. She offers a number of examples of new possibilities open to reference services and considers issues related to staff development and the work environment.

Although many online catalogs already offer the reference librarian search capabilities exceeding those of card catalogs, further improvements are possible. Charles R. Hildreth identifies shortcomings of current online catalogs and suggests a number of ways these can be extended to improve access and service potential. He convincingly argues that the catalog will continue to evolve with augmented functions and contents. Dana L. Roth provides specific examples of how the contents of the catalog can more completely represent the contents of library collections through the addition of analytics for book chapters, journal articles, conference proceedings, and technical reports.

Access to databases of various types is gradually becoming a more integral part of reference work. Betsy Baker presents a framework for discussing the integration of network databases, such as OCLC, into the reference setting. She points out that while such databases were originally developed to support technical services activities in libraries, they must now be evaluated to assess their reference effectiveness in verifying users' (sometimes garbled, often incomplete) citations. Two articles address the increasing use of databases as tools to answer ready reference questions. Virgil Diodato reports on a survey that indicates that online ready reference service is common in many academic libraries. In addition, he reviews planning issues that arise in the process of implementing such a service. Charles R. Anderson considers online ready reference from the perspective of public libraries, discussing both philosophical and practical aspects such as budgeting and staffing.

Among the sources that make up the electronic reference collection are a growing number of full-text databases. Dianne Rothenberg and Mima Spencer identify the types of full-text databases available and explore the implications for libraries. Such databases may be used both for document delivery and in answering reference questions. In addition to being available online, full-text databases may also be distributed on optical storage media such as CD-ROM (Compact Disc-Read Only Memory). Terry Noreault discusses the strengths and weaknesses of different optical technologies and suggests that this technology will create users who are more informed about advantages of electronic sources and thereby increase demand for all types of electronic information services.

This wide array of electronic sources is of little value unless searched effectively. While reference librarians have developed strategies for manipulating printed books to provide answers to questions, additional strategies must be learned for searching information in electronic form. In addition, if users themselves are to realize the potential for accessing such sources directly without the aid of librarians, support systems must be designed. Stephen P. Harter discusses online searching as a problem-solving process and describes useful classes of heuristics for online searching. He explains the implications of this perspective for education and training, for how librarians view end user searching, and for the design of expert systems for online searching. Charles T. Meadow suggests that the major way to make systems easier to use is to design systems around specific needs of user groups who share use of particular databases. He also identifies a number of ways in which search systems can be better tailored to users.

While describing the impact of automation on reference and information services in a particular library, the final set of five articles documents experiences that are likely to be quite valuable to other libraries as well. Beth S. Woodard discusses strategies for providing public service with the online catalog, both for answering reference questions and for assisting patrons in their use of the catalog. Sharon Clark outlines the development of the online catalog at Illinois and describes Illinet Online, a statewide online union catalog. Paula D. Watson presents the findings of a project that evaluated an online catalog on optical disc, assessing its value for reference and resource sharing. Karen Havill Bingham and Barton M. Clark discuss the library's experience with InfoTrac and assess the value of such in-house electronic reference sources. Finally, William H. Mischo and Melvin G. DeSart describe the features of customized microcomputer interface software designed to support end user subject searching of the periodical literature as an extension of the online catalog.

Taken together, the articles in this volume begin to answer some of the questions associated with the emergence of new reference sources in electronic form—e.g., how can each new type of source best be used? What are the administrative issues in the provision of new services based on the electronic reference collection? Tom McArthur's (1986) *Worlds of Reference* is a useful reminder that reference sources have evolved over a long period as compilers experimented with media, content, and arrangement. Likewise, the domain of reference services has evolved as librarians mastered the use of new sources and identified new ways to assist users. Reference librarians today face a dual challenge: to exploit fully the capabilities of the electronic reference collection answering a wider range of questions more efficiently and effectively than is possible using printed tools alone, and to assist users who seek to use these sources.

LINDA C. SMITH
Editor

REFERENCE

McArthur, T. (1986). *Worlds of reference: Lexicography, learning, and language from the clay tablet to the computer.* Cambridge, England: Cambridge University Press.

SHEILA D. CRETH

University Librarian
University Libraries
Iowa City, Iowa

Beyond Technical Issues: The Impact of Automation on Library Organizations

Automation is not new to libraries, but the scope and magnitude of the use of technology, and the pace at which technology is developing and affecting collections, communications, and services is overwhelming. As a profession, considerable time and attention has been focused on the demands of technology: how to make automation fit the unique needs of bibliographic records, how to connect local systems to national utilities and networks, and so on. While there is a need to continue to invest time in these important aspects of technological change, there must be a shift in focus to include consideration of the impact that this expanded automation will have on the organization. For the foreseeable future it is people that will continue to make libraries effective and not machines. Automation gives people in libraries a powerful tool to reach beyond present capabilities in providing users with information and thus knowledge.

What are the organizational issues that should be addressed as a result of expansion of automation in libraries? This article identifies issues associated with changes in the organization and with the impact of automation on the individual. Within this context, this author hopes to provide some sense of the opportunities and the problems that likely await librarians over the next decade.

CHANGES IN THE ORGANIZATION

New and Evolving Roles and Relationships
for Libraries and Librarians

What is exciting about automation is not that it will allow librarians to be more efficient (to do the same thing faster), but that it will provide opportunities to reconsider current activities, identify and design new services, and from this create new roles and responsibilities for the library and librarians. Rather than simply identifying these new activities as individual situations present themselves, librarians should instead step back and begin to envision a more global view of the library. A picture of the future should be drawn that is more comprehensive and far-reaching in terms of what we might become and how we might translate traditional values of service into new activities and roles within the library environment. Unless we can conceive of a future and move toward it, others will design the future; librarians will lose the opportunity to play a valuable and central role in the information society. This is of course a daunting task, even one that is not in the absolute sense doable. But what fun to be a visionary, to let the imagination wander around the edges of reality in order to try to see new directions. This is an important process if librarians are to take charge of the future that is suggested by the new technologies, new formats, and new methods for delivery of information, all of which will have to be designed and initiated while maintaining many of the traditional services, formats, and users.

The issue of the relationship between libraries and computing centers on campus has become a hot topic. We do have to be concerned with the possibility that the role of libraries in providing access to information could be lost to the computing center. There is no reason, for instance, that a computing center cannot provide access to database searching and training of end users in conducting their own database searching. The computing center (or another segment of the university) might decide that they will offer a service to faculty to assist them in organizing databases for personal collections or in developing personal catalogs online. What would be wrong with this and why should we care? Libraries should be the provider of such services not just to protect turf, but because organizing collections, developing bibliographies, and identifying and providing access to information resources are what librarians do well. Therefore, care should be taken not to let these opportunities slip away because of failure to consider emerging demands, priorities, and requirements that result from technology. Librarians cannot afford to be complacent. We should be prepared not only to respond to new demands (such as creating databases) but also to create the demand and suggest new opportunities within the organizational environment.

Technology already provides new and developing opportunities through integrated library systems and telecommunications. For instance, libraries will surely provide online reference service. What does this offer that differs from current direct reference service, phone or written reference? In the online environment there is speed and timeliness in assisting the researcher, but there is also convenience in avoiding telephone tag.

There is also the fact that the online question can be forwarded to the librarian with the subject expertise who will be able to provide the most knowledgeable assistance rather than having a question answered by whoever happens to be scheduled at the reference desk. Also, in a fully automated network environment, the librarian responding to a reference question will be more likely to use telecommunications to communicate with colleagues within the institution and nationally in responding to particularly complex reference questions. Librarians will also have the opportunity to initiate online conference or bulletin board systems over telecommunication hookups in order to encourage and participate in scholarly communication. This would allow librarians to maintain a higher level of currency on new publications and new fields of research while making scholars aware of publications that they may not have identified. Finally, librarians must grapple with the issue of materials that are made available online but not formally published (in the traditional sense). How will such materials be made available within the campus network, how long will they be stored, and what will be the access?

These new activities will lead to a new role and new relationships within the university and scholarly community. Academic libraries are often referred to as the "heart of the university," a tired phrase and often one that is pure rhetoric. But in a highly automated environment, libraries should indeed play a central role in such matters as: (1) assisting the scholar in adapting to new activities and tools; (2) providing leadership on the campus and nationally in establishing local area and national networks; (3) determining standards and exploring new means for providing access to information while managing the proliferation of formats for storing published and unpublished information; and finally (4) wrestling with myriad ethical issues that will surface from technology and access to information. The stature and the responsibility of librarians in this new environment are both challenging and staggering.

Communication Patterns

Research in the management literature suggests that the introduction of automation at all levels of an organization will have a profound effect on communication patterns. Computing is a social activity and therefore has an effect on the social relationships which in turn may alter or reshape relationships and the flow of information and decision-making within the organization. Several issues regarding the impact of automation on organizational communication should be of concern: (1) new communication patterns and channels open up; (2) the organizational structure becomes flatter; (3) change in structure and norms for communication occurs; and (4) communication among co-workers shifts particularly between supervisors and subordinates. Again it is difficult to identify which issue comes first because each is interrelated with the others.

What happens in an online automated environment? First, people throughout the organization have access—easy access—to information that may previously have been held by only a few—usually managers or specialists. People will be more likely in the future to communicate across departmental and divisional lines without going through recognized channels as displayed on an organizational chart. Because the computer provides an almost neutral means of communication—ignoring position and status in the organization—more people are likely to communicate in all directions—up, down, across. This may well increase the quality of decisions through the increased accessibility of information. Kiesler has stated that "increasing the pool of information and at the same time mitigating the effects of status could contribute to organizational strengths. It may also contribute to organizational instability" (p. 54). Some authors in the management field suggest that organizations will become flatter with so much information readily available. They predict that the middle management group will shrink since they have been the ones in the past that acted as the gatekeepers for much of the organizational information—acquiring it, organizing it, interpreting it, and so on. It is not clear that in fact this will happen, but because of the neutralizing aspect of computing, it is likely that managers will not hold the same power because information will be more highly dispersed. Finally, there is the important issue of communication between co-workers within the library organization. Currently library organizations are places where people interact with people to get their work done with a number of people also using terminals and technology as part of their work activity. In the future, there is going to be more reliance on automation to conduct librarians' work including interaction with one another. A major aspect of this is how supervisors will interact with the staff they supervise. Zuboff (1982) refers to this as remote supervision—i.e., the ability to assess performance through information obtained from the automated system (p. 147). How will this affect working relationships, morale, commitment, and turnover? This issue is addressed in more detail later in the discussion of automation's impact on the individual. Communication within the library organization is going to be fundamentally changed as will librarians' contacts with users and professional colleagues across the country and no doubt internationally. Attention must be given to the benefits that will be possible with automation and the problems that will be inevitable.

Organizational Structure

New technologies may call for organizational changes in the traditional library as would be expected from the impact on communication patterns, work responsibilities, and working relationships. Will it always serve libraries well to maintain the public and technical services divisional organization? Will the hierarchical and bureaucratic structure serve librarians well? Are there alternative organizational structures that can be examined before it is discovered that the existing work structure has become a dinosaur which is crushing librarians' ability to be responsive?

Most libraries maintain the traditional public and technical services divisions though there is considerable overlap so that clear distinctions are not always apparent. In this environment, reference librarians provide the primary, if not the exclusive, contact with users. In the online environment, technical services librarians, with their strong language and subject expertise, not to mention their experience with automation, should become increasingly a part of the user interface. Technical services librarians can respond to online reference questions and actively participate in the user education program. They can do this by assisting users in learning and making full use of the automated environment including the organization of personal databases. Meanwhile, public services librarians should continue to develop subject expertise, enhance communication with faculty through technology, and expand user education through tutorials, bulletin boards, and conferencing systems for scholars.

As local and national networks are established and proliferate, traditional communication networks among librarians, and among librarians and users, will alter. Librarians should begin to explore different organizational structures to support and enhance services that will increasingly build on the technology. For instance, teams may be identified to work within broad subject fields; there may be a team for humanities with responsibility for selection, cataloging, user education, direct reference, collection management, and so on.

Finally, there is the issue of how the hierarchical, bureaucratic structure of the library will be—or should be—affected by technology. Will the current structure serve the emerging new needs well? Veaner (1985) in his two-part article on academic librarianship in the next decade, suggests that the existence of microcomputers and networks is "already fostering the growth of a new kind of librarian—the entrepreneur who seeks out clients in an active 'marketing' mode rather than waiting for patrons to come to the institution" (p. 297). How will this type of individualized behavior work in the hierarchical environment? As librarians work even more closely and independently with faculty and students will conflicts arise? Or more important, will the bureaucratic organization stifle the opportunities that could be exploited? Will decisions in the library be reached more informally, ignoring the lines on the organizational chart and the roles and status of individuals that are currently acknowledged? Will this lead to greater innovation and better service or to conflict and chaos? Robbins-

Carter (1985) says that, "it will be extremely difficult, if not impossible, to foster productive competition and entrepreneurial attitudes if we maintain our present functional structure." She does go on to say, interestingly enough, that it is "ironic that the radical change in organizational structure that is required can be facilitated by the hierarchical bureaucracy that now permeates our libraries."

There is no single answer to what specific type of organizational structure academic libraries will end up with. After all, there are considerable variations currently within a somewhat standard structure. What is likely is that new means will have to be considered to bring about decisions and activities to encourage entrepreneurial behavior while maintaining some control over commitment of resources and policies. Certainly libraries will have to consider how to shorten the time line between idea and implementation. It is not enough to encourage innovation if ideas are always buried under an avalanche of study, debate, and committee investigation. Librarians are not known for risk-taking, but they will have to cultivate not only abilities to be analytical and good planners but also a good sense of when to move and when to take a chance. If librarians are always looking for "perfect" solutions or approaches, they will get bogged down and someone else will be at the gate and win the race before it is realized that they are no longer even in the race. Libraries and librarians only recently coming to terms with participatory management (with a move from an authoritarian structure) will now find that they cannot be leisurely in their discussions and analyses but must move quickly to keep up with today and be in step with tomorrow.

IMPACT OF AUTOMATION ON THE INDIVIDUAL

All of the issues raised thus far will have a direct impact on the individual but some specific areas of concern can be identified: (1) responsibilities and assignments of library staff; (2) training and development of library staff; and (3) work environment including the physical environment, work flow, and working relationships.

Responsibilities

Increasingly librarians will be expected to operate in a sophisticated, fast-paced environment with a new set of knowledge, skills, and abilities. Research conducted by Powell and Creth (1986) which focused on university librarians in the first nine years of their careers showed that librarians already recognize the need for the following knowledge and skills: management skills (specifically planning, personnel, and training) and automation. Other areas in which librarians perceived to have needs were in writing, systems analysis, program evaluation techniques, and inferential statistics. These indeed are going to be skills needed to some degree by all librarians. The new environment will also ask librarians to rethink the traditional, to let go of certain activities and standards, and in particular to strike from their vocabulary the phrase "because we've always done it that way." Librarians will have to cultivate a willingness to be risk takers, to be assertive, and to be visionaries. In addition, librarians have a responsibility to consider carefully the changes in duties and requirements for support staff because as the activities of librarians change so will those of the staff who work with them. Librarians should be careful not to exaggerate requirements for positions through exploitation of people who are available in the market in order to avoid the responsibility for training and developing people who meet basic requirements and who can grow and learn. Also opportunities must be provided for support staff so that they have a role in decision-making regarding their own work and operations and, as appropriate, the broader context of library services. Librarians in many libraries do not do a very good job of that right now, but it will become more critical to provide this opportunity if a mechanical response from staff is to be avoided because of a mechanical environment.

Training and Development

Another activity which will become increasingly demanding of library organizations but in which librarians have not yet excelled is training and development of staff. Somehow the financial and personnel resources to devote to training and development must be carved out; without highly skilled and highly motivated staff, librarians will have an albatross around their necks. Training will become an increasingly critical issue in the automated environment because it will be harder to cover up mistakes. After convincing the institutions to pour millions into these systems, there will be no sympathy if staff are inept in handling the system, display poor attitudes toward it, or lack creativity in expanding services through the technology.

New work patterns and new work will require new training approaches within the context of accelerated change. Training will have to accommodate both the traditional and automated environments for the foreseeable future, so librarians will be doubling training requirements rather than replacing current ones. An increasingly diverse staff will require greater flexibility and imagination in training. Supervisors will have to become more sophisticated in their understanding of the relationship between learning and performance and will have to devote the time and energy needed to respond to training needs in the electronic library. Equally important is that librarians will have to put far more effort—a sophisticated and polished effort—into educating and training the users: first, educating them to the advantages of the highly automated environment (after all librarians are asking that users provide, in some manner, the dollars to purchase these systems), and then training them to work within this new context. If training and development are approached with sufficient time and energy and a true commitment to staff, the issue of resistance to change will become a most mute one.

Work Environment

Work environment is an umbrella term for several critical issues facing librarians in a highly automated environment including physical environment, work flow arrangements, routinization of work and related stress, and working relationships within the library organization. To determine how the organizations will function within this new environment is going to be the most perplexing problem librarians face. As Kantor (1983) would ask, What is the organizational culture that we want to encourage?

Physical Environment

What does life at a workstation suggest? After all, people have sat hunched over paper and pen for centuries and in front of typewriters and calculators and hooked to phones for decades. So why this sudden increase in concern related to terminal use? Primarily it is one of scale: so many jobs in so many sectors of society will now have staff conducting their work at terminals. The health concerns identified so far include back and neck strain, eye strain from intense use of the monitor, and concern with radiation, particularly for pregnant women. There are ways to address these issues but costs are involved such as in rescheduling of work and possibly restructuring of jobs. Related to the obvious physical problems that have been identified, there is a secondary problem of stress associated with the highly automated environment. This is very much related to work flow and working relationships.

Work Flow

Clearly with an online integrated system available in a library, location of information and access will be literally at one's fingertips—not a room, a floor, or a building away. How materials are moved about should alter, and how records are created and maintained and by whom will be reconsidered and no doubt changed. The decisions that come out of this new environment will affect the location of staff and the way materials are or are not moved about the library as they go through the various stages of processing. A related and important issue, however, is one of routinization of work. While undoubtedly much work in the library is becoming more exciting and challenging, other work is becoming less interesting as it becomes even more controlled by technology. Because of the high control offered by technology, will librarians move increasingly toward an assembly-line approach to work? Malinconico (1983) indicates that electronic data processing technologies have allowed information work to take on "the characteristics of mass production jobs: mechanical pacing of work, repetitiveness, minimal skill requirements, predetermined use of tools and techniques, surface mental attention, and minute subdivision of labor" (p. 2222). The challenge for librarians will be to use technology to move into the information age effectively and efficiently and avoid the assembly-line environment with the all-too-familiar problems. After all it would be a shame if the joke about the automobile industry (never buy a car made on a Monday) was translated, in some form, into library services.

Work Relationships

Libraries have certain attributes that make them an attractive place to work despite low salaries. Libraries are viewed as people organizations both because they are labor-intensive (there are many people), and because they are service organizations. The library is seen as a place where social contacts and relationships are the way that work is accomplished. If library work increasingly involves people interacting with terminals rather than with other people, how will that affect people's desire to work in the library? The potential for alienation in the highly automated environment has been pointed out by researchers.

Of course there are already problems within the existing organizations that do not foster constructive working relationships and indeed create tensions between public and technical services staff and between professional and support staff. These existing situations will need to be addressed, as well as the difficulties that will emerge, from the highly automated environment in which staff will be more removed from interpersonal interaction with one another.

A very important part of the issue of working relationships has to do with the supervisor and his/her staff. Zuboff (1982) refers to this new environment as generating computer-mediated work; work in which supervision will, to a large extent, be conducted remotely. What does this mean for staff? One author has stated that:

> Continuously supervising every aspect of the job can destroy employee initiative and creativity. Workers who feel they are in an electronic straitjacket are reluctant to volunteer information to improve the system or respond more effectively in a crisis. One public employee remarked that, before monitoring, "when we had to meet a deadline, there used to be teamwork." Since computerized supervision there is little incentive to do anything but meet one's individual quota. (p. 144)

CONCLUSION

How do librarians minimize the negative impact that technology will have on the workplace? Part of the answer is to recognize the potential and take steps to prevent it from happening. Another is to look for benefits for individuals in the new environment: what useful skills will they learn that can be applied in other environments? How can staff access to electronic mail add a social contact into the workplace which would be worth supporting?

The future of technology is here; there's no turning back. As Kiesler (1986) has said: "Today we can perform more and more technical miracles with computers, but . . . [the real excitement] . . . will come from asking what social miracles we can perform with them" (p. 60).

REFERENCES

Kanter, R. M. (1983). *The change masters: Innovation & entrepreneurship in the American corporation.* New York: Simon & Schuster.

Kiesler, S. (1986). The hidden messages in computer networks. *Harvard Business Review, 64*(January/February), 46-60.

Malinconico, S. M. (1983). People and machines: Changing relationships? *Library Journal, 108*(December 1), 2222-2224.

Powell, R., & Creth, S. (1986). Knowledge bases and library education. *College and Research Libraries, 47*(January), 16-27.

Robbins-Carter, J. (1985). Reaction to "1985 to 1995: The next decade in academic librarianship, part II. *College and Research Libraries, 46*(July), 295-310.

Veaner, A. (1985). 1985 to 1995: The next decade in academic librarianship, Part II. *College and Research Libraries, 46*(July), 295-308.

Zuboff, S. (1982). New worlds of computer-mediated work. *Harvard Business Review, 60*(September/October), 142-152.

CHARLES R. HILDRETH

Chief Consulting Scientist
READ Ltd.
Springfield, Illinois

Extending the Access and Reference Service Capabilities of the Online Public Access Catalog

In a 1985 review of online catalog research and development activities spanning the years 1980-85, this author pointed out that two different questions were frequently posed in the literature on online catalogs: "Are these new systems really *library* catalogs?" and "Are they really online information retrieval systems" (Hildreth, 1985, p. 239)? In other words, do the early online catalogs match up to some set of fundamental criteria which define: (1) a genuine library catalog, or (2) an information retrieval system?

The online catalogs available in the early 1980s faced critical scrutiny from two different, unaligned segments of the library and information science community. Many traditional library catalog apologists looked upon the new online catalog as a dangerous impostor: friendly and popular but lacking the syndetic structure and functional properties (e.g., collocating and browsing features) required of a true catalog. On the other hand, online information retrieval specialists responded to the online catalog as if it were a new stepchild whose standing in the family was suspect at best. Actually, the new family member was little noticed and little respected by the information retrieval experts.

Proceeding along different paths, the developmental histories of online public access catalogs (OPACs) and conventional online information (or reference) retrieval (IR) systems differed in three respects: origins of system development, file and database content, and intended users. Early online information retrieval systems were developed into operational systems by government agencies or commercial firms for use in database searching by trained profesionals who came to be known as "search intermediaries." In the late 1970s, many libraries began major planning and development efforts to provide online public access to their catalogs. Several university libraries began their own development of patron access retrieval systems, and many other libraries encouraged the vendors of their turnkey automated circulation control systems to begin development of public access catalogs. Librarians and library system designers—not the search service vendors—were the first to focus on patron access to online library files. The files then available for direct patron access contained either shortened catalog records supplemented by item location and status data stored in the automated circulation systems or MARC (machine-readable cataloging) records acquired from one of the shared cataloging utilities such as OCLC or RLG/RLIN. Stand-alone, online library catalog systems were built by several universities largely to provide direct patron access to the library's MARC database.

One of my aims in the 1985 review article was to begin to bridge the wide gulf between the advances of information retrieval theory, research, and practice and the world of OPAC research, design, development, and use. Prior to 1985 there had been divergence and little crossover between these camps. Earlier forms of the library catalog were of no interest to IR specialists and researchers, and the new online form was viewed as little more than a mechanized card catalog. On the other hand, online catalog designers sensitive to the needs of untrained end users were reluctant to adopt the prevailing model of conventional, commercial online reference retrieval systems used almost solely by trained search intermediaries.

A close look at developments and opportunities as they existed in late 1985 led to the belief that we were at the threshold of a creative convergence of two separate movements. The advances in understanding the problems and needs of end user searching of IR systems seemed transferable to OPAC use, and some online catalogs, as they evolved, were beginning to incorporate the more sophisticated keyword and Boolean search methods common in the conventional IR systems. The transformation of the library catalog into a diverse, online information resource had begun. The promise was clear: OPACs could be better library catalogs than their predecessors, and OPACs could be both powerful and *usable* interactive retrieval systems.

Today, we must recognize that much of this promise is being fulfilled. Existing second-generation OPACs with their MARC catalog record databases can be viewed from a functional perspective as special purpose online reference retrieval systems. Some of them even satisfy Cutter's (1904) classic objectives for the library catalog:

1. to enable a person to find a book of which either the author, or the title, or the subject is known;
2. to show what the library has by a given author, or on a given subject, or in a given kind of literature;

3. to assist in the choice of a book, as to its edition, or as to its character (literary or topical). (p. 12)

Theoretical discussions of the proper content, structure, form, and function of the library catalog typically salute Cutter's objectives, thereby recognizing these objectives as foundational, first principles of the library catalog. While it is true that most twentieth-century library catalogs which incorporate Cutter's principles are largely monograph-oriented and provide no access to the periodical literature, Cutter's requirements, when fully understood, are a good place to start in achieving a good library catalog. However, if we are to provide the kind of access tool Quint (1987) describes as a "full-collection library catalog," we must advance beyond the Cutter catalog (p. 90). This can be accomplished without diluting or sacrificing Cutter's principles. Unfortunately, early OPACs came up far short of Cutter's ideal. These first-generation OPACs could be fast "known-item" look-up mechanisms when presented with precise author, title, or control number information, but they lacked the syndetic structure, linking references, and logical file organization necessary to function as a Cutter catalog.

In any area of science there is always some distance between theory and practice, some gap between institutionalized ideals (the conventional wisdom?) and actual accomplishments. In the past the available technologies of the library catalog accounted for the lag between actual library catalogs and the science and theory of the library catalog. Book, card, and microform catalog media were *constraining* technologies. Each had its inherent limitations, well known to every library science student who has had to learn the litany of the advantages and disadvantages of each "form" of the catalog. Ironically, the very existence of these early technology-based physical limitations has too often had a constraining influence on theory. More specifically, the old forms of the library catalog have limited how we dare to think about the potential of the library catalog as it may exist in an unconstrained physical environment. As we have passed irreversibly into the online access era with its wide availability of machine-readable bibliographic records for most items in any library's collection, we are witnessing something of a scientific revolution in our arena. Library catalogs in operation no longer have to fall short of the ideal because of the dead weight (maintenance) and costs associated with outmoded catalog technologies. In fact, the practice of developing, introducing, and extending the resources and capabilities of the online library catalog in our libraries and library consortia is outpacing academic speculation and theoretical discussions about what constitutes the "proper" library catalog. The technology of the online public access catalog has unleashed imaginations and has created an avalanche of possibilities for improving library catalog-based services. With a quickening pace, librarians are exploiting these possibilities to provide both deeper and more comprehensive access to the information and materials in their collections.

It is no longer fashionable to view the online catalog as merely a new form of the traditional library catalog, that is, as a sort of mechanized card catalog. Such a view represents a backward, unimaginative perspective. The best of today's online catalogs have transcended the limitations of the earlier forms of the library catalog (i.e., book, card, and microform). The unique characteristics of the online catalog account for this quantum leap forward: it is an interactive medium, it is infinitely expandable in function and content, and it is a public, self-revealing, self-tracking access instrument.

All of this makes it very difficult to define the ideal library catalog in the traditional manner, an approach which poses a theoretical construct imbued with the appropriate principles: the result being an ideal which actual catalogs should measure up to and could if only the costs were not prohibitive.

Accordingly, this discussion will not attempt a definition of the "extended OPAC." It will be pointed out that "extended" means, among other things, to enlarge the scope of, to make more comprehensive or inclusive, and to cause to move at a full gallop.

Today, library catalog analysts more commonly write about the *potential* of the online catalog or discuss its impact on library organizations and services. Malinconico (1984) has written:

> There is little doubt that we are standing on the threshold of changes that will alter the catalog and library service in ways that we can only dimly perceive. The library catalog will very likely change into something that bears little resemblance to the instrument we currently know. (p. 1213)

Recognizing the futility of defining the ever changing online library catalog, Hildreth (1985) suggests that even the name "online catalog" will soon be an inaccurate and outdated label for this new access phenomenon.

> It is time to start thinking of the online catalog as an intelligent gateway to diverse, integrated information resources for both the information specialist and the library patron or end user; a gateway accessible not only in libraries, but at places of work, study, leisure and the home. Perhaps someday the online catalog will just be called "my online library." (p. 246)

The remainder of this article will be devoted to: (1) a discussion of the present state of operational OPACs and highlight some recent developments, (2) an outline of certain problems and shortcomings of current OPACs, problems that illuminate the need for improvements and extensions, and (3) suggesting eight different ways today's OPACs can be extended to improve their access and service potential to library users.

SECOND-GENERATION ONLINE CATALOG

A few years ago, this author classified three generations of online catalog developments to chart recent history and to cast some light on the likely course of future catalog design (1984). This approach assumed we could identify qualitative stages of evolution in the design and production of online catalogs. Each of the three generations was defined by a characteristic set of features (see Figure 1).

The three-generation classification of online catalogs is useful once again, because it provides a framework for explaining precisely where online catalog development stands today. Almost without exception, we have moved beyond first-generation online catalogs. That is the good news. However, online catalog development has slowed to a snail's pace. Many of the commercial suppliers of second-generation online catalogs believe they have "finished" the job by adding online *public* access catalogs to their product lines. The danger exists that these commercial suppliers of online catalog systems will become stuck on the plateau of second-generation developments.

This period of developmental slowdown or complacency on the part of the commercial suppliers of online catalogs has its positive side. For librarians who will be involved in the evaluation and selection of online catalogs in the future, it provides time for learning and "catching up" on the state of the art, online access issues, and users' needs. It is necessary to understand how today's online catalogs have moved beyond the first-generation systems. First-generation online public access catalogs were characterized as being "known item" finding tools which provided few access points (typically only author, title, and control number) to short, nonstandard bibliographic records. They were either crude attempts to replicate the card catalog online or automated circulation database query systems masquerading as public access library catalogs. Many agree with Malinconico's (1983) astute analysis of circulation control systems as falling far short of any system deserving to be called a library catalog.

In first-generation catalogs, searching was initiated by derived-key input or by exact term or phrase matching on at least the first part of the term or phrase (as with heading searches in the card catalog). In addition to lacking subject access, including any keyword access to titles and subject headings, first-generation online catalogs provided only a single display format, a single mode of interaction with the system, and little or nothing in the way of online user assistance. Refining and improving a search in progress, based on an evaluation of intermediate results, was out of the question. Without subject access, authority-based searching with cross references, and meaningful browsing facilities, first-generation online catalogs were understandably criticized as inferior to traditional library catalogs.

KNOWN-ITEM FINDING TOOLS · · · · · · · · · ·> **INFORMATION RETRIEVAL SYSTEMS**

	1st Generation Features	*2nd Generation Enhancements*	*3rd Generation Enhancements*
I. SEARCH/ACCESS DIMENSIONS	Access points: author, title, standard/control numbers. Exact phrase or derived-key searching. Simple, constrained search paths.	Controlled vocabulary subject access via assigned headings. Keyword access. Interactive search refinement (Boolean logic, limiting, etc.). Index/headings browsing. Shelf list browsing/review. Search-term approximate-match routines.	Full authority-based/guided access. Automatic, point-of-need, search formulation guidance or search strategy aids. Integration of free text and controlled vocabulary search approaches. Expanded access via (1) augmented, subject-enriched bibliographic records and (2) linkages to multiple and/or multi-type databases.
II. INTERACTION/DIALOGUE MODES	Single dialogue mode for all users; either command language or menu selection.	Two or more selectable dialogue modes (novice, expert, etc.).	Ordinary language search expressions. Conversational, adaptive dialogue.
III. DISPLAY FORMAT/CONTENT	Single display format. Short bibliographic records. Circulation status data.	Multiple display formats. Full bibliographic records. Search results sort/print options.	Individualized, tailored displays. Abstracting/indexing information.
IV. OPERATIONAL ASSISTANCE	Coded, cryptic, uninformative error messages.	Informative error messages. Directory-based help facility. Search/display "how to" options prompting.	Context-based, automatic error correction or help displays.

Figure 1. Online catalog progress across generations

Today's second-generation online catalogs represent a marriage of the library catalog and conventional online information retrieval systems familiar to librarians who search online abstracting and indexing databases via DIALOG, BRS, DATASTAR, MEDLINE, etc. Improved card catalog-like searching and browsing (via headings and cross references) capabilities have been joined with the conventional IR keyword and Boolean searching approaches. Many online catalogs support the ability to restrict searches to specified record fields, to perform character masking and/or righthand truncation, and to limit the results by date, language, place of publication, etc. Also, bibliographic records may be viewed and printed in a number of different display formats.

Second-generation online catalogs should be viewed as bibliographic information retrieval systems. But when compared to their conventional IR forebears, these key differences should be kept in mind:

—the online public access catalog must be usable directly by untrained and inexperienced users (online assistance is usually provided to help with the mechanics of searching);

—records in the catalog database lack abstracts, the subject indexing is sparse and uses broad terms not representative of current terminology; and

—the catalog database, in covering a library's collection, includes information on a wide variety of disciplines and subject areas.

Designers of second-generation online catalogs have addressed these differences in two ways: by providing card catalog-like precoordinated phrase searching and browsing options (along with keyword/Boolean capabilities), and by providing more and more online user assistance in the form of menus, help displays, suggestive prompts, and informative error messages. On the other hand, postcoordinated keyword searching on subject-rich fields (e.g., titles, corporate names, series entries, notes, and subject headings) serves to alleviate the twin problems associated with the sparse subject indexing of most library materials by the Library of Congress (using its list of subject headings—"LCSH") and the users' unfamiliarity with the controlled indexing vocabulary.

A library catalog that fulfills Cutter's classic objectives for the catalog in the online environment is a significant accomplishment. It succeeds in at least two ways: users prefer the online catalog to either the card or the COM catalog, and the online catalog is easier to maintain and update than earlier forms. Designing a keyword/Boolean information retrieval system as an online catalog that is easier to learn and easier to use than the conventional, commercial IR systems is also a significant accomplishment. The traditional, well-structured library catalog has been joined with the power and flexibility of conventional IR systems. The prevailing temptation to be satisfied and to rest on our laurels is easily understood. We have come far and the journey has been costly.

The Need for Further Improvements

Experience tells us that second-generation online catalogs can be used effectively by library staff and by library patrons trained to use and understand their particular indexing and search idiosyncrasies. Most of these online catalogs are not yet effective, usable "self-service" information retrieval systems for a wide variety of untrained, occasional users.

The potential of the online catalog to provide improved access to library materials and the information they contain is still largely untapped. Eventually, the forces of innovation and market competitiveness will boost online catalog development off the second-generation plateau. However, we should not expect a giant, discontinuous leap forward to the next generation of online catalogs. Rather, progress is likely to be made in small, incremental steps. Some of the new developments will almost certainly be technology driven. Combinations of new hardware, especially more intelligent workstations, and software techniques will be applied to new and improved library catalogs and retrieval systems. We will see more "WIMPs" (Windows, Icons, Menus, and Pointers) at the user interface. Already, the CD-ROM-based online catalog is being touted as yet another new form of the catalog. The danger is that future design and development efforts will neither be "user driven," nor incorporate the knowledge learned from information retrieval research and experimentation to improve conventional Boolean retrieval systems (Mitev & Walker, 1985; Harper, 1980; Oddy, 1977; Hendry et al., 1986).

Online catalog research studies have uncovered a number of common problems experienced by users of second-generation online catalogs. Solutions to these problems should constitute the design agenda for improved online catalogs. In general terms, the major problems include:

—too many failed searches (search attempts that are aborted, that result in no matches, or that result in unmanageably large numbers of items retrieved) (Markey, 1986; Markey, 1984);
—navigational confusion and frustration for the user during the search process ("Where am I?" "What can I do now?" "How can I start over?") (Knipe, in press);
—unfamiliarity with or ignorance of the subject indexing vocabulary leading to the failure to match search terms with the system's subject vocabulary (Markey, 1986);
—misunderstanding and confusion about the fundamentally different approaches to retrieval and search methods employed in today's online

catalogs (e.g., precoordinate phrase searching and browsing, and post-coordinate keyword/Boolean searching) (Kranich et al., 1986); and
—partially implemented search strategies and missed opportunities to retrieve relevant materials (e.g., searches in which large retrieval sets are not scanned or narrowed in size, and title keyword searches that are not followed by searches on the call numbers or subject headings of the found records).

Chan (1986) points out that online searching is a process of extracting a subfile of useful documents from a large file, a process where "in most cases, a sequence of search statements is required for even minimally satisfactory retrieval" (p. 191). To optimize retrieval results in subject searching, more than one search approach may have to be employed in the overall search strategy: "Through combination, keywords and the [controlled] vocabularies, of DDC, LCC, and LCSH should offer far greater possibilities in search strategies than any one of them can provide alone" (Chan, 1986, p. 188. See also Croft, 1981). Markey (1986) has demonstrated, for example, that different records on a particular subject would be retrieved by using a classified approach from those retrieved using keyword or alphabetical subject heading browsing approaches.

Conventional IR systems place the burden on the user to reformulate and reenter searches until satisfactory results are obtained. This is typically the case with second-generation online catalogs as well. This approach assumes, however, that the user knows what he wants and can describe it in the language of the catalog database being searched.

Hjerppe (1986) quite correctly rephrases this problem as the fundamental paradox of information retrieval: "the need to describe that which you do not know in order to find it" (p. 14). Even the best second-generation catalogs do little to help the user transform an information need to explicit descriptions of the information understandable by the system. Nor do these catalogs lead the user from "found" information to related, linked information that has not yet been discovered. It is unrealistic to expect catalog users to know in advance the structure and language of library databases. It is equally unrealistic to expect online catalog users to be proficient in the various search approaches and techniques before they engage an interactive system in the retrieval process. Hjerppe (1986) reminds us that humans are much more adept at recognizing something than generating a description of it. Online catalogs could take advantage of this human facility by permitting requests such as, "Give me more like this!"

In summary, second-generation online catalogs fall short in that they:

—do not facilitate open-ended, exploratory searching by following pre-

established trails and linkages between records in the database in order to retrieve materials related to those already found;
—do not automatically assist the user with alternative formulations of the search statement or execute alternative search methods when the initial approach fails;
—do not lead the searcher from successful free-text search terms (e.g., title words) to the corresponding subject headings or class numbers assigned to a broader range of related materials;
—do not provide sufficient information in the retrieved bibliographic records (such as tables of contents, abstracts, and book reviews) to enable the user to judge the usefulness of the documents;
—do not rank the citations in large retrieval sets in decreasing order of probable relevance or "closeness" to the user's search criteria.

WAYS OF EXTENDING THE OPAC

Figure 2 lists eight ways the conventional library catalog is being extended in a variety of online manifestations in libraries. Most of these extensions involve adding data to the MARC catalog records, integrating related data files such as customized periodical indexes into the monograph catalog, or adding reference information files to the overall OPAC database or aggregate of databases searchable through the OPAC. However, functional and transactional performance extensions are also being made to today's second-generation OPACs. This is all to the good because research and experience have provided sufficient reason not to be satisfied with the performance of today's OPACs. Reflecting on all this creative, expansive activity to OPAC designers and librarians, it is clear that in practice no pre-defined "theoretical" boundaries for the proper library catalog (regarding its form, function, or content) are being respected or observed. We are witnessing a shift in emphasis from usual concerns for bibliographic control to expanding access to all the mateials and information in the collections. The promise is that the library's primary access instrument, the "catalog," will become its most used and most effective access and discovery tool.

FUNCTIONAL SEARCH AND RETRIEVAL ENHANCEMENTS

This author has written elsewhere about the opportunities for extending the OPAC's service potential through augmented MARC records and the integration of periodical indexes into the catalog database (Hildreth, 1987). Several OPACs are also extending access to local reference information files and, through gateways, to remote online database search services.

1. Functional Search and Retrieval Enhancements

2. MARC-PLUS Augmented Catalog Records (subject descriptors, headings from tables of contents, classification vocabulary)

3. Integration of Local Non-MARC and Pseudo-MARC Bibliographic Records (non-standard records and subject pathfinders, abstracts, book reviews, and research guides)

4. Advanced Database Syndetic Structure (defining customized sub-catalogs and subject-based trails and pathways)

5. Additional Self-Service Convenience Functions (self-charging, online ILL or reference service requests)

6. Created and Maintained Information Files

7. Remotely Published, Locally Stored and Accessed Information Files

8. Gateway Access to External Bibliographic and Information Files (online reference databases, other OPACs, and electronic union catalogs)

Figure 2. The extended OPAC

This article concentrates on the first extension listed in Figure 2: search and retrieval enhancements or how to create a smarter OPAC.

Improving second-generation online catalogs is a twofold challenge: (1) making them more effective retrieval systems, and (2) ensuring that they are usable and satisfying to a heterogeneous population of end users— some trained but many untrained; some knowledgeable in one or more disciplines but many at the initial learning stages in a discipline.

Much advanced (post-Boolean) information retrieval research and theoretical analysis has been directed to improving the search performance and retrieval effectiveness of IR systems in controlled, experimental environments. While the research has focused on system performance factors, actual human searchers have been excluded from most IR experiments. Information retrieval researchers and theorists generally have been critics of Boolean logic-based IR systems and have experimented with a variety of alternative approaches that either attempt to ameliorate the shortcomings of classic Boolean methods (e.g., "extended Boolean" processing and "fuzzy-set" retrieval) or offer radically different, non-Boolean retrieval operations (e.g., query and document term vector processing and statistical, probabilistic retrieval methods) (Bookstein, 1985). A consensus seems to exist among information retrieval theorists and investigators regarding the shortcomings of IR systems that rely solely on Boolean logic query expression and processing. Salton (1984) presents the following list of reasons why conventional Boolean retrieval methodology is not well adapted to the information retrieval task:

1. The formulation of good Boolean queries is an art rather than a science; most

untrained users are unable to generate effective query statements without assistance from trained searchers.

2. The standard Boolean retrieval methodology does not provide any direct control over the size of the output; some query statements may provide no output at all, whereas other statements provide an unmanageably large number of retrieved items.

3. The Boolean methodology does not provide a ranking of the retrieved items in any order of presumed usefulness, thus all retrieved items are presumed to be equally good, or equally poor, for the user.

4. The Boolean system does not provide for the assignment of weights to the terms attached to documents or queries; thus each assigned term is assumed to be as important as each other assigned term, the only distinction actually made is between terms that are assigned (with an implied weight equal to 1), and terms that are not assigned (with an implied weight equal to 0).

5. The standard retrieval methodology may produce results which appear to be counter-intuitive:

a. in response to an or-query (A or B or ... or Z) a record or document with only one query term is assumed to be as important as a document containing all query terms;

b. in response to an and-query (A and B and ... and Z) a document containing all but one of the query terms is considered as useless as a document with no query term at all. (p. 277)

Online catalog research and design has been directed to making post-coordinate Boolean library retrieval systems easier to learn and easier to use than the commercial models used by trained intermediaries. Little attention has been given to the performance limitations of Boolean OPACs, and no university-developed or commercially available OPAC uses any of the advanced post-Boolean retrieval methods which have been tested with some success in the retrieval labs by the probabilistic and fuzzy-set retrieval theorists.

The shortcomings of second-generation OPACs and Boolean retrieval systems are now well known. There is no doubt that a vigorous dialogue between information retrieval researchers and online catalog designers could lead to improvements in online catalogs and other IR systems intended primarily for use by the "everyman" end user rather than trained search specialists. Much is to be gained by a sharing of their separate insights and theoretical or design advances.

OUTLINE OF APPROACHES TO INTELLIGENT INFORMATION RETRIEVAL SYSTEMS AND OPACS

The fundamental problem of information retrieval (by now it should be clear that OPACs are being viewed here as IR systems and not just mechanized card catalogs) is achieving a degree of precision in a situation that is inherently variable and imprecise. The situation is commonly expressed using the terms *matching* and retrieval. The implicit metaphor is visually entertaining if you do not picture yourself as the fisherman at a poorly-stocked pond, using primitive reeling equipment. Something over there must be hooked and brought over here for display and evaluation. The "hook" in IR operations is some kind of matching mechanism. Of course the hook must have some suitable bait that will appeal to the kind of underwater specimen which is the object of the retrieval activity. A fair amount of knowledge and skill is required if one is to become a good fisherman.

In the IR/OPAC searching paradigm, the bait consists of query terms which attempt to express the searcher's information need(s), the document representations (citations, surrogates, catalog records, etc.) are the fish, and in automated systems the matching and retrieval software can be viewed as the rod and reel. At first glance the problem seems simple: match the user's query with the appropriate (relevant) document surrogates and retrieve them for the user's perusal and use. However, no matter the "type" of search query posed by the user (known item, topical), IR research has shown that the situation is loaded with variability and as a result uncertainty must be accepted as intrinsic to the retrieval process. From document description and subject analysis of texts to IR system design, efforts must confront the inherently probabilistic nature of the entire retrieval environment. The problem is complex and has many dimensions. No single "solution" is waiting to be discovered even with the coming of the "intelligent" interface. OPAC and IR research and development reflect this complexity and have taken a number of directions that may improve information retrieval in the automated environment.

So the problem is how to use the science and technology of automation to achieve the "best" retrieval for a given user query in an inherently imprecise and uncertain situation. Leaving aside the variabilities and complexities of subject cataloging/indexing, file structure, and matching and retrieval algorithms, the user may not know or be able to adequately express his need, or may simply change his mind during the retrieval process about what he wants or is interested in. In addressing the topic, "What is intelligent information retrieval?" Croft (1987) acknowledges the many advances made in the field of information retrieval since the arrival of the computer, but several basic issues remain unresolved. "To put it simply, we do not know the best way of representing the content of text documents and the user's information needs so that they can be compared and the relevant documents retrieved. We cannot even agree on a definition of relevance" (p. 249). Croft points to the small but significant improvements to the retrieval process where statistical approaches to the analysis of text and collections of documents have been applied.

Previous IR research has demonstrated that systems built on a probabilistic model outperform conventional inverted file, keyword/Boolean query-retrieval systems. Typically this approach exploits interpretations of queries and document records based on weighted terms and extended or "loosened" Boolean logic. Some rudimentary natural language processing, either of the user's terms or terms used in the document representations (especially subject descriptors), is usually applied in the "matching" operation. But progress has been modest and has come slowly. As Doszkocs (1986) points out: "Investigators have been confronted with the variability of ways in which the same ideas and topics can be expressed by different authors, abstractors, indexers, and searchers, the inevitable limitations of the query-matching procedures and the contextual subjectivity of users' relevance judgements concerning retrieved items" (p. 192). Doszkocs characterizes the common goal of most IR researchers: "to transcend the limitations of the basic keyword/subject heading/inverted file/Boolean logic search paradigm characteristic of the mechanized systems of the 1960's and 1970's" (p. 192). In the process, IR researchers have come to recognize the inherently uncertain and probabilistic nature of the information retrieval process.

Understandably, IR and OPAC researchers find it lamentable that most OPACs in operation have "advanced" only to become conventional IR systems mixing Boolean query features and word proximity search capabilities. Beneath a more palatable user interface, today's OPAC closely resembles the retrieval methods of the conventional systems like BRS, DIALOG, and ELHILL (Medline's software). Fortunately, many IR researchers have taken an interest in OPACs and related "end user" systems, seeing them as fertile ground for further experimentation and development. Their activities are moving librarians piecemeal but solidly into the next generation of OPACs and IR systems. These efforts can be grouped into three or four different but complementary approaches to making these systems more "intelligent" and usable. My point of departure must be kept in mind: intelligent IR/OPAC systems begin where conventional systems end with regard to functionality, usability, and performance. The case against the conventional Boolean retrieval systems will not be made here. It is well documented in the literature. Also, it must be pointed out that some researchers and writers have a more restricted and more specific view of intelligent systems. In addressing what makes a system intelligent, they may require that the system have a knowledge base and rule-governed inferential capabilities that can be used to make the appropriate connections between a request (typically in natural language) and a collection of documents. If the knowledge base, rules, and logic are based on the knowledge and decision-making capabilities of real experts, the system is called an "expert" system. Building expert OPAC systems is one approach to making OPACs more intelligent; like the other approaches to be described, it has exciting potential as well as inherent limitations.

Researchers have shown that the challenge of retrieving documents that will have the highest probability of being relevant to the user's information needs and/or interests is not one dimensional. Add to these the challenge of making the system accessible for direct use by a variety of patrons, both trained and untrained, experienced and inexperienced. Clearly this is the situation facing librarians with improving subject retrieval in OPACs. It is not surprising that several approaches and different techniques are being applied to making OPAC and IR systems more intelligent. The emerging consensus is that progress lies in the direction of a combination of these approaches, employing features of the probabilistic model, dynamic interaction with the user during the search process to gather evidence about relevance and preferences, plausible inference methods (including natural language processing), and vastly improved presentations of data and assistance at the user interface.

What is being done to improve subject retrieval in online library catalogs and similar retrieval systems? The scope of the answer is limited to automated system experimentation and design. The focus is on function, what OPACs should be able to do, and not on any specific cataloging or indexing practice or use of one thesaurus over another. The framework of the problem is this: generating (either the user or the system) an appropriate set of query terms that represent the concepts central to the user's information need (which may be vague or may change); terms that can match or can be linked or transposed to terms in the system's vocabulary used to represent names and topics in the document collection; joined by the best selection and use of available query-matching procedures and retrieval methods based on relevance feedback gained through the active participation of the searcher at key points in the matching-retrieval process. We have reached the limits of the metaphor of fishing by the waterside.

One approach is characterized by the use and evaluation of automatic or semiautomatic query/index term matching and retrieval algorithms. Included are various term stemming, term weighting, and document ranking techniques. Also in this research and development category are automatically applied combinatorial and combination search methods. These approaches attempt to find "closest" matches to query terms in a more flexible way than Boolean methods permit, or automatically pursue alternative search strategies when initial attempts fail or their results are rejected by the searcher. OPACs with these capabilities include CITE, OKAPI, LIBERTAS, and LCS/WLN at the University of Illinois.

Another approach involves some degree of automatic linguistic analysis of the user's query language at various levels (e.g., morphological, lexical, syntactical, semantic) and often further processing of this language against intermediate, special purpose dictionaries/thesauri linked or networked to the system's indexing language. This approach has been used by ERLI, the French firm that has developed a natural language "front-end" to RAMEAU, the online subject authorities file. In this category also is the Middlesex Polytechnic University OPAC research (sponsored by the British Library Research and Development Department) which is using PRECIS headings and words rearranged in a number of ways to serve as an end user "lead in" vocabulary/dictionary with appropriate linkages to the bibliographic records (mostly UK MARC).

Another approach focuses on improved display designs and user interaction devices including the use of windows and graphic presentations of structures of thesauri. The aim is to interpret and present complex file, record, and thesauri structures and arrangements in a way understandable to end users unschooled in the special practices and tools of the cataloger or indexer. The attempt is also being made to make displays function as discovery windows to the collection and related items for browsers. The efficient, linear path of searching through a precise name or subject term is seen no longer as the paradigm of searching but only one way of exploring the collection (Miller & Tegler, 1986).

Another approach, or an extension of the earlier discussion, uses navigation and relevance feedback methods and facilities that exploit the user's response to retrieved data or records to refine the search results, or to guide the user to additional, potentially relevant documents related in some way to one or more records already presented to the user. There are two assumptions underlying this approach: users know what they want more clearly after they see it, and authority or other linking data or mechanisms are better understood in the context of what they actually do. OPACs reflecting some part of this approach include CITE, TINMAN/TINlib, and SIBIL. Of particular interest in SIBIL is the tree searching capability and the "Tarzan" feature. Searchers can grab onto a data element in a displayed record and use it to swing over to predefined related records without having to reinitiate the entire search process.

Already mentioned is the expert system, rule governed, knowledge base approach. Work on library retrieval systems is slight and is confined to academic research at this time. Success has been limited to small, well-defined subject domains and a restricted set of queries. There exists some skepticism regarding the feasibility of expert systems in large, heterogeneous user/query/collection environments. As Croft (1987) reminds us: "Implementations of information retrieval systems, whether 'intelligent' or not, should address the important issues of IR, which include handling large numbers of documents in broad domains" (p. 253). Examples of special-purpose bibliographic/reference retrieval systems include the British Library's experimental PLEXUS system and Ohio State University's "EP-X" system. Theoretically, one approach to solving the large, mixed-subject domain found in library bibliographic database environments is to extend the concept of "parallel processing." A number of expert systems could be made available to assist different users bringing different search needs and requirements to the OPAC. Once the subject need and related information needs of the user have been established, automatic mechanisms could "switch on" the appropriate "expert." This would be something like placing a pool of reference librarians and bibliographers at the disposal of the OPAC searchers. Exploiting existing classification schemes and thesauri, the "experts" could even be made to communicate with one another when, for example, the information need is interdisciplinary. It appears that Croft's "I^3R" experimental system at the University of Massachusetts is testing this extended expert approach (Croft & Thompson, 1987).

By way of summary, advanced IR and OPAC systems have already demonstrated the feasibility and desirability of supplanting conventional inverted file, Boolean logic retrieval systems with systems that incorporate natural language query processing capabilities, linguistic analyses, closest match combinatorial or combination search strategies, ranked output based on term weighting or user feedback, and navigational features based on more flexible and diverse database design techniques. The latter makes it possible to pre-establish multiple, bidirectional links between any data element or record in the database. These links can be coupled with intelligent dialogue screens to guide or lead the searcher through any desired pathway or trail through the library database/collection. Far more is now possible than bringing all the works of a single author together or gathering all citations in which a particular subject heading is attached. These techniques represent early forms of collection navigation in a highly constraining physical environment, namely, the card catalog. State-of-the-art common sense and intelligent IR techniques can be employed to expand and diversify access to and use of today's bibliographic databases (taken in the broadest sense to include catalog records, classification schemes, thesauri, and other authority files). It is necessary for system designers to stop looking backward to the DIALOGs and ELHILLs and to heed the proven advances of IR and OPAC research.

CONCLUSION

The fully extended OPAC or even the "full collection access instrument" does not yet exist in a particular operational environment. In describing the extended OPAC, the summative aggregate point of view has been assumed. Each enhancement or extension mentioned can be found somewhere in one variation or another making synthesis by this writer an easy task. Demand, ingenuity, and the open-ended technology account for the recent rush of new access and service-oriented developments. The road to the common everyday extended OPAC will be traveled in time, but due to technical and economic obstacles, progress will probably occur in incremental stages. Overcoming all the obstacles will require considerable effort, and, in some cases, cooperation on the part of system designers, vendors, and librarians.

Among the "technical" problems to be resolved are:

1. A variety of incompatible record formats are found in different bibliographic databases. This presents a problem for the integration of acquired non-MARC bibliographic files into a MARC database. The database management software of today's OPACs is designed to perform optimally with MARC records.
2. There is inconsistency of indexing and access points across different data files. The OPAC may provide a uniform set of search protocols to be used across the data files, but what kind of data element is indexed and made searchable may vary from file to file. This presents a special problem for subject searching as different data files may employ different thesauri to control the subject vocabulary of the files. A short-term problem is, of course, that OPACs have no thesaurus handling capabilities and no thesaurus based searching features. It makes little sense to load Medline or ERIC files into these OPACs.
3. Most of today's OPACs are linked with a fully functioning circulation control system or come as a package of functions in the "integrated library system." However, the processing performance strengths of these linked or integrated systems are not associated with the special requirements of searching and retrieval activities in a large complex bibliographic database. Typically, these systems are fine tuned to optimize circulation transaction processing, not Boolean or full-text retrieval.

The extended OPAC will cost more. Some of the cost increases will be associated with the resolution of the technical problems mentioned. The increase in cost for additional data storage may be negligible, but acquiring the amount of computer processing power to maintain acceptable performance and response time in the extended OPAC will significantly increase the cost of the system. OPAC expansion will also incur major development and maintenance expenses. Integration of new functions and files into the OPAC is a complex matter requiring long periods of work by highly skilled individuals. Software maintenance rises proportionately with the increased complexity of the system. Lastly, data files acquired from commercial sources, such as the abstracting and indexing services, cost money, and special licensing agreements must be constructed. Some

OPAC owners and managers have the tools and resources now to integrate periodical and citation indexes into their catalogs but simply cannot meet the price demanded by the major commercial suppliers of index and book review data files.

These obstacles to the one stop, self-service, information access and delivery station (or the "scholar's workstation") will be overcome in time. Given a common vision and collective efforts it cannot fail to happen. The OPAC has truly created an avalanche of possibilities and unleashed our imaginations.

REFERENCES

Bookstein, A. (1986). Probability and fuzzy-set applications to information retrieval. *Annual Review of Information Science and Technology, 20*(September), 117-151.

Chan, L. M. (1986). Library of Congress Classification as an online retrieval tool: Potentials and limitations. *Information Technology and Libraries, 5*(3), 181-192.

Croft, W. B. (1987). Approaches to intelligent information retrieval. *Information Processing & Management, 23*(4), 249-254.

Croft, W. B., & Thompson, R. H. (1987). I^{3}R: A new approach to the design of document retrieval systems. *Journal of the American Society for Information Science, 38*(6), 389-404.

Croft, W. B. (1981). Incorporating different search models into one document retrieval system. *ACM SIGIR Forum, 16*, 40-45.

Cutter, C. A. (1904). *Rules for a dictionary catalog* (4th ed.). Washington, DC: Government Printing Office.

Doszkocs, T. E. (1986). Natural language processing in information retrieval. *Journal of the American Society for Information Science, 37*(4), 191-196.

Harper, D. J. (1980). *Relevance feedback in document retrieval.* Ph.D. dissertation, Cambridge University.

Hendry, I. G.; Willett, P.; & Wood, F. E. (1986). INSTRUCT: A teaching package for experimental methods in information retrieval. Part 1: The user's view. *Program, 20*(3), 245-263.

Hildreth, C. R. (1987). Beyond Boolean: Designing the next generation of online catalogs. *Library Trends, 35*(4), 647-667.

Hildreth, C. R. (1985). Online public access catalogs. *Annual Review of Information Science and Technology, 20*, 233-285.

Hildreth, C. R. (1984). Pursuing the ideal: Generations of online catalogs. In B. Aveney & B. Butler (Eds.), *Online catalogs, online reference: Converging trends* (proceedings of a Library and Information Technology Association preconference institute, 23-24 June 1983, Los Angeles, CA), (pp. 31-56). Chicago, IL: American Library Association.

Hjerppe, R. (1986). Project HYPERCATalog: Visions and preliminary conceptions of an extended and enhanced catalog. In B. C. Brookes (Ed.), *Intelligent information systems for the information society* (proceedings of the sixth international research forum on information science (IRFIS6), Frascati, Italy, September 16-18, 1985), (p. 221). New York: North Holland.

Knipe, N. (In press). Hands-on: User-directed system evaluation. A paper presented at the Conference on Integrated Online Library Systems, 23-24 September 1986, St. Louis. To be published in the proceedings of the conference.

Kranich, N. C., et al. (1986). Evaluating the online catalog from a public services perspective: A case study at the New York University libraries. In J. R. Matthews (Ed.), *The impact of online catalogs*, (pp. 89-140). New York: Neal-Schuman.

Malinconico, S. M. (1984). Catalogs & cataloging: Innocent pleasures and enduring controversies. *Library Journal, 109*(11), 1213.

Malinconico, S. M. (1983). Circulation control systems as online catalogs. *Library Journal, 108*(12), 1207-1210.

Markey, K. (1986a). *Dewey Decimal Classification online project: Evaluation of a library schedule and index integrated into the subject searching capabilities of an online catalog: Final report to the Council on Library Resources.* Dublin, OH: OCLC (report no. OCLC/OPR/RR-86/1).

Markey, K. (1986b). Users and the online catalog: Subject access problems. In J. R. Matthews (Ed.), *The impact of online catalogs* (pp. 35-69). New York: Neal-Schuman.

Markey, K. (1984). *Subject searching in library catalogs: Before and after the introduction of online catalogs.* Dublin, OH: OCLC.

Miller, C., & Tegler, P. (1986). Online searching and the research process. *College & Research Libraries, 47*(July), 370-373.

Mitev, N. N., & Walker, S. (1985). Information retrieval aids in an online public access catalogue: Automatic intelligent search sequencing. In *Informatics 8: Advances in intelligence* (proceedings of a conference organized by the Aslib Informatics Group and the BCS Information Retrieval Specialist Group, 16-17 April 1985, Wadham College, Oxford) (pp. 215-26). London: Aslib.

Noerr, P. L., & Bivins Noerr, K. T. (1985). Browse and navigate: An advance in database access methods. *Information Processing & Management, 21*(3), 205-213.

Oddy, R. N. (1977). Information retrieval through man-machine dialogue. *Journal of Documentation, 33*(1), 1-14.

Quint, B. (1987). Journal article coverage in online library catalogs: The next stage for online databases? *Online, 2*(January), 87-90.

Salton, G. (1984). The use of extended Boolean logic in information retrieval. Computer and Control Abs. 1985. *SIGMOD Record, 14*(2), 277-285.

DANA L. ROTH

Head, Science and Engineering Libraries
California Institute of Technology
Pasadena, California

Extending the Online Catalog

Future plans of the California Institute of Technology Libraries (Brudwig, 1984) include an online analytic catalog of books, serials, journals, and technical reports. In an attempt to avoid the observation of Mandel and Herschman (1983) that "new technologies are often adapted to traditional uses without exploiting added capabilities" (p. 148), a number of innovative cataloging approaches are being developed. Encouraged by the work of Petersen (1983), Cochrane (1978), Hoffman and Magner (1985), and Quint (1987), staff members are developing procedures to augment the basic MARC records available through OCLC.

One of the serious drawbacks of currently available MARC records is that they generally describe physical items while many library users are interested in retrieving intellectual works or specific data (the contents of the items). This is particularly troublesome in science and engineering libraries where serials and journals are the primary data source and are much more likely to be consulted than read cover to cover. Striking examples of this dichotomy include: (1) a student looking for Mulay's work on "Analytical Applications of Magnetic Susceptibility" that was published as a chapter in the *Treatise on Analytical Chemistry;* (2) a faculty member looking for vapor pressure-temperature curves for a series of hydrocarbons that can be found in Landolt-Börnstein; or (3) a postdoctoral research fellow looking for a recent review article on "Electronic Processes in Thin Films and Novel Conductors" that appeared as a chapter in *Annual Reports on the Progress of Chemistry.*

These examples are, unfortunately, only indicative of a much greater problem. Science and engineering libraries are becoming progressively much more difficult to use due to: (1) the dramatic increase in publication of multiple works in volumes that continue to be cataloged as individual items, and (2) the need to use various databases to access information in serial and journal articles and technical reports.

For example, a number of comprehensive reference items are, in a very real sense, a collection of individual monographs (i.e., each chapter has a monographic character). Some examples include Landolt-Börnstein, *Treatise on Analytical Chemistry* and *Advances in Physical Organic Chemistry*. Unfortunately the *Anglo-American Cataloguing Rules* do not easily provide for added entries for chapters even when they have distinctive authors and titles or when they have been reprinted as monographs. Thus there is the dilemma of cataloging what amounts to monographic sets under the set title while users are searching for information that can be found only under the "monograph" (chapter) title (see Figure 1).

Another area of concern is retrieval of information in journal articles which is most easily accomplished by locating a relevant review article and some recent references. Users requiring access to very recent information, however, are usually stymied by the normal four to eight months gap between the most recent journal issues on the shelf and coverage in an online database. A partial solution is to download citations to articles in a library's journals from the *Science Citation Index* (source index) database to narrow the gap (see Figure 2). Deleting or backfiling these online records as each issue of the printed *Science Citation Index* is received will offer the opportunity of maintaining a relatively static file and avoid overwhelming the user with information better presented in review articles or books.

CHEMICAL EQUILIBRIUM AND THE THERMODYNAMICS OF REACTIONS.
LEE, T.S.

BOOK CHAPTER

TREATISE ON ANALYTICAL CHEMISTRY; Pt. 1, V. 1, pp. 185-275.
REF 543 KO pt. 1, v. 1, pp. 185-275.

Figure 1. Sample analytic entry for book chapters

CATALYSIS BY HUMAN LEUKOCYTE ELASTASE.
STEIN, R. L.

JOURNAL ARTICLE

BIOCHEMISTRY 1987, 26, 1305-1314

Figure 2. Sample entry for journal articles

Online searching through a database vendor is another solution. However, given the relatively large number of users who prefer to "do it themselves" and the fact that index-mediated retrieval is not equivalent in efficiency and usefulness to immediate retrieval via the library's catalog (Hoffman, 1981), an approach integrated into the library's online catalog would seem mandatory. As an aside, unless one has a database such as MEDLINE that is continually being restructured to reflect changes in terminology, printed indexing/abstracting publications are a necessity. In general, end user online searching remains, at best, a quick and dirty approach that if used extensively could easily exceed the annual cost of the printed counterparts. At worst, because of the inherent inefficiency of inexperienced searchers, it could have an adverse effect on the quality of research performed.

Another problem area involves publishers who are using journal issues for publishing an increasing number of conference proceedings and collections of review articles that, in the past, would have been published as monographs. Reviewing each issue as it is checked in identifies items requiring analytic entries (see Figure 3).

Access to individual technical reports is another concern since these are not generally represented in library catalogs because many are, in essence, journal articles and are abstracted and indexed in detail in the NTIS or NASA RECON databases. There are, however, a significant

---

INTERNATIONAL CONFERENCE ON CRYSTAL GROWTH (8th: 1986: YORK)
CRYSTAL GROWTH 1986: proceedings

JOURNAL ISSUE

Cockayne, B.
Journal of Crystal Growth; v. 79, nos. 1-3

Figure 3. Sample analytic entry for conference proceedings in a journal issue

---

Gasification of refuse derived fuel in a paired fluidized bed pyrolysis unit.
JONES, R. L.

TECHNICAL REPORT

NBS special publication; 664

Figure 4. Sample brief record for technical reports

number of monographic reports that deserve individual cataloging and, again, the time lag between publication of a report and its retrieval from an online database suggests that a procedure analogous to the one described for journal articles be adopted for selected items (see Figure 4).

At first glance, the costs associated with an analytic catalog would seem prohibitively expensive. However, just as MARC tapes are supplemented by input from member libraries to create the OCLC database, WORK-MARC records (Hoffman, 1981) could be created by member libraries and linked to the existing ITEM-MARC records. Thus, at a cost little more than what is being currently spent on shared cataloging, libraries could usher in a whole new age of information retrieval.

REFERENCES

Brudwig, G. L. (1984). A look at technology and the future of the CalTech Libraries. *Engineering and Science, 47*(3), 15-19.

Cochrane, P. A. (1978). *Books are for use.* Syracuse, NY: Syracuse University, School of Information Studies.

Hoffman, H. H. (1981a). The analytic catalog. *Technicalities, 1*(3), 12-13.

Hoffman, H. H. (1981b). ANALIST: An analytic online library union catalog. In M. W. Williams & T. H. Hogan (Comps.), *Proceedings of the 2nd national online meeting* (pp. 275-82). Medford, NJ: Learned Information.

Hoffman, H. H., & Magner, J. L. (1985). Future outlook: Better retrieval through analytic catalogs. *Journal of Academic Librarianship, 11*(July), 151-153.

Mandel, C. A., & Herschman, J. (1983). Online subject access: Enhancing the library catalog. *Journal of Academic Librarianship, 9*(July), 148.

Petersen, T. (1983). The AAT: A model for the restructuring of LCSH. *Journal of Academic Librarianship, 9*(September), 207-210.

Quint, B. (1987). Journal article coverage in online library catalogs. *Online, 11*(January), 87.

BETSY BAKER

Head of Reference Library
Northwestern University
Evanston, Illinois

Reference Services and the Networks: Some Reflections on Integration

Reference uses of the "bibliographic utilities," as the networks were most commonly referred to in the early years, were recognized by reference librarians almost from the moment these services went online. Richard Blood (1977) published a pioneering article that explored the reference potential of OCLC.

In rapid succession, other works appeared in the literature describing the usefulness of WLN as a reference tool and praising RLIN's value as well. All of these writings enthusiastically endorsed the use of the utilities in reference (Farmer, 1982; Woods, 1979). In fact, this body of writing might best be characterized as being nearly evangelical in nature: "Spread the word that RLIN (or OCLC) works well at the reference desk; look at what we have done and what you can do; join the revolution" (Bennett, 1986, p. 476). Of course, the literature did offer some genuinely informative and helpful searching advice which enabled novice searchers to build confidence in using these tools. However, very little evaluation was offered or assistance provided in determining how these new tools could be or should be integrated into the reference process.

Today we seem to take for granted the two largest networks—OCLC and RLIN are adequately integrated into reference services. It seems to be assumed, since reference librarians are aware of the services of the networks and have ready access to their databases, that the integration process is complete. It may be useful to examine this assumption in a broader context.

Initially, evaluation of the networks by reference librarians for reference purposes was not viewed as being particularly necessary since the decision to implement a particular bibliographic utility was based on technical service considerations. For many the evaluation question did not arise because by the time reference became involved, a system had already been adopted and was in place. Why spend time evaluating a tool that you knew was going to be yours anyway? Reference librarians adopted a "Let's make the best of it" attitude. And "the best of it" was surely going to be better than capabilities offered by existing manual systems. With the arrival of the technical service system of preference, the evaluation question appeared to be a moot point. In reality it was not and has yet to be resolved.

How do the networks fit into the reference setting? For that matter, what is it about any of the numerous new technologies that makes them good or useful resources for reference work? Integrating a new resource into services appears to be a simple and straightforward procedure—it is done constantly. The physical activity of integration is easily understood. However, the mental, almost subconscious evaluation performed when using a new tool is less easily described and yet extremely important. Evaluation, both formal and informal, is important because it ultimately determines service choices. The fact that reference was not involved at the selection stage with the utilities does not take away a responsibility for reference to carry out both formal and informal evaluations of how and where the utilities can be used effectively in service design and delivery.

In this discussion, a framework will be presented for the integration of the network databases into the reference setting. In addition, while particular events associated with the networks will be highlighted, the framework itself may easily be applied to assess how any form of new information technology is integrated into the reference setting. The general principles involved in assessing the integration process transcend the particulars of specific tools and include: identifying the value of a resource; assessing its unique and useful properties; establishing its level of availability; learning; diffusion of knowledge among reference staff; and policy decisions. The final step is a formal evaluation and a reassessment with a formalized policy decision informing the public.

In order to place this framework within a historical context, the discussion will begin by briefly tracing the evolution of the networks' focus on reference concerns. As reference use of the networks has increased, the focus of support services offered by networks has broadened. Just as the network perspective on support services to libraries has expanded, so too should reference librarians rethink their views of how to integrate the networks into the public service environment. The almost obligatory summary of why the networks are useful in reference will not be offered for this is readily available in the literature.

THE EVOLUTION OF FOCUS

In 1980, North America had four bibliographic utilities—all not-for-profit—and about two dozen regional library networks specializing in providing access to information for libraries through the use of information technologies. In all of these, the initial focus was on shared cataloging followed later by interlibrary lending, serials check-in, and acquisitions. Identification of these systems as having reference value occurred almost simultaneously with their invention. However, attention was focused on stabilizing telecommunications equipment and software to support a growing interstate database and its users. The systems were busy responding to searching questions, technical questions about cataloging, and the mechanics of using online files for cataloging. Loading LC authority tapes was an issue as was index regeneration. The mechanisms for user governance and input were also being shaped at the time. RLIN and OCLC both were concerned about internal operations and administrative structure; a formidable task considering that there were no guidelines upon which to model their structures (Martin, 1987).

Establishing regular system availability was of prime concern. In the case of OCLC, it was not that corporate author searching only after 4 PM was seen as acceptable; this type of search required such a vast amount of CPU time that already tenuous system response time was endangered. Public service issues were not being neglected on purpose, they just were not seen as crucial to the operations of the systems. Also, when public service questions were being addressed at all, it was indirectly to assist users in refining searches to make efficient use of the systems. A casual look at issues of *RLG Operations Updates* between 1981-83 confirms this focus of attention by its numerous examples of searches done in a variety of ways emphasizing those that were inefficient and thus costly. Systems development focused on efficiency and reliability first before a move could be made to provide more flexible searching options.

THE PICTURE TODAY

In 1988, the profiles of the networks can no longer be described in similar terms. OCLC and RLIN have begun to take on a role influenced to an extent by the profit motive, in order to support more sophisticated development needs reflected by their user communities. As stated by Sara How (personal communication, March 1987), Program Officer of Research Libraries Group (RLG), virtually all of the early feedback RLG received regarding command language, search options, interface issues, and response time came from public service staff—users for whom the systems were not initially intended. As the systems grew in size and diversity, so also did their reference value and usefulness. Now that the systems have been in place for nearly two decades with early programs well established, strong memberships, and financial stability, they are expanding the scope of their operations beyond the basic cataloging and interlibrary lending functions for libraries to a role that is increasingly multifaceted.

Rowland Brown (1987), president of OCLC, in a report entitled *The Nationwide Network: A Vision and a Role,* summarizes OCLC's shift in perspective:

> What I see as the major change in OCLC's fundamental structure is a role in networking. As others have noted, bibliographic control on a national scale was one of the earliest goals of OCLC and its membership. Academic administrators, public library trustees, and particularly library users, however, are interested in network operations that focus on access, economics and other issues in addition to bibliographic control. In recognition of this broadening of interests, OCLC will move beyond (not away from) bibliographic control. (p. 4)

The utilities have evolved from systems with very distinct functions into communication networks with more diverse functions. Within the past several years, as networks have moved beyond bibliographic control, they have increased the overlap between their primary functions (cataloging and interlibrary loan) and new directions to support more public service needs. Visible evidence of this broadening of interest can be seen in OCLC's cooperative work with BRS to provide subject access to a cross-disciplinary database of OCLC records available using BRS's searching software. Other OCLC products that address reference needs include subject-oriented subsets of the OCLC database on CD-ROM, gateway searching access to BRS databases from the OCLC terminal, and improved dial-access capability (Online Computer Library Center, 1986-1987).

Similarly, within the Research Libraries Group, initiatives have been taken to improve reference use of RLIN. A public service committee, specifically charged to provide the RLG president with advice on projects relevant to the public service functions in member institutions, has been in place for a number of years. Other reference services include recent development of a gateway link that enables users to access DIALOG through a direct RLIN connection. A reference librarians network has been established which uses RLG electronic mail to allow reference colleagues around the country to communicate with one another. Several special subject databases are also available through RLIN and include SCIPIO, ESTC, and the AVERY Index. Most recently an RLIN Clearinghouse of user produced publications has been created to facilitate the sharing of documentation and user aids (RLG, 1987).

With this increasing overlap, it is natural for reference librarians to play an important and growing role in shaping the future of systems which can no longer be seen simply as "utilities."

CONVERGENCE OF REFERENCE CONCERNS
AND NETWORKS' FOCUS

From this brief summary, it is clear that considerable efforts are now being directed toward a reference and public service market. Since the evolution of the utilities into networks did not happen in isolation, the concurrent path being paved by reference librarians to bring these systems into their service programs will now be traced. As mentioned earlier, the first step in any integration process is an identification of the value of a new resource. The literature referred to in the opening comments of this discussion served as the first step on the path. It pointed out areas of reference where the networks might be used, described why the tools might succeed where printed tools might fail, offered moral support for thinking about using the tools, and suggested concrete searching guidelines which in many cases exceeded those offered by the systems themselves. Most importantly, the early literature helped public service librarians articulate initial notions of what it was about the networks that had potential for reference and ultimately facilitated the learning and building of the knowledge process.

As these initial notions were borne out, the networks quickly became useful components in reference service. However, by which criteria were they being assessed? Generally, they were assessed as reference tools in much the same way as traditional reference tools are assessed. These techniques include outlining the possible questions a tool might be expected to answer, and then experimenting with the tool to see how effectively it responds to the questions. As James Rettig (1987) has written, a new reference tool is tested by "relating its strengths and weaknesses to the situations that arise day in, day out, in dealing with the information needs posed by the individual library's clientele" (p. 470).

This stage of evaluation is where much of the interest that is reflected in the literature ended. The assessment of the networks that was taking place at this time involved the same criteria used for traditional or printed reference sources. These criteria addressed some of the core reasons for using the networks in the reference setting. However, as noted earlier, the networks offered services which began to move beyond the scope of traditional reference tools. At that point reference librarians may not have recognized the need to update assessment criteria so that they would also encompass new and innovative uses of the utilities. Many were dazzled by the quick retrieval of information normally sought in disparate locations. However, efforts to test new roles for the utility databases or to evaluate how the networks contribute to traditional reference roles have not been forthcoming. Some individuals were exploring innovative uses of the utilities, but it took some time for these to be shared within institutions and on a broader scope in the literature (Froessler & Rhodes, 1983).

Overall, the depth of these initial assessments was limited because they only described the technical possibilities of a system. There was little attempt to determine how these technical possibilities would translate into reference effectiveness in the real world of the reference librarian. This failure to examine the service effectiveness of network systems limited the value of the assessments; they stopped at description and thus did little to inform the policy-making aspects of integration.

LEVEL OF AVAILABILITY

The physical setting for any reference tool will certainly affect its patterns of use; only in unusual circumstances will a librarian return to a tool that is inconvenient to access. Thus a third and most influential step along this path of integration is examining the level of availability of the new tool for reference purposes.

Although the value of the utility was widely recognized, many reference librarians had, at best, inconvenient access to the system which likely limited its full integration into the reference setting. To explore the availability issue, a colleague and this author initiated a study of the availability of OCLC as a reference tool in sixty-three Association of Research Libraries (ARL) libraries. The survey was conducted by telephone interviews with the head of the reference department in each of these libraries.

Several levels of OCLC availability were identified. Of the sixty-three departments surveyed, over half relied on availability through technical service terminals for their OCLC access. A smaller percentage shared an OCLC terminal with the interlibrary loan department. Twelve departments were also equipped with their own dedicated terminal for searching OCLC. Only three departments reported that OCLC was not used for reference purposes.

Those twenty-four departments relying on technical service access were then queried about their knowledge and use of dial access as a means of interacting with OCLC. It was anticipated that those librarians with less convenient access to dedicated terminals—those going through technical service units—would be more likely to supplement this access with dial access. In 1981, OCLC was not publicizing the dial access option because of its probable negative impact on OCLC's dedicated line users in technical processing. This lack of emphasis probably contributed to the low level of dial access use in the reference setting, an area where there was normally low use of dedicated lines. Most of the twenty-four units had the necessary hardware for online searching, but only four were using the dial access option for the utilities. The unsolicited but overwhelmingly positive comments about OCLC from many participants in the study reinforced the value of the system for reference. However, as one librarian noted, "the difficulty in batching OCLC searches so as not to inconvenience cataloging staff prevented it from reaching its true potential" (Baker & Kluegel, 1982, p. 382).

Today there is high use reported of RLIN as a reference tool. In March 1987, this author contacted thirty reference departments in RLIN institutions via electronic mail to determine their type of access to RLIN. Of the thirty contacted, fourteen responded; all but two had direct access to an RLIN terminal. A few libraries were also using the dial access option to supplement this use. While the degree of physical access to a system may influence how often it is used, it is only one aspect of the overall process of integration.

INTELLECTUAL INTEGRATION

Integration involves much more than description and physical access. Intellectual integration also occurs, which involves learning and diffusion of knowledge. This is an abstract concept that is difficult to define. One can think of intellectual integration as a qualitative index of the range and authority of a tool, logistical ease of use, combined with the individual's perception of its effectiveness and the inclination or incentive toward using it. Tools that are relatively easy to use, comprehensive, up-to-date, and authoritative, such as *The Statistical Abstract of the U.S.*, achieve a very high level of intellectual integration. Tools that are less easy to use, less authoritative, which cover only a limited topic or number of sources, or with which reference librarians are less comfortable or confident, achieve a lower level of intellectual integration. Frequency of use, physical distance, logistics, and level of individual skill all interact to determine the intellectual integration of a particular tool (Baker & Kluegel, 1985). In the process of assessing the intellectual integration of bibliographic utilities, physical distance from the terminals, logistical difficulties in dial access, and a lack of confidence about the content of the files represent primary obstacles.

PERSONAL ATTITUDES AND INTEGRATION

Closely related to personal attitude is the initiative that is needed by the individual librarian first to learn a new system and then to keep current with changes. Perhaps the most important process in integrating *any* reference tool involves the intellectual assimilation of the content of the new tool by the individual reference librarian. In regard to the utilities, it seems that many reference librarians have delegated this responsibility to the online search coordinator. In many libraries the online search coordinator becomes, by default, the coordinator for all database and electronic services. Including the utilities under the technology umbrella is a logical extension of the online coordinators' role. While no one would argue against the need for a coordinated approach to handling passwords, logon procedures, news updates, and other hardware and software issues, such technical concerns do not overshadow the importance of individual learning of the content of all reference sources regardless of their format. However, in the case of utilities, it seems that this abdicating of responsibility is due to more than simply the electronic nature of the tool. It is a combination of the hardware and software obstacles that are encountered when attempting to use the networks that separates the utilities from the mainstream of reference sources. While the utilities are online databases, they differ from those available from BRS or DIALOG in that their content is not of a "known" nature. For example, reference librarians know the intellectual content and merely learn new data access and data manipulation techniques in such databases as ERIC, SSCI, etc. The content of the utility databases is less clear since it involves such a vast and diverse body of information.

Relying on one's colleague to know a subset of the reference collection represents a fundamental shift in the reference librarian's role. James Rettig's (1987) analogy between the process of what goes on every day as reference librarians respond to information requests across a reference desk and the process a reference book reviewer engages in when reviewing a new reference work indicates that a long-standing assumption concerning reference responsibilities is the ability to use informed and critical thinking in matching an information need with an information source (p. 467). Reference librarians who do not have this sort of knowledge either run the risk of providing incomplete service or becoming prescriptive in their delivery of service (Sandore & Baker, 1986). Further, the reference department as a whole provides inconsistent service when arbitrary decisions are made about which reference department personnel are privy to certain categories of knowledge. The possibility of limited service is especially true with respect to the networks since they are more used in a ready-reference service style. By establishing two classes of librarians, the computer literate and those without computers, we are also communicating an administrative or policy message that online reference tools are not a permanent part of the reference collection. Reference librarians are expected to be able to evaluate and use virtually any printed reference tool. Why should online sources be different if we have a commitment to integration?

The public policy aspects of integration are also critical. For example, use of the database is sometimes perceived as a workload shift from the user to the librarian. This is most often the case in those instances where a public terminal is not available, and the search of the utility becomes a search of last resort for the user. Unresolved issues about the function of the databases also come into play. Are RLIN and OCLC searches conducted for the general public or only for those associated with the university? In a public institution this may not be an issue, but in a private setting, where levels of clientele are more clearly delineated, it can be a divisive issue.

THE LINK BETWEEN EVALUATION AND INTEGRATION

In order to take the final step along the path of integration, reference librarians must become critical and evaluative in their thinking about the systems. Such critical thinking involves knowing the strengths and weaknesses of the databases. Critical evaluation allows one to clearly define the reasons for using a tool; the rationale behind using a tool should be clear to the librarian in order to establish its place in the reference process. This does not imply that the reference process is a linear one, but rather that critical thinking simply allows one to use information in planning a search strategy, and that the role of various tools within the process is understood.

The process of evaluation assumes, however, that one has defined what it is that is to be measured or assessed. Not all evaluation projects need be undertaken with the objective of gathering data to measure an activity. Some projects that measure the frequency of systems use are helpful because they describe what is actually operational in the field. However, it is not difficult to go one step beyond measurement to evaluation of the services and resources in place. Truly useful research combines measurement with qualitative evaluation in order to determine how less tangible factors such as attitudes, policies, and current practice affect the choice, use, and ultimate integration of resources. Of course a key component in evaluating reference effectiveness of the bibliographic networks is a shared agreement by reference librarians on what constitutes effectiveness.

MEASURING THE EFFECTIVENESS OF SYSTEMS

Research projects carry with them different motives and the results differ in value. For example, in the published literature there is considerable variation in the reported success rates of the network databases. It has been found that success rate depends on the nature of the material being searched. Elizabeth Groot (1981) examined the effectiveness of many bibliographic tools in verifying recently published monographs. She found that OCLC had a 97.5 percent success rate and that its closest competitor, *Micrographic Catalog Retrieval System (MCRS)*, had a 95.5 percent success rate. In the matter of time spent trying to verify an item, OCLC required an average of 1.15 minutes per item. *MCRS* averaged 1.31 minutes per verification. In comparison, the *National Union Catalog* averaged 2.94 minutes per search.

In using speed as a measure of a tool's effectiveness, OCLC certainly seems to perform best. This study, as with most comparative studies done among the three bibliographic utilities, was done in a technical service setting based on technical service factors. However, evaluation of bibliographic networks for reference effectiveness cannot be extrapolated from studies done for technical service capabilities. The technical service studies drew upon bibliographic data which were complete, accurate, and recorded. A study which is based on a shelflist, for example, is clearly working from a population of items which is known to exist and for which the information available to the searcher is complete and accurate. A study which is based on books in hand is again working from known data—i.e., the item exists—it has a title which is known, persons associated with the item are identified, corporate bodies associated with the item are identified, and so on.

In all of these respects it is readily apparent that technical services staff work with a different world of information from that most commonly encountered by reference librarians. As we are all aware, bibliographic information supplied by a user is often incorrect or incomplete. A patron may be fairly certain that a work exists but is unsure of the publication format, the persons associated with the work, the title, language, and publication date. A reference librarian, when faced with the task of verifying these citations, relies very heavily on bibliographic reference tools.

The weaknesses of a particular tool are readily identified in the heavy demands a reference librarian places on that tool. The ability of a bibliographic utility to use effectively user-supplied bibliographic data as retrieval keys is the real test of a system's reference effectiveness. That is to say, any system available can probably find an item when the LC card number is known and is therefore effective at using that piece of bibliographic information. A more reasonable test of the reference effectiveness of a system is if it can find "That book by Johnson and Jones on system design." It is "that book" that reference librarians are trying to find. In the early 1980s, Kathleen Kluegel and this author investigated how successful WLN and OCLC were at finding "that book," and the factors affecting the searching process. We had hoped to include RLIN searching as well, but system difficulties at the time made it impossible.

Briefly, the following is a description and discussion of the methodological considerations in this project. In evaluating bibliographic utility services as reference tools, two sets of criteria were seen to be important. The first set of criteria were those factors used to evaluate more conventional reference tools such as size, scope, reliability of information, and comprehensiveness of bibliographic coverage. Evaluating the quality of the indexing, the clarity of the entries, and ease of use is likewise part of such an assessment process. An effective reference tool must provide multiple access points. Included in the definition of multiple access points is the concept of cross-references. Therefore, a subject catalog or index must provide either multiple subject headings or multiple cross-references to be an effective reference tool. The effective reference tool must be organized in comprehensible, systematic ways. A catalog in which entries are arranged by size of volume, for example, would not meet this test of effectiveness, although such a catalog might overcome its organizational oddity through multiple access points.

An effective reference tool links inquiry to answer with a minimum of intervening steps. A reference tool which requires two steps is a more effective tool than one which requires four. An effective reference tool displays the information in a readily identifiable and usable format. A tool in which the entries are over-abbreviated is less effective than one which has entries with fuller information. In this respect it might be said that the *Handbuch der Organischen Chemie* is less effective than *Chemical Abstracts*. An effective reference tool must have reliable information. A tool which provides an answer which is not believable is not an effective reference tool. An effective reference tool is timely and current. Obviously an abstracting service which is regularly three years out of date is not as effective as one which is more current. In some fields, or for some bodies of information, timeliness is less of a factor. An effective reference tool is comprehensive within its stated boundaries. In using a tool, a critical factor is knowing that it covers the desired topic completely. Such criteria applied to the networks provide one measure of their effectiveness.

Other criteria were used involving factors associated with online interactive systems such as size and composition of the database, the displayed record format, the ease of use, the response speed, the overall reference retrieval rate, the costs, the differential retrieval rate for different categories of materials, and record completeness. In comparing the effectiveness of reference tools, no one factor outweighs another. The size of one tool may be counterbalanced by the difficulty of use. Another tool, more modest in scope, may be extremely effective because of its organization, design, and access points. In this study, it was expected that similar patterns would emerge with one system's design compensating for a smaller database size.

Method

In brief, over 500 requests that had been submitted to the University of Illinois Interlibrary Loan Department were searched on OCLC and WLN. This sampling universe was selected in preference to other sources of bibliographical citations because it was generated by patrons and felt to more closely approximate the bibliographic queries handled at a reference desk. (At the time of this study, the Interlibrary Loan Department of the University of Illinois Library accepted uncited, unverified requests so most of the information represented patrons' beliefs rather than exact citations.) If the bibliographic information provided permitted searching in more than one way, then it was searched in as many ways as possible. However, an absolute number of search combinations for the study was established. For example, an item may have joint authors. This item would be searched in all systems under both authors and under both author-title combinations. The number of operator steps required and the amount of time per search were also counted to determine how simple or complex it was to retrieve each item from each database.

This methodology allowed a two-stage analysis of the reference capabilities of these systems to be conducted. The first stage showed overall effectiveness for each system—i.e., the success rate or retrieval rate based on the entire sample. The second stage analysis provided a measure of the differential effectiveness of these systems for different categories of bibliographic materials. This two-stage analysis was preferred given the likelihood that the first stage analysis might indicate similar overall reference effectiveness across both systems. The second stage analysis might then reveal systematic gaps in one system's retrieval pattern. These gaps, whether in database composition or in system retrieval features, can be significant in evaluating the reference capabilities of that system.

Findings

Briefly stated, the findings of the study indicated that utilities are of benefit in helping locate information for which a patron may or may not have a full and accurate citation. In 1982, when this research was completed, well over half of the 500 requests (63 percent) were located in OCLC. WLN, on the other hand, had a lower retrieval rate of 35 percent. Understandably, it was the size of each database which played an important role in retrieval success. A repetition of this study today would probably result in higher percentages for both systems. In addition, the findings suggest that the utilities may be efficient to use for verification purposes because most of the searches were short and required very few commands to retrieve the desired information. Of the items found on OCLC, 84 percent required three or fewer commands. For WLN, 89 percent of the successful searches were found with three or fewer commands. It is important to consider how efficient and successful these systems were for verification purposes given the very rudimentary command structure available expecially in the OCLC database. Clearly the factors examined here point to the fact that the networks should be a logical choice for verification needs. However, taken in a broader perspective, it is clear that other factors, less easy to quantify, can influence decisions to use the networks.

What is the value of this research today? Why did we scrutinize the online files using measures by which we normally do not evaluate printed files? Would we make choices about the utilities based on the findings presented here? This research confirmed some early notions by showing that the networks indeed perform well as verification tools. A further analysis of the data might reveal categories of materials for which each network displays a particular strength. Although the specific percentages of retrieval are no longer accurate representations of the content of the databases, the method developed is as useful now as it was five years ago. Printed sources have always been an accepted basis for everyday reference service—there is no difficulty reviewing their function. With networks, as with other online sources, there is still the tendency to focus on the tool as an electronic (as opposed to print) source, and, as a result, we have not fully integrated their function into reference services. The knowledge that OCLC or RLIN are available for use is meaningless unless it is examined as to what makes them attractive for our purposes. Also the primary way of judging value is to determine effectiveness. When measuring effectiveness, or assessing effectiveness less formally, it is done with the aim of identifying the points in the reference process where this tool is most appropriately used. No one tool is appropriate for all reference inquiries. The key to reference effectiveness is to select the best tool for the question at the right point in the reference process. Based on the inquirer's information, we must determine the best tool available at that time and then use it competently. Errors on the part of the inquirer about the nature of the item and incorrect assumptions on our part can lead very quickly down the wrong branch of the reference process. With the results of reference effectiveness in mind, the likelihood of correct tool selection and appropriate reference searching can be maximized.

The criteria for examining effectiveness are useful today as we evaluate other technological tools for selection. However, as new tools emerge, it is important that the criteria for judging them are continually assessed. The intended uses of tools vary; one set of criteria will not serve all purposes. Perhaps it was this increasing awareness of the diversity in formats of reference tools that caused Eugene Sheehy to omit the long-standing preface on "Reference Work and Reference Books" from the 10th edition of the *Guide to Reference Books*, which outlined how to evaluate a reference book (Mudge, 1982, pp. xiii-xv).

This is not to suggest that we wait until a tool has been thoroughly evaluated in the literature before considering it. After all, different institutions have different needs. Rather, it is suggested that we actively evaluate the uses of a tool instead of passively awaiting the results of someone else's work. The first step in this process involves articulating how and where it might be used. Final judgment is withheld until its value and place among the other resources in reference collections is considered.

STRATEGIES FOR OVERCOMING BARRIERS

Which strategies might be used to make decisions about how effectively network databases are used in a reference setting? The evaluation study mentioned here is only one means of determining the relative value of a tool within a reference setting. A key element in evaluating resources is one's approach to evaluation—i.e., passive or active. Earlier in this discussion, it was noted that perhaps public service librarians began as, and have continued to be, rather complacent users of utilities. For a number of years reference and public service librarians considered themselves nonprimary users of networks. Therefore, they did not actively pursue improvements that might make networks more useful in this setting. Granted, the decision about which utility is adopted by a library is often made without consulting reference librarians. Should the lack of involvement at the selection level preclude an active role in evaluating a potentially rich information source for reference use? Consider the change in perspective regarding access to the network databases now compared to five years ago. One can now obtain dial access to search any of the network databases without significant technical processing investment. In this respect, reference librarians are not entirely limited as to choices; they may opt for search-only accounts to more than one network. As we now operate in a different relationship to the networks—i.e., not nearly so reliant on the choice of the technical services department, the importance of evaluation should increase. This author's proposal is that an active role be assumed in evaluation to assure effective integration of networks into mainstream reference service. It is now clear that a number of factors may influence one's decision to use network databases. The individual perspective of reference librarians plays an important role in how actively a tool is used. To facilitate informed perspectives and a further diffusion of knowledge, it is important to return to the obstacles mentioned earlier in using these files and focus on removing such obstacles from the work setting. In order to do this, a number of strategies can be employed.

First, examine physical and logistical access to the systems. If the department has a dedicated terminal, is it conveniently situated for quick access? If not, what is the possibility of obtaining dial access? Consider the use of script files available within one's telecommunication software to increase easy access to databases by all reference librarians. Is there adequate training and support channeled to enable librarians to become proficient in using the systems? Or is the decision to search based on individual initiative?

Second, take advantage of current communication mechanisms. Both OCLC and RLIN publish regular updates and newsletters that encourage user input, questions, and suggestions about their systems. Make a point of routinely reading and actively incorporating these as vital information into departmental routines. Since there is a tendency to become lost in a sea of paper, one librarian reported that she provides a regular newsletter of newsletter updates summarizing particular points of concern for her colleages (D. Cheney, personal communication, September 1987). Both OCLC and RLIN have established mechanisms for regional training workshops which offer invaluable periodic refreshers for long-time users.

Third, consider the overlapping relationship that is developing between user education coordinating functions and database coordinating functions within a library. User education efforts now focus increasingly on database applications as a teaching vehicle. The technical and conceptual information that these two positions can share will be useful not only for staff training but also for user awareness.

CLOSING REMARKS

This discussion has focused on the value of looking at integration as a multidimensional process. This process of integration has a time dimension, a personal dimension, and a professional development dimension. There are practical, space, equipment, and economic dimensions as well. Each reference service finds itself at a unique and ever changing point in this integration process.

After two decades of experience in using the networks, it is not surprising that they are taken for granted; it is easy to take for granted that which is familiar. It is also human nature to become enamored with other newer technologies such as microcomputers and CD-ROM products that enter the library and promise to make specific reference tasks more productive and interesting. The newer tools often provide information better tailored to reference needs than was the information provided by the utilities. It appears that the momentum in public services has moved on to other technological products and issues. Is it that we are complacent about the networks because we have already used these tools and there are so many new tools to learn? Are we complacent because we may possess a thumbnail sketch of their value and likely potential but have not truly integrated them? Or are we complacent for a combination of these reasons?

Every new development requires substantial attention and financial support and may necessitate making choices. Older tools, the utilities, are no longer new and exciting, so they are taken for granted. However, this complacency toward the networks by reference librarians is occurring prematurely. Their value has not been examined systematically. There has been little analysis of the integration process or answers to questions about the effectiveness and efficiency of the tools for reference, and little resolution of the many public service policy issues associated with integrating technology. In this environment of rapidly proliferating information sources, public service librarians are currently being inundated with new products. Consequently, it is becoming increasingly difficult to match an information need with a potential product's name and function let alone arrive at a point which allows for formal evaluation or assessment for reference use. This is not to suggest that an in-depth evaluation of every potential product is required. It is suggested that reference librarians should assume a personal responsibility, both individually and institutionally, for integrating new tools into service patterns.

Concurrently, the networks are taking steps to change their image. Significant changes are being made in the search options, services, and files being offered by the systems. Networks themselves have recently begun to reach out to reference users and have been making strides to accommodate this use. The crucial question is, however, are reference librarians still there to be reached?

We are at a window of opportunity. As discussed here, there is the potential of a convergence of two paths. One is the evolution of the networks to more full service library systems. Major networks are at a point now where they have begun to address a broader scope of library use including the traditional functions of interlibrary lending (ILL) and cataloging as well as working to meet the information-seeking needs of reference librarians. Are reference librarians receptive to these overtures and are they also making steady progress on the path so that they can provide meaningful input into the use of the networks? If so, they will be able to serve as a positive change agent in the development of reference tools that better meet their individual needs as well as addressing broader professional interests. Reference librarians can contribute a different perspective of the networks, one that is based on their own use and evaluation as opposed to incidental or secondary use after cataloging or ILL.

Within any industry, windows change. It is a fundamental human belief that if we do not change, the future will not change. However, if we do not accept the role afforded us now, the future will simply move on without us, and we will forfeit an opportunity for taking a leadership role not only in the public service development of the networks but also in the general area of information system design.

ACKNOWLEDGMENT

I began my career in the reference department of the University of Illinois Library at Urbana-Champaign and much of my interest in the issues addressed in this article was sparked by colleagues and friends in the library. I particularly wish to acknowledge Kathleen Kluegel's contributions to my thinking on this topic and her role in the projects described here.

REFERENCES

Baker, B., & Kluegel, K. (1985). Assessing bibliographic utilities for reference use. *Technical Services Quarterly, 2*(3/4), 103-113.

Baker, B., & Kluegel, K. (1982). Availability and use of OCLC for reference in large academic libraries. *RQ, 21*(4), 371-383.

Bennett, G. (1986). RLIN: Mud and starts—A bibliographic essay on the use of the research libraries information network at the reference desk. *RQ, 25*(4), 476-482.

Blood, R. W. (1977). Impact of OCLC on reference service. *Journal of Academic Librarianship, 3*(2), 68-73.

Brown, R. (1987). *The nationwide network: A vision and a role.* Dublin, Ohio: OCLC.

Farmer, S. C. (1979). RLIN as a reference tool. *Online, 6*(September), 14-22.

Froessler, J. B., & Rhodes, J. M. (1983). Online services at the reference desk: DIALOG, RLIN and OCLC. *Online, 7*(6), 79-86.

Groot, E. (1981). A comparison of library tools for monograph verification. *Library Resources and Technical Services, 25*(2), 149-161.

Martin, S. K. (1987). *Library networks, 1986-87: Libraries in partnership.* White Plains, New York: Knowledge Industries.

Mudge, I. G. (1982). Reference work and reference books. In E. Sheehy (Ed.), *Guide to reference books,* 9th ed. Chicago: American Library Association.

Online Computer Library Center. (1986-87). *OCLC reference service fact sheets.* Dublin, Ohio: OCLC.

Reference Libraries Group (RLG). (1987). *RLG operations update.* Stanford, CA: RLG.

Retting, J. (1987). Every reference librarian a reviewer. *RQ, 26*(4), 467-476.

Sandore, B., & Baker, B. (1986). Attitudes toward automation: How they affect the services libraries provide. *Proceedings of the American Society for Information Science Annual Meeting, 23*(September), 291-299.

Woods, R. (1979). The reality and the dream for WLN reference librarians. *RQ, 19*(1), 32-43.

VIRGIL P. DIODATO

Assistant Director for Information Services
University Library
Governors State University
University Park, Illinois

Online Ready Reference in Academic Libraries: Current Practices and a Review of Planning Issues

How does the staff of an academic library plan the introduction of online searching for ready reference services? A purpose of this article is to answer that question by describing the planning issues that appear in the literature of online ready reference. The article also reports on a survey that indicates online ready reference service has become common to many academic libraries.

Definitions

Online ready reference is the use of online searching services to answer ready reference questions. An example would be the use of a microcomputer at the reference desk for contacting DIALOG or OCLC for quick verification of an article title or the name of an author. It is possible to refine this definition so that it fits local interpretations of online searching and of ready reference. Thus, online searching in some libraries might mean only the searching of computerized indexing/abstracting services like those available on the DIALOG and WILSONLINE systems. In some libraries, online searching also might include the searching of what are called bibliographic utilities such as OCLC and RLIN. Searching for information in a computerized circulation system or even on a compact disc could be, for other libraries, an activity very much like online searching. The important point is that online searching involves looking for information in a computerized database. "Online" also usually implies that the database is in a computer that the user has access to only by using telephone lines to connect his/her own computer or terminal to the database. However, this author is willing to accept definitions of online ready reference that involve databases housed right in the library such as in some circulation and compact disc systems. If the definition becomes broader, it might be useful in the future to consider a term like *automated ready reference* as a substitute for *online ready reference*.

Ready reference, whether or not it is online, is the supplying of brief factual information to a patron. As Katz (1974) has said about the service: "Average time to answer: one to five minutes. Average difficulty: nil ..." (p. 9). Online ready reference is the answering of brief information needs through the computerized systems mentioned earlier. Automating ready reference seems to add a facet to the definition of ready reference. Whereas a definition like the one by Katz has relied on time as a characterization of ready reference, a definition of online ready reference could mention location. The literature says that online ready reference takes place at or very close to the reference desk because that is where the computer or terminal is. For example, Brownmiller et al. (1985, p. 321) report some of their online ready reference terminals to be in offices adjacent to or in library reference areas. Root and Glogowksi's (1983) definition places online ready reference "at the reference desk while the patron waits" (p. 5), and Hitchingham et al. (1984) say the questions are "presented at a reference or information desk" (p. 45). Note that the latter two definitions leave open how far away from the desk the terminal or computer is. This author feels that characterizing online ready reference by the briefness of the service is much more important than where the searching equipment is. In a given library, a service deserves to be called online or automated ready reference if it is indeed online or automated, as discussed earlier, and if it handles questions of the type traditionally felt to be ready reference questions. One can accept the service as being online ready reference even if the searching terminal or computer is not right at the reference desk.

Later in this article it will be necessary to compare online ready reference with other online searching. The term *formalized online searching* suggested by Hitchingham et al. (1984) is used for online searching that is not done for ready reference. The word *terminal* is used to refer to the searching equipment that might be either a terminal or a computer with communications software.

Surveying Online Ready Reference Practices

When planning for a library service, librarians sometimes investigate whether the service is offered at other libraries. The literature reports very few surveys of online ready reference in academic libraries. Yet one can read that "it was likely that a number of libraries were involved" in online ready reference (Hitchingham et al., 1984, p. 44); "many libraries are now attempting to integrate at least brief and specific online searches with traditional reference desk service" (Miller, 1982, p. 270); "databases are extensively used in ready reference" (Rice, 1985, p. 301); "many academic... libraries now have terminals or microcomputers at the reference desk for online ready reference services" ("Lapsize Microcomputers," 1984, p. 2). The lack of surveys and the claims of use led this author to create a survey to test those claims.

Previous Survey Results

The one previous major survey of online ready reference came about because "there have been relatively few reported uses" of online ready reference (Hitchingham et al., 1984, p. 44). In 1981, Hitchingham et al. (1984) found that 219 (44 percent) of 495 respondents "had used online databases for reference activities 20 or more times in a six month period..." (p. 45). In 1982 the same authors received 180 responses from these users who told about the nature of questions handled, the length of searches, the success of answering questions, and other matters. About half of the libraries surveyed by Hitchingham et al. were academic libraries.

Other surveys have been quite limited. Mosby and McKinney (1983) found that twenty-five of fifty-nine academic libraries in Georgia offered online services, and sixteen (27 percent of the fifty-nine libraries) had online ready reference (pp. 4-6). Root and Glogowski (1983) found that of fifty-two academic libraries in New York state, nineteen (37 percent) offered online ready reference (pp. 6, 14).

The Present Survey

Academic reference librarians were asked if they performed online ready reference searches. In particular, the survey investigated whether the percentage of use was at least equal to the 44 percent obtained in 1982 by Hitchingham et al. Such a result would seem to support a claim that online ready reference is a rather common activity especially since Hitchingham et al. surveyed all library types and the present survey included only academic libraries.

A postcard survey was sent to 554 libraries. Selection of the libraries was according to a stratified random sample based on the number of academic libraries in each of fifty-four areas of the United States: the fifty states, District of Columbia, Pacific Islands, Puerto Rico, and Virgin Islands. The 554 libraries represented about a 10 percent sample of the 5,592 academic libraries listed in the thirty-ninth edition of the *American Library Directory* (1986). Data for the area by area stratification came from the thirty-first edition of *The Bowker Annual of Library & Book Trade Information* (1986, pp. 396-97). For example, the 1986 annual reported that academic libraries in Alabama comprise 1.9 percent of all those in the United States. Multiplying 1.9 percent by a planned sample size of 559 determined that eleven Alabama libraries received surveys. (The planned sample size was 559; applying the stratification method and rounding off multiplication products resulted in a total of 554 libraries being sent the survey card.) A random number table helped determine which eleven records in the Alabama section of the *American Library Directory* were to be the recipients. A failing of the method is that the annual and directory count libraries differently, probably at least because of the manner in which they total departmental libraries. Thus, the directory listed 5,592 academic libraries in the United States (pp. x-xi), while the annual reported that there were 3,249 academic libraries (p. 396).

Survey Questions

In January 1987 each library in the sample receivd a three-question postcard survey and a cover letter. The postcard asked: (1) if the library had performed online ready reference in the past six months; (2) if so, which vendors or systems were used; (3) if not, whether the library, in the past six months, had performed any online searches. The cover letter consisted mostly of a definition of online ready reference. The definition drew from definitions by Hitchingham et al. (1984) and Root and Glogowski (1983). Borrowing parts of previous researchers' definitions enabled some of the results of this survey to be compared with those of Hitchingham et al. Thus, although this author felt that using compact disc services for ready reference could be included in a library's online or automated ready reference work, he followed the intent of Hitchingham et al.'s definition and required the survey respondents not to consider compact disc systems. However, Hitchingham et al.'s definition was extended by including bibliographic utilities like OCLC and RLIN as well as online catalog and circulation systems as sources for respondents' ready reference service. Access to such systems is indeed online.

According to the formal definition for the survey cover letter, online ready reference is the use of online search services to answer questions at a reference or information desk while the patron waits. The search often takes only a few minutes. The service usually, but not always, is used to retrieve or to verify a specific item of information related to the patron's question. Typical online ready reference vendors are DIALOG, BRS, OCLC, RLIN, WILSONLINE, and others. Another online ready reference source can be a library or library system online catalog/circulation system.

The Respondents

Of the 554 libraries in the sample, 440 (79 percent) responded by March 15, 1987. The responding libraries, arranged according to the *American*

Library Directory (1986, p. x) categories, were: 123 junior college nondepartmental, nonspecialized libraries; 234 university and college nondepartmental, nonspecialized libraries; and 83 departmental or specialized academic libraries. (For the remainder of this discussion, "junior college" libraries and "university and college" libraries will mean nondepartmental, nonspecialized libraries. The article will refer to departmental and specialized libraries simply as departmental libraries.) Among the eighty-three departmental libraries were twenty religious, thirteen medical, three law, and forty-seven other libraries.

Results and Discussion

Of the respondents in the sample, 213 of 440 (48 percent) reported that they had performed online ready reference between July and December 1986. This finding was similar to the 44 percent of the 495 respondents that Hitchingham et al. found to be using online ready reference. Online ready reference was most common in university and college and in departmental libraries, with more than half of the respondents in each of those two groups providing online ready reference services. Only about one-quarter of the junior college respondents used the service, however (see Table 1).

Does having had formalized online searching service commonly lead to a library providing online ready reference? This seems to be the case if one assumes that a library with both services introduced the formalized service before the ready reference service. All categories of libraries in this survey reported that 70 to 80 percent of those offering any kind of online searching also offered online ready reference.

Why do some libraries not offer online ready reference? The only possible answer the present survey could test was that such libraries simply did not offer any form of online searching services. That indeed seemed to be true for about two-thirds of the respondents not offering online ready reference. The author had no indication from his results as to why of 282 respondents offering any online searching that there were sixty-nine libraries also not offering ready reference searching.

What are the most commonly used online sources? With one exception, all library categories using online ready reference relied far more heavily on DIALOG and OCLC than on any other system. Of 213 libraries providing online ready reference, 155 searched DIALOG and 147 searched OCLC at least once for ready reference during the six months covered by the survey. The exceptions to this trend were the eight medical online ready reference users for which the most commonly used vendors were DIALOG and the National Library of Medicine which were used by five libraries each.

So those planning for online ready reference service should know that the service is one common to many academic libraries, and apparently the

Table 1
Academic Libraries Offering Online Ready Reference Services
July-December 1986

Service Offered	123 Junior College Libraries	234 College & University Libraries	83 Departmental Libraries	440 Total Libraries
Any online searching	45	179	58	282
Online ready reference searching	31	136	46	213
Online ready reference via the following vendors or systems:				
DIALOG	18	110	27	155
OCLC	16	100	31	147
BRS	8	52	15	75
WILSONLINE	8	25	6	39
Online catalog and circulation systems	2	19	8	29
Research Libraries Information Network	0	14	10	24
National Library of Medicine	1	6	6	13

Other vendors or systems and the total number of libraries (in parentheses) using them for online ready reference: VU/TEXT (9), Mead Data Central (7), SEARCH HELPER (7), Western Library Network (7), Dow Jones News/Retrieval (6), DataTimes (4), System Development Corporation (4), WESTLAW (4), STN International (3), Classification and Search Support Information System (2), Agricultural Computer Network (1), Chemical Abstracts Service (1), CompuServe (1), EasyNet (1), Electronic Legislative Search System (1), NASA/RECON (1), Pergamon InfoLine (1), and Questel (1).

Also, 6 libraries reported using online ready reference systems that might not satisfy the definition of online ready reference given in the cover letter: ERIC on compact disc (1 library) and miscellaneous local systems (5 libraries). The author has included these 6 libraries in the "Any online searching" and "Online ready reference searching" lines of this table.

number of libraries offering it is growing. Hitchingham et al. found that 44 percent of libraries receiving the *BRS Bulletin* offered online ready reference, for that publication was their means of reaching potential online ready reference users (Hitchingham et al., 1984, p. 45). And the present survey found that 48 percent of respondents used online ready reference. This is an important increase at least because the population surveyed extended beyond those known to be users of online searching services, and still the percent of libraries using online ready reference increased.

Planning for Online Ready Reference:
A Literature Review

Reading the literature of online ready reference is a way for reference staff to plan for it. Learning how others have planned and implemented the service can help in decisions about the service including whether or not even to offer it.

The very size of a body of literature can give readers a feeling for how popular, commonplace, or untried a service might be. Rice (1985, p. 301) reports that in the early 1980s a "rash" of articles discussed online searching as an aid to reference work. However, as the reference list at the end of this article indicates, since that time the literature has grown slowly. This is so even though a comparison between surveys done by Hitchingham et al. (1984) and by this author indicates a growth in the service itself.

The small size of the recent literature could imply that formal planning for online ready reference (and hence article writing by those who do such planning) has not been widespread in academic libraries. Hitchingham et al. (1984, p. 47) reported that about half of the 177 respondents let online ready reference services evolve out of formalized online searching. Evolution of a service implies little formal planning. It suggests that the service comes into existence very naturally because it is so much like what a library already had done before the new service existed. Perhaps online ready reference evolves out of formalized online searching as the time between some formalized requests and the actual searches gets shorter and shorter; perhaps a terminal used for searching gets closer and closer to the reference desk; perhaps some of the questions answered online require briefer and briefer pieces of information to be retrieved; perhaps there are more and more occasions of a reference desk staff member hurrying to the formalized search service terminal to do a quick search for a waiting patron. At some point, formalized online searching has evolved into a service that permits some searching to be done at or near the reference desk while the patron waits for brief, factual information. The evolution can happen without planning. It does seem to require, however, a library environment that permits staff members to try new things, even if what is new is only somewhat different from what has taken place previously.

If online ready reference evolves as a service, then it is not surprising that an increase in use of the service has not been accompanied by an increase in related article production nor by an increase in formal planning. Evolution rather than formal planning for the service might be especially common in libraries that had done detailed planning a decade or so ago while preparing for formalized online services. Why plan today for a service that, in part, was planned for a decade ago? Awareness of online services today could be so common even for libraries still without their own online services that planning, in general, is rarely as intense as it had been for those libraries that introduced online services when the technology and the service were new.

Guidelines for an Online Ready Reference Service

Almost any article on online ready reference discusses guidelines because even those who do not formally plan for online ready reference searching can develop guidelines for its use, whether the guidelines be written or implied, whether or not the guidelines evolve as informally as the introduction of the service. Guidelines cover such issues as: deciding whether to use online ready reference to answer a reference question, cost of the search, which patrons are eligible for the service, length of the search, the amount of information retrieved online, how soon to do the search, and which vendors and databases to use.

Deciding to Do the Search

Online ready reference is appropriate if doing the search satisfies all or many of the guidelines discussed in this section. But a first consideration, according to some authors, is deciding that online ready reference is to be preferred to a manual search. Online ready reference is appropriate if the library has inadequate or no appropriate paper resources to answer a question (Brownmiller et al., 1985, p. 321). For small libraries, online ready reference simply might be a method to increase the level of reference services (Rice, 1985, p. 301). Or the service can be appropriate if it is the most efficient way to use the reference staff's time (Chenoweth, 1982, p. 123).

Expectations can affect the decision on whether to do an online ready reference search. Whether such reasoning is logical or proper, expecting to do much online ready reference could lead the reference desk staff to such searches even when only a few of the guidelines are met. Lower expectations perhaps force the staff to be demanding about guidelines being met. But it is not clear what the expectations of search frequency should be. Hitchingham et al. apparently have been unique in providing data on how frequently to expect online ready reference searches. They found that online ready reference questions in academic libraries amounted to only 1.31 percent of the general reference questions handled in those libraries (Hitchingham et al., 1984, p. 49). If these findings are typical of academic services today, reference staff expectations should be that, although online ready reference is a service common to many libraries, it is a relatively infrequent activity. That information ought to help the staff plan for the service or even decide that not much effort need be expended in planning.

Cost

Some authors consider the estimated cost of a search to be a guideline. If the topic of a request makes it a candidate for an online search, then the reference desk staff member who handles the question can attempt to predict how much the online cost will be for the search. If this predicted cost is above some limit, the search is referred to the formalized online search service. Assistance for making this decision and even the basis for establishing a specific guideline comes from the few reports of actual online ready reference costs. Such average costs for an online ready reference search have ranged from $3 (Chenoweth, 1982, p. 122) to $4.51 (Brownmiller et al., 1985, p. 322).

Eligibility

The literature says little about which patrons are eligible for online ready reference service. This implies that the service is so clearly one provided at the discretion of a librarian that deciding to do the search because it saves the library time and money or simply replaces inadequate print sources outweighs any consideration of the status of the patron. Chenoweth (1982) is probably typical of those who think about eligibility guidelines saying that the service is available to students, faculty, and staff of the college or university served by the library (p. 123). For libraries that perform online ready reference only for patrons who meet an eligibility test, it is not clear what happens when a patron is ineligible but online ready reference is otherwise appropriate. Perhaps the search is not done at all. Alternatives to omitting the search would be to refer the patron to the formalized search service (if eligibility requirements are less stringent for that service) or to do the online ready reference search and charge the patron for the service. However, none of the literature read by this author suggested that there ever was a charge for online ready reference.

Search Length

An estimate of the online time it would take to answer a user's question helps the searcher decide whether or not online ready reference truly is to be preferred to a manual search or to a formalized online search. If the estimate for a potential search is more than, say, five minutes online, then the reference desk staff could decide to handle the search manually or refer the patron to the formalized search service. Search length is a guideline even when it already has been decided to do the online ready reference search for this provides an estimate of when to stop if the required information is not being retrieved online. Such a time limit affects other characteristics of the service such as limiting the number of databases there is time to search and the number of references or amount of information there is time to retrieve. If the search ends without retrieving any or all of the needed information, a formalized online search and/or a manual search still are options.

Search length, either as recommended by guidelines or as determined by timing individual searches, has been reported by Brownmiller et al. (1985) to range between one and five minutes (p. 321), by Chenoweth (1982) to be four minutes (p. 122), and by Hitchingham et al. (1984) to average 6.6 minutes in their survey of various library types (p. 49).

Amount of Information

As implied earlier in this discussion, an online ready reference search often retrieves a small amount of information. The literature expresses this by counting citations retrieved during a search thereby reminding one of the dominance in online searching of bibliographic databases—i.e., databases that correspond to printed indexing and abstracting tools. Suggestions and actual counts of search results report that patrons often receive no more than ten citations per search (Chenoweth, 1982, p. 123; Brownmiller et al., 1985, p. 321), with the limit sometimes being only one or two citations or a few good references (Friend, 1985, p. 25).

However, counting citations is not the only way to measure the amount of information retrieved. Because online ready reference sometimes requires retrieving a specific piece of information, like a date or a definition (Chenoweth, 1982, p. 123), the guidelines can state that obtaining that piece of information signals the end of the online search. Certainly finding one piece of information can extend rather than end a person's information needs. But online ready reference probably is not meant to be the means to such extended searching of topics related to the original information need. So, if information found via online ready reference sparks an interest in the patron for further searching, that patron might be able to pursue the research manually or through a formalized online search.

How Soon to Do the Search?

It seems that an online ready reference search occurs almost immediately after the reference desk staff decide a search is appropriate, for rarely does the literature say otherwise. However, Chenoweth has suggested that when the reference staff is very busy, immediate service might only be possible if one reference staff member can deal with other patrons while another does the online search. Delaying the search, say for an hour or more, and then leaving the results at the desk is also a possibility for the busy reference staff member who has no colleague to handle other patrons (Chenoweth, 1982, p. 123).

Thus, how soon to do a search often depends on how the staff decide to share services between types of patrons. This contention for service between the ready reference patron and other patrons sometimes is actually a contention for equipment. As will be discussed later, one terminal might be available both for online ready reference and for searching of the library online catalog or circulation system. If so, the staff might postpone an online ready reference search because the search would tie up reference desk access to the online catalog during a busy time of day (Chenoweth, 1982, p. 123).

Which Vendors and Databases to Use

As Hitchingham et al. (1984) found out, reference staff place "relatively few restrictions" on which vendors and databases to use for online ready reference (p. 47). Friend (1985) did suggest that experienced searchers have ready reference access to BRS, DIALOG, OCLC, and WILSONLINE (p. 25), and Brownmiller et al. (1985) reported their most frequently used databases to be ERIC, NTIS, DUN'S MARKET IDENTIFIERS, GPO MONTHLY CATALOG, and AGRICOLA (p. 323), but deciding which vendors or databases not to use for ready reference probably is simply a matter of avoiding online sources that violate the guidelines listed earlier. For example, searches in expensive databases, like some of those that provide business and financial information on companies, would be more appropriate for the formalized searching service than for ready reference despite the need for specific information about a single company. The staff might decide that potentially expensive searches, even if they are brief, deserve a less hectic atmosphere for preparation and patron negotiation than the reference desk. Searches in a large database during the vendor's busy time of day might also be avoided at the reference desk. For example, looking for a single citation via title words that occur frequently through all of an online version of *Chemical Abstracts* during a busy period might take so much processing time by the vendor's computer that the search surely would violate the guidelines for length of search. In this case, it might be wise to postpone the ready reference search for a less busy time or refer the patron to the formalized search service.

Question Types

Planning for online ready reference can go beyond setting up guidelines. Being aware of the nature of the service and of the support it requires helps a staff to decide if and when to introduce the service.

One of the most straightforward ways to characterize online ready reference is to describe the kinds of information needs or questions it responds to. Reports on the types of questions answered by this service also provide a means to decide whether or not online ready reference is appropriate for a given patron's information need, for question types often handled by the service probably are the questions that tend to fit the guidelines listed earlier. These commonly occurring question types tend to require short periods of online time, small amounts of online costs, and brief retrieval of information.

The online ready reference literature most often mentions the following question types or information needs: bibliographic verification (Brownmiller et al., 1985, p. 325; Friend, 1985, p. 25; Hitchingham et al., 1984, p. 48), current information, obscure information, complex information, information that requires coordinating several search concepts or terms, information for which no printed sources exist in the library (Brownmiller et al., 1985, p. 325), definitions, directory information

(Friend, 1985, p. 25), and material written by given authors (Hitchingham et al., 1984, p. 48). Hitchingham et al. (1984) grouped many of these question types and reported that the "fact/subject" search was most common with bibliographic verification the next most common (p. 48).

Bibliographic verification refers to, for example, retrieving the complete citation to an article for which the patron only remembers a small part of the citation like a few words from the title. Searches for current information can satisfy needs for references to articles published too recently to have been indexed by any of the printed sources on the library shelves. Obscure topics, such as those on which very little has been written, might require online ready reference to retrieve quickly the one or two references that do exist. It is possible in this case that the online search would find quickly that nothing relevant seems to be available on an obscure topic; that information is useful to the patron, too. Complex topics that require coordinating several concepts—such as finding information on the tendency of hyperactive children to become substance abusers as adults—might be much more feasible online than in a manual search. However, there remains the question of whether a complex topic would result in a search that is brief enough for ready reference status.

Record Keeping

If online ready reference is a brief activity, it makes sense that logging the activity should be brief too. Complex logging would offset some of the time savings attained by doing the search online. In any case, there might not be time to keep detailed records at the busy reference desk. Record keeping for online ready reference might need to provide only enough data to enable the staff to reconcile vendor invoices and to evaluate the service. The logs reported in the literature might well be more extensive than those at libraries not described in the literature since preparation for writing the article about the service might have required data not needed for day-to-day operation of the service. Brownmiller et al. (1985) included the following in their logs: search number, date, searcher initials, vendor, file(s), total costs, and question type (p. 326). However, at the author's library, only the date and searcher's name are required with costs and file name(s) recorded only if there is time to do so.

If record keeping is needed solely for verification of vendor invoices, vendors' interfaces or in-house software added to the communication software at the reference desk might be sufficient for collecting log data (Friend, 1985, p. 26). This author suggests that libraries having multiple passwords consider devoting one password to the ready reference area so that when invoices arrive, all online ready reference searches might be listed together on the invoice thus easing verification of the bills.

Rice (1985, p. 302) has asked if tallies of reference desk interactions ought to include online ready reference searches. One could also ask if these searches should be included with formalized online search statistics. The basic question seems to be: is ongoing data collection needed to evaluate online ready reference services? If so, then online ready reference interactions should be tallied separately from other reference desk statistics. The staff still could add the online ready reference data to tallies of interactions at the desk and/or to the number of formalized searches performed.

Search Aids

Surely many libraries that have separate areas for online searching have one or more shelves loaded with vendor manuals, thesauri, and other searching aids. Some of these items would be helpful at the reference desk for online ready reference (Friend, 1985, p. 25). Room for and maintenance of these materials could be a chore for some, and so reference staff might feel comfortable with no more than vendor catalogs to help decide which databases to use. Manuals and thesauri might not be necessary if searches are very simple and if only a small collection of databases is being used at the desk.

Reference Staff and Change

Brownmiller et al. reported the fears of a reference staff that is about to change from manual ready reference to manual and online ready reference. There is the fear of being inundated with inappropriate requests. For Brownmiller et al. (1985), the staff was not inundated at all (p. 325). For Friend (1985) the "very visibility" of this service could result in some "inappropriate demands from patrons" (p. 25). There is the fear by reference desk staff who have not been formalized search service searchers of how well they will recognize a given patron's need for an online ready reference search (Brownmiller et al., 1985, p. 325). There is even the fear of the very process of doing the search. This last fear could exist when the online ready reference searcher is a novice and infrequent searcher—i.e., being one who does not do formalized online searching. Fear of the search process itself could exist also for experienced searchers because of the thought of doing a search at the busy reference desk.

Some fears might be groundless, especially if reference staff are quite able to distinguish among reference questions that do not need online searches, those that do need formalized online searches, and those that require online ready reference. Some fears can be allayed, perhaps by regular update training sessions for the desk staff. Hitchingham et al. (1984) suggested that such sessions could engender a "feeling 'at ease' with online ready reference" (p. 46). However, it is not clear if ready reference searchers' training needs differ from those of formalized online searchers.

Online ready reference and other automated services not only have the potential of eliciting fear in some, but they can also do just the opposite and increase reference staff pride and confidence. As Miller (1982) has suggested, online ready reference "enhances the image of the librarian," who can now quickly answer some questions that might have been impossible to respond to before introduction of this service (p. 277).

Equipment

Online ready reference can occur at a reference desk terminal, or near the desk, or even remote from the desk. At the desk the ready reference service might share a terminal with some other piece of library automation such as an online catalog or circulation system. Indeed, at the desk the reference staff certainly can satisfy some ready reference needs, like bibliographic verification for books, by using online catalogs and circulation systems. When the library adds to automated catalog or circulation services the ability to do ready reference via online vendors like DIALOG and OCLC, it might be necessary to add a separate terminal to handle communications to these vendors. An alternative to separate terminals for the catalog or circulation system and for communicating with off-site databases is to have a physical or software switch that permits the reference staff to use one terminal for other tasks (Friend, 1985, p. 24).

Online ready reference done at a terminal that is not at the reference desk was typical at least at the time of the survey by Hitchingham et al. (1984) who found that this searching seldom occurred at the desk and at best occurred at a place "easily accessible to" the reference desk. According to that survey it was likely that this remote terminal had a primary function other than online ready reference (p. 47). Root and Glogowski (1983) confirmed this, for their survey of New York academic libraries did not even ask if the ready reference terminal was at the reference desk; instead it asked if the terminal was "near" the desk. Most libraries doing online ready reference answered "yes" to that question (p. 14).

Security

The reference desk is a public place. Passwords that appear on the terminal screen or that are observed as a patron types might compromise the security of vital information (Friend, 1985, p. 25). Some automated logon procedures prevent seeing password information at the desk.

Effects of Online Ready Reference

Miller (1982) wondered how online services "at the reference desk affect public services staff, patrons and the overall reference operation" (p. 273). This is an important planning issue because examining the probable effects of introducing a service is one means of deciding whether to offer the service or deciding in what form to offer the service. This is an important planning issue even if there is no doubt that the service will soon be introduced because it enables the staff to prepare not only for the service itself but also for its effects. One such effect could be a change in the physical patterns of searches done by the reference desk staff. For example, there might be less walking between the reference desk and paper resources. Verification of subject headings, authors, and titles could occur first at the desk terminal before sending or going with the patron to the card catalog, shelf, or other paper resource (Chenoweth, 1982, p. 122). A conceptual rather than physical effect on searching patterns could be a change in the point at which one stops helping a patron. Perhaps the availability of online ready reference will lead the reference staff to not give up as soon as before online ready reference when faced with needs for brief but obscure or difficult to identify information. The effect here is a raising of expectations, and it could affect both patrons and reference desk staff. Patrons served by online ready reference once could be more likely than ever before to put reluctance aside and take even the most obscure needs to the reference desk. Raised expectations might create frustrations that would not have existed before online ready reference. Patrons and some reference desk staff might perceive the service as a panacea and be disappointed when it does not satisfy an information need.

Of academic libraries in Hitchingham et al.'s (1984) survey, 30 percent claimed that "availability of online databases had been a direct factor...in the cancellation of subscriptions" (p. 48), but it is not clear if availability, especially via online ready reference, was an important factor. Because this service apparently accounts for such a small portion of reference transactions, it probably is unlikely that online ready reference by itself causes many journal or index/abstract cancellations. Yet online ready reference might be an important factor in deciding against beginning a subscription to a printed source. If the advantages and disadvantages of paper versus online formats are otherwise balanced, online ready reference availability could lead to a decision not to subscribe if one of the disadvantages is low potential use of the printed tool.

Finally, as implied by Brownmiller et al., introduction of an online ready reference service can affect the entire online searching service. It can lead to the entire reference desk staff becoming able to do at least some online searching (Brownmiller et al., 1985, p. 325).

Evaluation

Rice's (1985) review found that "no reports of evaluations of ready-reference searching have appeared as part of collection of services evaluations" (p. 302). So, the study by Hitchingham et al. was unusual in that it asked for ratings of how well questions were answered by online ready reference services. Apparently some responding libraries performed these evaluations only because the survey requested it. Two-thirds of the 413 online ready reference questions evaluated by all library types were reported as successfully answered. The other one-third of the questions were almost equally divided among questions answered somewhat successfully and those answered unsuccessfully (Hitchingham et al., 1984, p. 49).

Evaluating the service is like record keeping for the service because time and effort spent on either process could overshadow the savings obtained by using the service. Evaluating especially a new service is important, but reasonable methods are needed like doing the evaluations during sampled time periods rather than all the time, and using the staff's opinions and reactions to the service in addition to collecting statistics.

REFERENCES

Brownmiller, S.; Hawbaker, A. C.; Jones, D. E.; & Mitchell, R. (1985). On-line ready reference searching in an academic library. *RQ, 24*(Spring), 320-326.

Cattell, J. (Ed.). (1986). *American library directory* (39th ed.). New York: Bowker.

Chenoweth, R. (1982). The integration of online searching in reference service. *Reference Librarian*, (5/6), 119-127.

Friend, L. (1985). Access to external databases: New opportunities to interface. *Wilson Library Bulletin, 60*(November), 24-26.

Hitchingham, E.; Titus, E.; & Pettengill, R. (1984). A survey of database use at the reference desk. *Online, 8*(March), 44-50.

Katz, W. A. (1974). *Introduction to reference work* (vol. 1, 2d Ed.). New York: McGraw-Hill.

Lapsize microcomputers for libraries. (1984). *Information Intelligence: Online libraries and microcomputers, 2*(8-9).

Miller, J. E. (1982). OCLC and RLIN as reference tools. *Journal of Academic Librarianship, 8*(November), 270-277.

Mosby, A. P., & McKinney, G. (1983). *Status and future directions of online search services in Georgia academic libraries.* Atlanta, GA: Georgia State University (ED 245 709).

Rice, B. A. (1985). Evaluation of online databases and their uses in collection evaluation. *Library Trends, 33*(3), 297-325.

Root, C., & Glogowski, M. (1983). *Online searching in SUNY libraries.* New York: State University of New York Librarians Association (ED 242 323).

Simora, F. (Ed.). (1986). *Bowker annual of library & book trade information.* New York: Bowker.

CHARLES R. ANDERSON

Assistant Director for Public Services
Evanston Public Library
Evanston, Illinois

Online Ready Reference
in the Public Library*

Online computer databases can serve as excellent and cost effective resources for ready reference in public libraries. In the following discussion some philosophical and cost factors as well as staffing patterns connected with online searching will be examined. The primary source for this information comes from a three-year attempt to maximize usage of online searching, given existing cost constraints, in a medium-sized public library.

Database Usage in Public Libraries

The Northbrook (Illinois) Public Library is a member of the North Suburban Library System (NSLS)—one of eighteen state-funded locally-governed library systems in Illinois. There are forty-four public libraries in NSLS. As of January 1987, twenty-two of these libraries besides Northbrook offered online database searching. Eighteen of the twenty-two responded to a brief informal questionnaire regarding current search activities, although one of these eighteen declined to furnish any information. Comparing these responses to comments in articles and at online meetings suggests that the forty-four NSLS libraries probably represent in microcosm the continuum of database usage in public libraries. The NSLS libraries that offer online searching are not all large or even medium-sized libraries—some of the smallest libraries have added online databases. Nor

*Portions of this article were published in an article by the author entitled "The Public Library." In J. Lee (Ed.), *Online Searching: The Basics, Settings, and Management* (pp. 106-11). Littleton, CO: Libraries Unlimited.

are all the NSLS libraries affluent North Shore institutions. Total budgets range from $86,000 to $3 million. Although there are a number of libraries with budgets over $1 million, fourteen libraries have total expenditures of less than $500,000 ("Illinois Public Library Statistics," 1986). Among the libraries responding to the questionnaire, amounts budgeted for online searching ranged from $1,000 to $10,700 (mean = $4,388). The number of searches done in the past year ranges from 1 (for a library that began searching several months ago) to more than 1000.

Two libraries do not have a separate budget for online searching; they simply pay the costs out of general funds. Most libraries restrict cost free searching to residents of their community. In some cases there are additional dollar limits on the searches with $25 being the most common amount. Several libraries allow only a fixed number of searches per year—usually equaling one per month—although one library will do only three searches per year per patron with a maximum of $20 per search. Another common policy is to search free if the librarian initiates the search but charge if the patron requests a search. Several libraries require the patron to sign a statement to pay all costs above a fixed amount. These statements also include the equivalent of a "hold harmless" clause disavowing any warranty or liability on the part of the library for the information found. Given the nature of the online policies and the number of searches reported, it seems likely that only a few of these libraries are using online databases very often for ready reference. The Northbrook library does use online sources for ready reference and does so frequently.

The Northbrook Public Library began online searching in October 1981. Searches were done by the head of reference and patrons were required to pay all search costs. Six searches were done from October to December 1981 and thirty-nine more in the following year. January through September 1983 produced an additional forty-seven searches. At this point a new policy was adopted. All full-time reference librarians received search training from a new department head, and the library began subsidizing the first $20 of search costs for any registered North-brook patron. Searches were done at the discretion of the librarian on duty. Total searches in 1983 equaled 132 and by the end of 1986 amounted to 729 for that year.

A further liberalization of search policy took affect in July 1986. Online databases were truly integrated into the regular pattern of reference source use. They are now chosen (as they have been since 1983) when considered the most appropriate source, but the staff member is no longer required to ask whether the person has a Northbrook library card before answering the question using a database. Since the provision of reference services is not restricted to Northbrook residents, it seems unethical to treat one source for reference service—online searching—differently. An enlightened board agreed to try this policy on a six-month basis to study the effect on costs. The policy was renewed when no demonstrable effect on long-term growth in costs could be found. It is now permanently in effect.

Ready Reference Use of Databases

It seems fairly certain that a basic reason why search costs have not gotten out of hand lies in the way online databases are used at Northbrook. In almost all cases (over 95 percent), the librarians are using online searching as a ready reference tool—not as a response to patron requests for extensive literature searching. Therefore, it is important to have a common understanding of the difference between ready reference use and literature searching of databases.

Ready reference is a term in such common use that a definition is almost superfluous. However, as one begins to investigate what various librarians mean when they speak of ready reference online searching, it becomes apparent the words may be used to define a wide range of activities. Katz (1987) makes a distinction between specific search questions, usually looking for general information on a topic, and ready reference questions, seeking quick facts about dates, persons, statistics, and the like. He goes on to state that 40 to 60 percent of questions other than directional questions in an average library will be of the former variety and 30 to 40 percent of the latter. In some respects, this distinction becomes blurred in the use of online databases at a busy public reference desk. When the question is: "I need anything you have on the Universal Widget Co.," and the librarian retrieves a summary financial printout on the company using DIALOG's file 516 (D&B's MARKET IDENTIFIERS), spending two minutes and forty-eight seconds on the search, does this qualify as ready reference because it is providing quick facts (statistics) or as a specific search question because it is providing general information on the topic? When a large library with over $30,000 budgeted for online searching says it is using online databases for ready reference but takes down the questions to be searched later, is this really ready reference?

If the primary characteristic of ready reference is being able to find quick facts, most reference work in a busy public library probably qualifies as ready reference. Even Katz's specific search questions requiring general information on a topic—e.g., "I need a simple explanation of how a grain elevator works"—are difficult to distinguish from ready reference with an experienced librarian who goes directly to something like *The Way Things Work*. Librarians who have only three to four minutes to spend on each question rarely can afford to get into in-depth reference searching— manual or online. Therefore, if an online database is to be used at a busy public reference desk, it almost has to be used in a ready reference mode.

Three elements are essential if online databases are to be used for ready reference:

1. The terminal must be at the reference desk and the connection to online vendors must be at least as convenient as the connection to a copy of the *World Almanac*. That is, the computer or terminal is turned on and a communications program is either loaded and ready to run or is accessible at the press of several keys from a menu.
2. There is someone who is capable of searching online scheduled at the reference desk at all times the library is open.
3. If the library does not charge for looking up the name of a president of a company listed in Standard and Poor's *Register of Corporations,* then the library also does not charge for looking up the name of the president of a small company that can be found only online in D&B's MARKET IDENTIFIERS database.

Given these parameters, there exists an obvious difference between ready reference searching in public libraries and the use of online databases for literature searching. Literature searches—i.e., comprehensive bibliographies on a topic often requiring subject competence in a field to compile—have seldom been a feature of public library service unless the library offers a fee-based information service. Online computer databases do make marvelous tools for compiling lengthy bibliographies on topics for doctoral dissertations or extensive academic or special library research. However, public libraries have never had the budgets or time to do literature searching when only manual sources were available, and few can afford this even now with computer databases.

The most effective use of online databases in ready reference is found in two areas: faster access to information that might be findable in manual sources if the time to search were available and access to facts in sources that either cost too much for the library to obtain or simply are not available in a print version. If print sources are available, the library may choose not to purchase them because online searching is more cost effective. Deciding when online becomes more cost effective than a print counterpart can be a difficult process. With some investment of time, however, it is possible to develop an "Online/Manual" ratio that reflects the relative costs of accessing data online or through manual sources (Anderson, 1987). Of course, with heavily used print sources there is still no way that online searching can be an economical substitute.

The question that has provided a topic for a number of articles—i.e., whether a library should offer online searching—is the wrong question to ask. We are in the business of providing information. Clients may not care how that information is supplied as long as they get what they need. Using online or print sources is a matter of choosing the channel through which the information is to be supplied. Downloading, a term for capturing facts from an online database, can equally well be applied to photocopying some pages from a reference book. Both cases facilitate the transfer of needed information from some stored form to the user. Librarians should be the facilitators of this transfer, choosing the most effective channel to download requested information. If an online database is the best choice in a particular situation, then the reference department should not be deterred from using it just because the cost appears at the end of the search. It is almost ironic that probably the major factor in preventing a widespread acceptance of online searching—i.e., the clear cost figures supplied by the vendor—is something reference librarians have been seeking for years—a way to provide accurate costing for their services.

Cost Factors

Several factors make up the online cost equation. Although individual cost figures usually appear at the end of each online search, it is not easy to compare costs of competing sources for online databases. Another factor influencing ultimate cost may be differing levels of expertise among the searchers on the reference staff. Questions about these costs may arise when making initial decisions regarding adding online sources to the reference collection. One can find in the literature some studies of cost comparisons of experienced versus inexperienced searchers or comparisons of different online vendors. However, these studies usually deal with extensive searches on fairly complex questions. Generalizing from these studies to the environment at a public library reference desk may not be warranted.

One study at Northbrook analyzed cost factors in a ready reference situation based on a year's collection of search data (Anderson & Weston, 1987). Comparisons of average search costs for searchers with experience ranging from four months to seven years are reported. The average amount spent online per question by the most experienced searcher was $3.95. The newest searcher averaged $5.39. This is a 36.5 percent difference. However, in the total cost perspective of providing information services, the difference is not particularly significant. First, the more experienced searchers probably cost the library more in salaries if for no other reason than simple longevity in the field. Second, using online sources for ready reference, as stated earlier, implies that the sources are available anytime the library is open. To have only experienced searchers present at all hours is probably physically impossible or at least very costly. In the Northbrook study the net result in savings, if the most experienced searcher had been able to do all the questions of the newest staff member, would have been $102.24. This was 2.6 percent of the money spent for online searching in the year studied, or about twenty-six more questions searched at the least expensive average rate.

When it takes a novice reference librarian thirty minutes to find an answer to a question in a print source that a long-time veteran would find in five minutes, the labor cost may be as much as ten times higher for the novice given differing salary levels. However, there does not appear to be very much interest in worrying about manual question answering costs based on experience levels of reference librarians.

Another cost variable discussed in articles is the choice of an online vendor. One study reported discounted cost differences ranging from zero to 45 percent between BRS and DIALOG on identical searches on both general and specailized databases (Hoover, 1979). The Northbrook study referred to earlier extrapolated from searches on BRS to calculate search costs on DIALOG for the same connect time and number of citations printed. While there was a 22.6 percent differential between the full BRS cost and DIALOG (in DIALOG's favor), when BRS was accessed through a consortium such as the Bibliographic Center for Research, it was 4.06 percent less expensive than DIALOG. The only time significant cost differences are found is when searches are concentrated on a few specialized databases that have widely varying royalty charges depending on the vendor used.

Hidden Costs of Online Searching

Utilizing online databases to answer ready reference questions may also generate additional costs not readily apparent from the sign-off tabulation at the end of a search. In addition to staffing, training, and documentation costs, there may be effects on other aspects of library service. For example, some librarians have speculated about increased costs in requests through interlibrary loan to obtain photocopies of articles located through an online search. Possible additional heavy use of in-house magazine collections may also be considered as a hidden cost factor. Online databases expand the individual library's horizons enormously. Locating previously unavailable information bibliographically does not do much good if one cannot also provide the actual details when needed.

In the North Suburban Library System, photocopy requests are handled through the Central Serials Service (CSS). Detailed statistics are kept of Northbrook Public Library's requests to CSS as well as statistics on in-house use of the periodical collection which is shelved in a closed stack area. This makes it possible to study use patterns over a period of time to look for correlations between database usage and periodical requests.

Chi-square analyses of annual totals for CSS requests, in-house use of periodicals, and database searches for the years 1982 through 1986 were performed. Pearson's correlation coefficient and regression equations were also calculated, using the EPISTAT statistical program for an IBM PC, on monthly totals for these three variables. Checking for a relationship using individual months from 1986 and CSS requests/database searches as the variables produces a chi-square of 99.64506 with 28.869 required to reject the null hypothesis (that there is no relationship between the variables) at the 5 percent level. In all cases there was a significant correlation between the number of searches, the number of CSS requests, and the in-house use of periodicals.

Correlation does not necessarily imply causality. Just because the correlation exists, it would not be fair to conclude that online searching was responsible for increasing serials use. There may be very little significance to the correlation because of the time/linear relationship of the data. The same positive correlations were found between reference questions and database searches, in-house use of periodicals and interlibrary loan, and reference questions and interlibrary loan.

The only reasonable conclusion is perhaps obvious (and somewhat Gestaltian)—i.e., all elements of service provided contribute to and affect the total level of service. If users are pleased with the reference services provided, they will no doubt be more likely to come to the library for other services and vice versa. And increasing services increases costs, but there is no particular reason to single out database searches any more than any other area of the library as creating significant cost increases for other services.

Budgeting for Online Searching

Of interest to reference managers and library directors is a related question—i.e., what is a reasonable amount to set aside for online searching (if indeed it is necessary to segregate online costs from other reference costs). In an attempt to derive a cost predictor, the correlation between total number of reference questions asked and number of database searches was used to develop a regression equation. As noted earlier, a correlation does exist between these two factors ($r = 0.59$), even though there may be no causal relationship. In this case, the equation for predicting Y^1 (number of online searches) based on X (number of reference questions) is:

$$Y^1 = -4.237 + .013859X$$

As an illustration of how this equation might be used to predict amounts needed for searching in a future year, a month-by-month calculation was done using 1985 reference data to predict the number of searches for 1986. These figures were then multiplied by the long-term mean cost per search of $6.50. As illustrated in Table 1, this would have underestimated the actual 1986 expenses by $53.99 (1.1 percent) at the $+1s_{est\ y}$ level. In other words, in 68 percent of the cases, the cost would not be expected to exceed $4,860.36 (the true cost was $4,914.35). At $2+s_{est\ y}$ (95 percent level), the equation would have overestimated expenses by $1,160.44 (23.6 percent). It is not suggested that this regression equation can be used directly as a guide by other libraries to predict searching costs. However, additional studies of this nature under other searching conditions would be helpful in testing the possibility of predicting search costs.

Question Analysis

To provide some idea of how online databases are being used for ready reference in one library, a subject analysis of Northbrook searches during the period January through December 1986 was conducted. The search logs included a space for "question." This disclosure is not intended as an invasion of privacy (see later discussion), rather it has been used to increase knowledge about how this new tool is being used. Instead of attempting to allocate the questions to traditional Dewey subject areas, they have been grouped into what is believed to be a more meaningful categorization corresponding to the kinds of databases available (see Table 2).

Of significance is the dominant position of business related questions. Searches for financial data on specific companies (primarily on Dialog's File 516, D&B's MARKET IDENTIFIERS), searches for general business information as well as background information on companies from business news databases (such as File 148 and TRADE AND INDUSTRY INDEX), and general business news stories from the *Wall Street Journal* and *New York Times* accounted for 52.3 percent of the online dollars spent in 1986 and 50.2 percent of the total number of searches.

Consumer product information, on the other hand, accounted for only 0.64 percent of the money spent. (This is probably due to the existence of alternative sources such as the microfilm and InfoTrac II versions of *Magazine Index* in the library.) Other than business questions, there were only a few significant categories of questions searched over a fraction of a percent of the time. General news stories, education, medical, and psychological topics accounted for 28.28 percent of the cost and 26.9 percent of the number of searches.

Table 2 also illustrates the effect of price differentials between scientific databases, more generalist databases such as ERIC, and basic bibliographic or biographical sources. If one makes a somewhat unfair assumption that each access of an online database resulted in information of some sort being retrieved (even negative information), some interesting questions can be raised about the relative costs and benefits of information in different fields.

Art questions appear to be the best bargain of all. At $1.59 average cost per search and a 3-to-1 ratio of the percent of total questions versus percent of total dollars spent, this was clearly the cheapest searching done in this

Table 1
Predicted vs. Actual Search Costs

Month	Predicted 1986 costs based on 1985 data	Predicted 1986 costs based on 1985 data (+1s est y)	Actual 1986 costs
1	$326.31	$427.51	$376.38
2	$307.19	$408.40	$383.67
3	$369.34	$470.54	$396.29
4	$260.72	$361.93	$326.77
5	$343.16	$444.36	$337.24
6	$233.09	$334.30	$213.89
7	$232.64	$333.84	$394.83
8	$224.40	$325.60	$360.40
9	$297.41	$398.61	$494.55
10	$380.93	$482.13	$643.06
11	$395.97	$497.17	$650.50
12	$274.76	$375.97	$336.77
Total	$3,645.92	$4,860.36	$4,914.35

Table 2
Subject Analysis of Online Searches
January-December 1986

Category	Average cost	Percentage of total cost	Percentage of total searches
Art	$ 1.59	0.10	0.30
Bibliographic	1.84	2.47	6.50
Biographical	3.67	2.81	3.70
Business info	9.69	9.41	4.70
Company (financial)	4.42	27.38	30.00
Company (news)	4.23	8.83	10.10
Consumer info	3.88	0.64	0.80
Dissertations	7.45	0.46	0.30
Educational	4.38	4.17	4.60
Engineering/Science/ Biology	8.15	3.87	2.30
Foundations	7.13	1.18	0.80
Government	5.67	0.59	0.50
Hardware/Software reviews	10.03	2.69	1.30
History	2.52	1.41	2.70
Legal	4.52	0.28	0.30
Library Science	6.21	0.64	0.50
Medical	3.44	5.69	8.00
News stories	5.59	11.91	10.30
New stories (business-related)	5.99	6.68	5.40
Psychological	7.88	6.51	4.00
Sociological/Political	5.26	2.28	2.10
Statistical/Demographic	5.89	0.97	0.80

year. However, these art questions provided only negative intelligence—
i.e., no information on the individual artists being searched was found—
which is the reason the searches were so inexpensive. But the value of this
negative information to the patron (and in terms of librarian time) could
possibly be quite significant. If someone was thinking of buying a paint-
ing by an artist who was represented as being of some importance, learning
that nothing had appeared about the artist in ART BIBLIOGRAPHIES
MODERN or ART LITERATURE INTERNATIONAL could be quite
valuable. To manually cover many years of *Art Index* for the same negative
information would be considerably more costly for librarian or patron.

The most expensive searching in terms of average cost per search was
for reviews of computer equipment or software programs—$10.03 per
search. And the relationship between total dollars spent on this category
and number of searches was the opposite of the art example—1.3 percent of
the searches accounting for 2.69 percent of the costs. But these searches
provided knowledge on software frequently costing in hundreds of dollars
and computer equipment worth thousands of dollars.

Searches in the business area, while usually moderate in average cost,
can produce extremely valuable benefits. For example, how does one
measure the worth to someone who goes into a job interview armed with a
detailed financial background about a company only obtainable through
an online search? And other users have reported that information from a
database search resulted in their company being awarded expensive con-
tracts. In the nonbusiness sector of reference services the average $3.67
biographical search for students who were unable to find needed information in printed indexes is equally important.

Problem Areas

Privacy Considerations

Just as accounting control must be exercised in the library acquisition
process, amounts expended on online searching must be recorded in some
fashion. The usual method in an online search service is to use a manual
logging process or some type of software to accomplish the same task.
Commercial programs such as ProSearch or DIALOG LINK can provide
detailed cost accounting. Alternatively, a simple Basic program can be
written to ask the searcher to input the needed facts at the beginning and
end of the search with the online times being recorded automatically
through the DOS time and date commands if using PC-compatible
equipment.

However, when the library is required to maintain some control over
individual patron usage of the online system because the searching policy
puts some restrictions on the amount of free searching, privacy issues may

come into play. In the search log used at Northbrook, space is provided for the general subject of the search. This knowledge can be very helpful in later studies of database usage, but it does have a potential for creating a breach of confidence. One safeguard is to never record any specific details such as the name of a company. For example, the subject for a patron researching True Fidelity Products, Inc. will be logged as "Company Info." The same process can be used to make the subject in other searches as general as possible while still recording enough to be useful. Care is always taken to protect the confidentiality of the search log just as circulation records are protected.

Cost Overruns

Does the kind of free and open database use described in the preceding discussion create a potential for disastrous budget overruns? Probably no more than exists for any library that assigns book ordering responsibility to more than one librarian. The same sound principles that control over-spending on book budgets can also control overspending on database searching. Just as one must monitor the amount of money encumbered for books and stay within the allotted budget, the online services coordinator (or department head) must closely monitor the amounts being expended for online searching. A computer spreadsheet is a very useful item for doing this budget record keeping and is highly recommended. If the library charges patrons for searches exceeding some fixed amount, then reaching an understanding with the business office to ensure reimbursed searches are put back into the online budget, not into the library's general fund, is also very important.

The primary mechanism for controlling costs before the fact is a workable searching policy that is clearly understood by staff members involved and easily explainable and justifiable to patrons. In developing a policy for public library use of online databases, the first step requires resolving some philosophical issues. As a frequent columnist on the subject has pointed out: "A library needs a consistent policy based on a sound philosophy of service rather than a policy that discriminates either by category of resource or by the financial resources of the patron" (Roose, 1987, p. 65).

The following policy (with editorial comments in brackets), while not suggested as a model for all situations, represents the best compromise the staff at Northbrook has been able to produce.

Database Policy

Online databases are an integral part of reference services and, like other resources, are used when most appropriate in the professional judgment of the reference staff. [Primary importance is attached to fully integrating online searching in the reference process. In order to control usage, decisions about when to use this source are made by the professional involved.] To make this service available to the maximum number of patrons, individual users will be limited each month to a total of $20 online search time at no charge. [To equalize the budget over the maximum number of users, a cap on the amount for any one patron is set. This is similar to limiting manual staff research time on any one question.] If it appears the cost of a search will exceed the monthly maximum, the patron will be offered the option of terminating the search below this limit or paying for all charges above this amount. Payment by cash or check at the termination of the search (before delivery of the results) will be required.

Depending on frequency of use and financial constraints as determined by the head of information services, nonresidents who specifically request database searches may be required to pay the full online cost—i.e., the library will not subsidize the first $20 of search costs. [To ensure primary service to the taxing area should budget problems develop, the department head retains the right to reevaluate service to nonresidents.]

The other important factor in controlling costs is the training and abilities of the searchers. If a commitment is made to include online searching in the reference process on the same level as any other reference source, it will be necessary to have people at the reference desk who can use the online databases. Any librarian working at a public reference desk is expected to be familiar with the tools of his/her trade. An online database is just another tool, but, except for librarians who have graduated in the past few years, the techniques of online searching are probably not within most staff members' repertoire. Consequently, some form of training will be required.

While public library usage may not require the expertise of literature searchers in academic or special libraries, all searchers must have some basic competencies. Typing is an elementary prerequisite since the keyboard is the primary communication device with a computer. Searchers must be able to log on to an online vendor, select the desired databases, input search terms, print out results, and log off. It is important that at least every full-time reference librarian be able to use the computer easily. The two methods normally used are either vendor training, which can be costly, or in-house training, which depends on the skill of the trainer for its success. The best combination, as one writer points out, is probably a combination of vendor and in-house training (Tenopir, 1984, p. 871). Online experimentation time is essential for new searchers. While DIALOG offers a number of ONTAP files (scaled-down versions of full databases at a reduced cost), these often prove less than satisfactory because the material coverage is so small. Vendors, with their training experience and limitless access to online time, are probably in the best position to provide the introductory training for completely new searchers. However, if the person has had some exposure in library school or elsewhere, in-house training can be satisfactory if the trainer has a good background in search-ing. If possible, attendance at database producer workshops (if the cost is reasonable) can help maintain search skills.

Continuous reading in the field of online searching is also important. The major vendor newsletters offer searching tips, and there is a continu-ally increasing flow of "how to" articles in library magazines. Attendance at conferences can also be helpful. Local user groups with searchers shar-ing problems and solutions can be an important factor in the flow of professional searching information. Simple tricks like maximizing the use of database indexes (DIALOG's DIALINDEX and BRS's CROS databases) can save significant amounts of money. Temporarily saving search results to disc or a RAM disc while printing is a form of insurance, and will almost assuredly save money at some future point when the printer runs out of paper or the ink cartridge goes dry halfway through an expensive search.

Conclusion

It is possible to theorize that had online vendors hidden their individ-ual search costs by selling online searching in the way that major business services—e.g., the Standard and Poor's investment packet—are sold, then the newly available precise cost data might not have produced such feel-ings of shock that many libraries experienced and which may have pre-vented them from getting into online searching. The vendors of CD-ROM versions of online databases seem to have taken a lesson from the business services providers and are selling the product on a subscription basis. This may reflect a market realization that too much knowledge about individual usage may be unhealthy for the vendors.

Librarians should be grateful that costs of information services can be identified so precisely. It is also very helpful to know that one is paying for information, not something that will gather dust waiting for some poten-tial future use. Nothing in the earlier discussion should suggest that online searching can replace manual sources. Rather, the argument has been that both have a place in the reference department just as the microfilm version of the *Magazine Index* (or InfoTrac II) and the old green *Readers' Guide to Periodical Literature* can both be utilized effectively in reference. Online ready reference does expand the horizons of a reference librarian and offers new ways to locate information. However, *Poole's Index to Periodical Literature* also expanded horizons and offered new access to material in 1882. It is hoped that more public librarians will begin to take advantage of online searching just as librarians were able to adapt to the intricacies of *Poole's.*

In some cases, an online search is the *only* way a question can be answered. In other cases, *Famous First Facts* is the only way a question can be answered. As information providers, librarians need to have and use the right source to answer the question and not worry about whether that source is electronic or paper.

REFERENCES

Anderson, C. R. (1987). Budgeting for reference services in an online age. *The Reference Librarian*, (19), 179-194.

Anderson, C. R., & Weston, A. (1987). The costs of online searching. *Library Journal*, *112*(6), 44-47.

Hoover, R. E. (1979). A comparison of three commercial online vendors. *Online*, *3*(1), 12-21.

Illinois public library statistics, 1984-85. (1986). *Illinois Libraries, 68*(3), 130-152.

Katz, W. A. (1987). *Introduction to reference work* (5th ed., Vol. 1). New York: McGraw-Hill.

Roose, T. (1987). Free versus fee reexamined. *Library Journal, 112*(1), 65.

Tenopir, C. (1984). In-house training & staff development. *Library Journal, 109*(8), 870-871.

DIANNE ROTHENBERG
MIMA SPENCER

Co-Directors
of ERIC Digests Online
Associate Directors
ERIC Clearinghouse on Elementary and Early
Childhood Education
Urbana, Illinois

Full-Text Databases: Implications for Libraries

The dramatic increase in the amount and kinds of information available online in full-text databases has implications for all users of online information systems. The increase in the number of full-text databases is related to recent technological advances in condensed data storage, a sharp rise in the number of people accessing online services with microcomputers and modems, and a long-standing user demand for online document delivery.

Defining the Full-Text Database

In comparison to bibliographic databases, full-text databases are still in a formative stage. Design, content, format, and definitions are still evolving, leading to some confusion among users. Current definitions of full-text databases tend to emphasize different kinds of database characteristics. As early as 1984, for example, Carol Tenopir described the availability online of the complete texts of journals, books, legal documents, newspapers, and other materials. She noted that when these texts are made available on free-text systems (where every word of the text is searchable), they are referred to as full-text databases (Tenopir, 1984, p. 216).

DIALOG's *Database Catalog: 1987* describes full-text databases as composed of "complete text records" that "contain the entire or full narrative text of a journal article or source publication," and then goes on to classify directories and textual-numeric databases—which frequently contain minimal amounts of narrative text—as full-text databases (DIALOG Information Services, 1987, p. 58).

The *1987 BRS Full Text Syllabus* defines a full-text database as a "file that contains the entire contents of journal articles, encyclopedias, textbooks, or other print publications. While bibliographic databases provide structured citations, full-text databases often provide many paragraphs of unformatted text" (BRS Information Technologies, 1987, p. 1). Since few, if any, full-text databases truly contain the "entire contents" of a print publication, this definition is misleading.

Clearly, new or more comprehensive definitions of full-text databases will continue to emerge as additional types of publications become available in full-text databases.

Full-Text Databases Available Online

Most widely available full-text databases contain the content of publications available as printed products with some notable exceptions. Database producers generally claim that more frequent updating of the online versions of their products creates added value for the online user of their products. A selective look at some of the kinds of full-text databases reveals a number of differences from the print products from which they are derived, and many of these differences have important implications for searchers of full-text files.

Newspapers

VU/TEXT, with approximately thirty-two regional newspapers, and DataTimes, with forty-five papers expected online and searchable by the end of 1987, are currently the most prominent vendors of full-text newspaper databases. The full-texts of approximately 150 newspapers, regional and national, are currently available online and used primarily by the business community. Most newspaper database producers are careful to describe their databases as containing the "editorial" content of a newspaper. As full-text databases cannot cost-effectively store and transmit pictures and graphics, the advertisements, graphs, and pictorial information are omitted. Syndicated columns, letters to the editor, and news of primarily local interest may or may not be included depending on the newspaper and the vendor. For example, while some vendors carry the Capitol Edition of *The Washington Post*, others carry the "electronic edition" which contains primarily national news. It is essential that searchers understand what the vendor has included online. The words *electronic edition* should be a clue that there are significant omissions from the printed newspaper edition.

Encyclopedias

According to Grolier, the full-text "electronic edition" of its *Academic*

American Encyclopedia provides added value for the online searcher—quarterly updates of the online edition compared to yearly updates of the print version. Again, no graphs, pictures, or captions are included. One problem with these omissions is that it may be difficult to understand an entry if the information normally contained in the graphics has not been repeated in the text. The ACADEMIC AMERICAN ENCYCLOPEDIA DATABASE is currently carried by at least thirteen vendors, with home and library users ranging from elementary school students to adults.

Journal Articles

Many of the most familiar full-text databases contain the narrative text of journal articles such as the HARVARD BUSINESS REVIEW database on DIALOG. Recently DIALOG listed nearly 400 journals in its "Full Text on DIALOG" list and indicated that this is only a partial listing. The growth in usage of readily available journals online indicates the willingness of the business community to pay for the convenience of using full-text online. It is likely that full-text databases will become substitutes for on-site collections of at least some journals in corporate settings. But business users are not the only ones interested in the convenience of online. Recent conversations with BRS Customer Service representatives indicate that in some instances members of the medical community also use full-text databases in lieu of medical journals available in the same building.

Directories

Directory databases are generally classified as full-text databases by BRS and DIALOG on the grounds that the user is given the complete text of each entry rather than a surrogate bibliographic record. Many directory databases are updated more frequently than the print products can be and represent true added value for the user.

"Conglomerate" Databases

For lack of a better term, this label may be attached to a small but growing number of databases that contain information from several different kinds of print sources, reflecting the trend toward diversification of database content. HAZARDLINE on BRS, for example, contains the full text of selected book chapters, journal articles, and court decisions concerned with toxic chemicals. CCML, the Comprehensive Core Medical Library on BRS, contains selected full-text information from textbooks and journal articles for physicians.

Databases with No Widely Available Print Counterpart

In the long term, the full-text databases that provide information that is difficult or impossible to find in print may prove to be more useful than other kinds of full-text databases. For example, a new file named DIO-GENES, soon to be mounted on DIALOG, will contain news stories and unpublished documents relating to U.S. regulations of pharmaceuticals and medical devices. MAID (Marketing Analysis and Information Database), available on Pergamon's INFOLINE, contains the full text of over 30,000 market research and company reports, digests of advertising expenditures, and information on company brand names. MAID's news reports contain stories from foreign trade publications, often in translation, that are difficult to find in U.S. libraries.

Databases carried by end-user oriented services such as CompuServe and The Source, which view themselves as providers of full-text information, must also be considered in this context. When the authors asked how many full-text databases were mounted on CompuServe, the immediate response was that it would be easier to determine how many were *not* full-text databases. Most librarians need to know more about vendors and databases not traditionally used by the library community. For example, CompuServe and The Source provide financial, personal, entertainment, travel, and shopping information, and both vendors also make available hard to find information on computers through bulletin boards of special interest groups that often contain databases. SPECIALNET and ED-LINE are examples of sources of information on education which have pioneered electronic communications for educators and made full-text information available online to their user groups.

Implications for Libraries

The option to retrieve the full text of a document (rather than a bibliography) as a search result will inevitably lead to increased searching of full-text databases by librarians and patrons in the next few years. In an era when library budgets are reduced, and library journals are heavily used, and too often vandalized or missing, many libraries already recognize the online "copy" of a journal or journal article as the ultimate archive for the patron who must have an item immediately.

Different allocations of funds will be possible—and necessary—as full-text database usage grows in libraries. Instead of four subscriptions to a popular journal, for example, an academic library may be able to maintain just one or two and use the online full-text database as an always available reserve copy from which articles can be downloaded and printed out.

Ready reference or online searching initiated by a librarian to answer a reference question will increase as the efficiency of retrieving from full-text databases is measured against staff time required to search indexes and sources manually (Diodato, 1986). In fact, libraries will be able to provide better service as full-text databases containing information not available elsewhere become available to answer questions.

Increased searching of full-text databases is also likely to reduce the number of interlibrary loan requests for items which are available full text online. For many libraries, the cost of fulfilling interlibrary loan obligations should be reduced significantly; some libraries already will not provide interlibrary loan of items that can be retrieved online by the requesting library.

Another advantage of full-text databases is that their use provides access to the full text of documents for patrons in locations which do not have extensive on-site collections. School libraries, for example, will be able to have access to the latest editions of encyclopedias, scientific reference works, and directories of all kinds.

Funding for use of full text online continues to be a major problem. As Diodato (1987) points out, there may be a great deal of merit in thinking of the book budget as part of a general information services budget that includes funds for online access. Online funds are used to purchase information directly requested by patrons, while book funds often buy information based on an expectation that patrons may request it (pp. 49-50).

Unfortunately, libraries will find that the costs for online training for staff, hardware and software, and increased online connect time will more than offset any anticipated savings. Improved service is therefore a more realistic goal than reduced costs.

Another cost-related issue is the provision of access to online information for those who do not have ready access to computers or sufficient funds to use online resources—particularly full-text databases—which tend to be more expensive. The growing segments of the population whose information needs are underserved (or unserved) must be considered in the context of equity issues in income and education and the empowerment of traditionally underprivileged segments of society. Libraries have a special responsibility to make information available for everyone and to work toward making online access possible for all library users. Increased budgetary support and reallocation of the library budget, subsidized services, use of new storage technologies like CD-ROM to reduce costs, and other creative approaches are needed.

End Users as Searchers

In designing and offering databases to their clientele, producers and vendors in the past have taken for granted a certain level of user education and training, including a disposition to read manuals and database documentation, and hands-on experience. This kind of user knowledge and experience can no longer be taken for granted, and the design of the vendor's user interface therefore becomes a challenge of greater proportions. The existence of a large group of end users searching for information from their homes or offices is bringing about changes in the user interface.

The number of end users is growing dramatically. Fully 80 percent of the new subscribers to DIALOG in 1985 were individuals rather than organizations (DIALOG Information Services, 1986, p. 1). It is likely that BRS statistics for this same period equal or surpass DIALOG's figures since BRS markets heavily to end users. Despite the training sessions, end user oriented materials, and technical support provided by vendors, many experts see a greatly expanded role for librarians in advising inexperienced online searchers.

Vendors view end users as a new and practically unlimited market for online services, while the library market is finite and becoming saturated. Most experts forecast that librarians will play a major role in advising end users on such issues as selecting vendors and databases, developing search strategies for full-text and bibliographic databases, and downloading. Ongoing training and updating of librarians' skills will clearly be necessary to satisfy end user needs.

Many factors have contributed to the dramatic increase in the number of end users searching databases. Consumer-oriented services such as CompuServe, The Source, and topically-focused vendors like DELPHI (political science) and ED-LINE (education) are demystifying online searching for thousands of end users who will consequently be more interested in using other online information services.

The growing number of students learning to use online services will also enlarge the population of end users. DIALOG's fast growing Classmate Instruction Program is helping to create the next generation of end users. Hundreds of high school and even some junior high and elementary school teachers and librarians are using the database Classmate's specially targeted training materials and lower-priced online connect time charges to teach information retrieval skills to students and faculty (A. Caputo, personal communication, March 1987). Dow Jones NEWS/RETRIEVAL also offers special rates for schools but requires that a surcharge be added to its hourly rate for full-text database usage. The concepts involved in online searching are also being taught in a number of other ways. Students are using computer programs that include searchable databases of facts in history, science, and other subjects and are learning to create their own databases.

Vendors are aware that more full-text databases—especially on previously neglected subject areas—are necessary to encourage growth of the end user group. The increase in the number of "niche databases" which concentrate on a fairly narrow topical area provide evidence that as the user base diversifies and grows, so will database coverage. The KING JAMES

BIBLE full-text database on DIALOG, for example, is one of several recently added databases of little apparent commercial value but great research value. SPORT and CINEMA are other examples. These two databases, which index primarily the scholarly literature on these popular topics, are probably of most interest to those who have an academic or career-related interest in these subjects.

The development of user-friendly software such as Sci-Mate and Pro-Search that simplifies logging on and the mechanics of searching are also important. Already in place are subsystems, often menu-driven, designed for generalist end users, such as BRS/After Dark and DIALOG's Knowledge Index.

Among those subsystems structured for users in specific professions is BRS/COLLEAGUE, intended for use by physicians and researchers. COLLEAGUE currently represents approximately one-fourth of BRS's business. Major features of BRS/COLLEAGUE are full-text databases of the medical journal literature and the full-text AIDS KNOWLEDGE BASE. Other full-text databases in a variety of subject areas are planned. BRS profiles its typical end users as people familiar with computers who have immediate information needs and who work in environments where other people are using computers.

Menus, which most vendors believe are easier for inexperienced searchers to use than command languages, moved to prime time on the standard DIALOG system with the 1987 addition of AMERICAN BANKER NEWS, a full-text database that offers menu-driven access to its contents as well as keyword and full-text searching of individual database records. The implications for special librarians who serve these new end users of databases are numerous: an increased advisory and training role, staff access decisions, and online costs as they impact on other library services.

The Future of Full-Text Databases

Deterrents to the increased use of full-text databases include the small number of databases available and the high costs of full-text retrieval. As more databases cover subject areas previously neglected, the user base will grow. The growth of subject specific "niche" databases is a good indication that the number of users for all online services is increasing. Niche database development seems to contradict earlier speculation that full-text databases in commercially important subjects would be among the first to be developed.

Another trend is the development of databases created by organizations for the purpose of making their own print products available to online users. For example, FIND/SVP originally produced market reports which are now available online full text. Similarly, the ERIC system has taken short articles on education called "digests," which are produced by the sixteen ERIC clearinghouses, and created a database called ERIC DIGESTS ONLINE.

While the number of full-text databases is increasing, the production of full-text databases has proved to be labor-intensive and expensive. Only a few years ago, for example, Information Access Corporation (IAC), a major full-text database producer, was still keyboarding text from published journals to produce its databases. Vendors also are affected by the growth in the number of full-text databases; they continue to invest in new software features intended to make these databases easier to search. Inevitably the increased production and marketing costs are passed on to the user. Therefore, full-text database usage costs are frequently higher than those associated with bibliographic retrieval.

Over time, database production costs are likely to decrease and the number of users to increase. If these changes result in lower prices, full-text databases can be expected to fulfill the promise they hold to improve library services. More immediately, since most information providers' profit derives from print and online versions of their products, the income lost in one sector may have to be recovered in the other, sometimes resulting in rising online costs. Libraries may find that local storage options can help to meet these rising costs. For example, full-text databases are candidates for CD-ROM or alternatives such as Grolier's Storage On-Site Program, which plans to offer access to Grolier publications and other databases for a fixed fee by storing them on campus data processing facilities and networking these databases to the library (Grolier Customer Representative, personal communication, April 1987). CD-ROM in particular has the potential to make full-text databases available to end users in libraries, such as the full text of popular journal articles.

Despite revisions already being made by vendors in search software, more improvements are needed. Database vendors and front-end software designers could make full-text database usage more attractive to users by creating user friendly interfaces specifically for full-text files. Such interfaces could deal with the special problems of full-text searching with the goal of minimizing false drops by combining a keyword-in-context approach with a full-text search of user-specified terms.

Conclusion

Full-text databases are changing the way libraries "package" and store information for their patrons. The implications for libraries range from staffing and equipment issues, to reallocating budget funds, to finding ways of providing equal access to information for all patrons. In a recent television advertising campaign, *The Wall Street Journal* claimed that "information isn't power; knowing where to find it is." The answer to "where" is more likely to be "full text online."

REFERENCES

BRS Information Technologies, Inc. (1987). *1987 BRS full text syllabus.* Latham, NY: BRS Information Technologies.

DIALOG Information Services, Inc. (1987). *DIALOG database catalog: 1987.* Palo Alto, CA: DIALOG.

DIALOG Information Services, Inc. (1986). From the director. *Chronolog, 14*(1), 1.

Diodato, V. (1986). Eliminating fees for online search services in a university library. *Online, 10*(6), 44-50.

Tenopir, C. (1984). Full-text databases. In *Annual Review of Information Science and Technology,* New York: Knowledge Industry Publications, Inc. pp. 215-246.

TERRY NOREAULT

Database Department Manager
OCLC, Inc.
Dublin, Ohio

Optical Publishing:
Effects on Reference Services

Recent technological developments are having a major effect on the delivery of reference services. The most recent of these, optical storage technology (specifically CD-ROM), has been touted as the most important development in publishing since the printing press. While this appears to represent a level of hype that is most probably not deserved, it now appears clear that reference services are beginning to be changed in significant ways. This technology does not represent a qualitatively different service, but it will have a very dramatic effect on the economics of delivering certain types of services.

Before concentrating too heavily on optical storage, attention should be paid to an older technology which is a vital part of this revolution—i.e., the microcomputer. The advent of low cost personal computing in the last decade is an important part of the equation in allowing these new services. Presently the focus is on the newest technology, CD-ROM, but the computer is the most important element of the equation. The computer is useful in the delivery of information with the CD-ROM, but the converse is not true.

One of the immediate effects of this new publishing medium is to accelerate the trend toward end user searching. The personal workstation, without its need for telecommunication costs and with the low production cost for CD-ROM discs, is allowing libraries to offer access to electronic reference sources in much the same way that access is provided to print reference material. The term *electronic reference sources* is being used here in place of online services since CD-ROM is certainly not online.

Optical Technologies

While optical technology is having dramatic effects, it is not a panacea. This discussion will explore this new technology with attention to the strengths and weaknesses of the different optical technologies. There are four basic optical technologies: CD-ROM, WORM, erasable, and video. The first three are digital technologies and the fourth is an analog technology developed for use with television.

The video disc technology has been adapted for use with digital computers, but it has few advantages compared to the digitally based technologies. It is the oldest of the four and achieved a great deal of early interest as a publishing medium but has been mostly discarded in favor of the CD-ROM.

One of the very important aspects of the CD-ROM technology is how quickly the CD audio has been adopted by the consumer market. The audio version of the CD has been the most successful consumer product ever. Its adoption has been faster than either the telephone or television. The success of the CD in the consumer market is important for two reasons—economics of scale, and availability of the hardware and mastering services. Because the consumer market is buying millions of the drives, and much of the manufacturing process is common to both, CD-ROM drive purchasers are gaining the advantage of economies of scale which would not be present in a device useful only in the computer market. In addition, the mastering facilities for CD-ROM discs cost in the tens of millions of dollars to construct, and if they had to recover the cost from data applications alone, the cost of producing the discs would be much higher. The acceptance of the CD by the consumer market also increases the life span of the technology by the shear number of people who own CD audio drives. This is a huge market which will not be easily walked away from.

The WORM (Write Once Read Many) drive allows data to be written to the drive but not erased, hence the "write once" in the name. The WORM drive appears to be most useful for archival purposes, a replacement for magnetic tape.

The erasable drive will allow data to be erased after it has been used and therefore makes the disc reusable. The first beta test versions of this technology are just coming to market.

CD-ROM

One of the prime advantages of CD-ROM is the de facto standards that exist for the hardware, software, and file structures. The Sony/Philips standard defines the characteristics for both the reader and the physical properties of the disc. There are three Sony/Philips compact disc standards, referred to as the Red, Yellow, and Green Books. The Red Book describes the CD audio system and specifies media size, layout, and mechanical characteristics as well as the organization of information on the disc, the encoding scheme, play back signal characteristics, and so forth. The Yellow Book governs the use of the CD medium as a CD-ROM, specifies sector layout and an additional layer of ECC. The Green Book describes the use of the CD medium for CD-Interactive (CD-I) and describes the functions required on a CD-I player. None of these standards is publicly available; they are available only to licensees of the standards (essentially drive and media manufacturers), but the contents are widely known. Some of this material may be made public in order to facilitate file format standards. National standards need to be able to reference the Sony/Philips standards but cannot unless they are publicly available. This means that a disc manufactured by any mastering facility will work on any CD-ROM reader. The CD-ROM technology appeared in reference products only a short time after its introduction. In fact, the first commercially available CD-ROM product was a reference product, the *Academic American Encyclopedia* from Grolier. It was well received in the marketplace, and now there are many products available.

The other important standard is the one originally developed by the High Sierra Group and adopted by ECMA (European Computer Manufacturers Association) and NISO (National Information Standards Organization). (The High Sierra Group was formed by the major CD-ROM suppliers to produce a draft file format standard. The Fall 1985 meeting produced a draft upon which ISO, ANSI, and ECMA standards are based.) This standard specifies how the files are to be structured on the disc. Software which is developed to this standard will work with any of the CD-ROM hardware on any computer which provides a driver designed to the standard. This is important to the library community in that it increases the likelihood that one hardware configuration will be able to run software packages from different vendors.

There are two primary advantages of the CD-ROM technology—i.e., low cost and high storage capacity. At the present time, the price of a CD-ROM reader is about $700. It is likely that the price will drop in the near future, but it still will remain several hundred dollars higher than the CD audio drives. The higher cost is due to the cost of the interface card and special requirements of data applications. When looking at possible technologies which could replace CD-ROM, it is important to remember that one of the important reasons for the low cost of CD-ROM is the huge success of CD audio. This means that a replacement technology would find it difficult to compete on a cost basis without also finding a consumer niche.

The storage capacity of the CD-ROM (600 million bytes) opens up the publishing of large databases at low prices. At present most of the mastering facilities are only capable of placing 550 million bytes on the disc, but this is still a large database. This means that with complete indexing it is possible to place 500,000 to 700,000 MARC records on a disc. Of course this depends on the size of the records, the overhead of the particular indexing package used, and whether data compression is used.

While the capacity is large, it is of fixed size. This places limits on the number of records which can be placed on the disc and forces the system designer to make packaging decisions when the database size exceeds the capacity of one disc. It is possible to build multi CD-ROM reader applications, but at some point the size of the database becomes too large to be manipulated by a microcomputer if Boolean queries are performed. It is unlikely, with today's technology, that a CD-ROM-based microcomputer system will be used to search the entire MEDLINE database since it would occupy approximately fourteen discs.

Another important advantage of CD-ROM is that the variable production costs of the discs are very low—about $5 each. It is likely that this cost will still drop a little. This low unit cost is important in something which is basically a publishing medium with a large market. While the variable costs are low, the fixed costs of production are a slight barrier. These are large databases and the cost to prepare the original data, put it in machine-readable form, and index it, are quite substantial. In addition, there is a cost to prepare the master. In the past two years the mastering charge has dropped from $15,000 to under $3,000. This trend should continue and even lower prices can be expected.

What these advantages mean is that the CD-ROM is best for fairly large databases with many potential subscribers. The databases need to be large enough to require this technology, but not so large that they exceed its practical limits. If the application will only have a few users, then each user must be willing to pay a large share of the fixed production cost. An application with many users can be offered at very attractive prices.

The CD-ROM readers are, by computer standards, quite slow. Drives are now offered with average access times from 250 milliseconds to 1,000 milliseconds. This may seem fast, but when compared to the Winchester disc technology used on today's microcomputers it is almost 20 to 100 times slower. The slowness of the drive is noticeable in information retrieval applications. This slowness places more demands on the software developer and is a very real limit on the performance of such systems. The CD-ROM drives will not, due to technological limits, match the performance of magnetic drives.

Write Once Read Many

Another optical technology which shows promise for some applications in the reference area is WORM. As the name says, each area on the disc can only be written to once. It can be read repeatedly, but once data are written to a part of the disc, it can never be rewritten. The most obvious use of this medium is for archival storage—i.e., as a replacement of magnetic tapes. Compared to tape, it is more durable, easy to store, and it can provide quicker access to archival data when placed in a jukebox.

One of the major advantages of the WORM disc is that there is a low fixed production cost—no mastering is required. The WORM will be cheaper for applications where only a few copies are to be distributed. Given the cost reductions in CD-ROM mastering, this gap is becoming very small. The problem with WORM is that the variable costs are much higher than CD-ROM. The disc itself costs $100 or more and each copy of the disc must be written on the computer and not pressed as in the case of CD-ROM. This means that more labor is involved in the production of the disc.

The WORM technology has faster access speeds—more like magnetic discs—than CD-ROM. It was designed with data applications—not audio—in mind. The readers are also more expensive—from $1,500 to over $10,000. The capacity of the drives is much larger; the range is from 150 million to over 3.5 billion bytes per disc.

One of the most serious drawbacks of this technology is the lack of standards. There are no standards for the format of the disc, the way data are encoded on the disc, or even on the size of the disc. This means that it is very likely that a reader purchased for one application cannot be used for other applications. This is not a great problem for archival purposes, but for reference uses it is a definite problem.

It does not appear that WORM technology will have a major impact on reference services. It will be used primarily in those cases where only a few copies of the database are needed such as a database of local material. But if the mastering charges for CD-ROM keep falling, even these applications may not be justifiable when the cost of the reader is included.

Applications for CD-ROM

It is important to remember that CD-ROM is primarily a publishing medium. The important attributes in evaluating a potential CD-ROM application are: (1) size of the database; (2) number of potential users; and (3) types of access required for the information. Each of these factors will be discussed in turn.

The database must be large enough to require a CD-ROM but not so large as to make its use impractical. A database of a few hundred thousand bytes can be distributed on floppy discs and would not require the users to purchase additional hardware for their microcomputers. In contrast, a database of 5 billion bytes, which cannot be logically segmented, would be difficult to use because of the number of CD discs involved in a complete search of the database—between eight and sixteen depending on the level of indexing.

The number of potential users has a great influence on the per unit cost of the product. The high fixed cost and low variable cost associated with the production of CD-ROMs mean that applications which have only a few users will have a high cost for each user. Successful applications will have a large user population—the larger the better.

Information which does not benefit from the more flexible searching available on the CD might be better suited to print. The primary advantage of print media is that no hardware investment is required. One disadvantage of CD-ROM is that it requires the user, or the user's library, to purchase a workstation. The cost of this purchase will certainly discourage some potential users from purchasing CD-ROM products.

Given these characteristics, it seems that there are a number of areas in which the technology can be successfully applied—e.g., as a supplement to online searching, for reference material, and for full text.

The CD-ROM is initially being viewed as an alternative to online searching but will eventually lead to an increase in online searching activity. The advantage of CD-ROM over online searching is the lack of telecommunication and connect charges. This technology allows access to the database to be sold on a fixed cost basis enabling end users to conduct their own searches. Increased use of information systems by end users will lead to increased demands by these users to access online systems since online has advantages over CD-ROM for some applications. The online systems will be the access method of choice when: (1) the databases are large; (2) currency of the information is important; or (3) the database is not highly used. The last of these points is important to remember; an organization or individual is not going to purchase a database which is only used a few times a year. This technology will create users who are more informed about advantages of electronic sources and thereby increase the demand for electronic information services.

Another important application of CD-ROM technology, in addition to bibliographic databases, is that of reference material. As noted earlier, the first CD-ROM product was a reference work, Grolier's *Academic American Encyclopedia*. Microsoft has recently announced a product which is a writer's workbench of reference material: a thesaurus, dictionary, and quotations. This is a natural progression for libraries, which are providing access to bibliographic databases, to purchase electronic versions of reference material.

The last type of information to become CD-ROM products will be full text—both serials and monographs. While publication of these materials on CD-ROM is not ideal for reading the material, it does open up the possibility of full-text searching. It now becomes possible to treat books or journals as reference material. With full-text searching available, it is possible to look in a journal to find the answer to a specific question.

The distribution of full-text material, and some reference material, presents special problems. The main problems are graphics and an acceptable level of readability of hardcopy output. OCLC has been working for a number of years on these problems and its Graph-Text project has developed solutions to both of these problems. It is possible to scan the graphics from journals and to use computer typesetting languages—such as TeX— to allow the workstation to produce a copy with print quality almost identical to the original.

Future Reference Services

As was stated earlier, CD-ROM is not a panacea for the delivery of reference services. While it is going to have a major impact on their availability, it will actually increase the demand for already existing electronic reference sources. In the future—and for universities the future is not very distant—there will be access to three major sources of electronic information: (1) CD-ROM, (2) local online, and (3) remote online. The distinction between the last two is who provides the machine.

The CD-ROM is well suited for medium sized databases where single user access is acceptable. If the databases are small, it is cheaper to distribute them on floppy discs unless there is a large number of small databases. Very large databases require a substantial number of CDs making it impractical to use for a complete search. The single user is really the limit of the technology. The CDs are not very fast and will not rival magnetic technology for speed. If there are multiple simultaneous users, the response time is going to be slow.

There has been a great deal of interest in providing access to CD-ROM readers on Local Area Networks (LANs). This appears attractive for three reasons: (1) providing remote access, (2) saving on hardware costs, and (3) saving on subscription costs. The first of these is a definite advantage and may allow users to access the database from a remote site. The savings on the hardware would only be relevant if the network is already in place. At present prices, the cost of the CD-ROM reader is about equal to the necessary network access hardware. The saving on subscriptions is driven by what the vendors charge for multiple copies. In addition, there are some operational costs of maintaining multiple readers. This system will also have to have either one CD per reader or a jukebox. If a jukebox is used, then some scheduling will need to be done.

If remote access by multiple users is desired, the better approach is to use local online access. In this arrangement, a minicomputer or mainframe with magnetic storage provides access to multiple users through either a telecommunications line or LANs. The major drawback to this approach, at present, is the need to maintain the database locally. This requires a staff and a large amount of computer resources for database construction. One of the byproducts from the CD-ROM database production is a fully indexed database. Manufacturers of CD-ROM databases can sell the software and premastered databases to local sites to mount on their own machines. This would mean that bringing a new database up would be similar to installing a new software package.

The last source of electronic reference information is the remote online system—the current technology. This source is still best for very large databases, infrequently used ones, or where currency is required. If the user demands the most current information available, remote online sources will still have to be used to satisfy the demand. It is unlikely that either of the other local alternatives will be inexpensive enough to allow a user to have all the databases that will be required. To get access to these databases, remote online systems will still have a very significant cost advantage. The very large databases, as has been previously stated, will be most convenient to access remotely. Databases the size of *Chemical Abstracts* or *MEDLINE* will not make sense for local mounting for most institutions.

Conclusion

Optical storage media are going to have a much larger effect on the delivery of reference service than their direct applications might indicate. Users are going to become more aware of the benefits of electronic information sources and expect to have access to them for all their information needs. CD-ROM, while not appropriate for every information need, is going to educate end users about what is possible and thereby increase the demand for all forms of electronic information sources. CD-ROM will not cause the death of online services but will lead to increased use in the future.

The decreased cost for both storage and computing will lead not only to making searching of bibliographic sources more accessible but also to whole new areas of information searching and delivery. It is now possible, using desktop publishing systems, to do on demand printing of very high quality. This kind of system could be a very cost effective replacement for microforms. It is possible to set up such a system so that items stored in the library on CD-ROMs can be transmitted over a Local Area Network to be printed on remote systems in the user's office or department. The quality of such printing, using a $2,000 laser printer, is much closer to typeset material than to facsimile.

Full-text searching will become very popular. The first applications will be in reference material. It obviously meets the requirements of size and high use. The offerings now lack graphics and color, but there are no major technological barriers to supporting those capabilities. The next step is in offering books and journals in CD-ROM. This form of distribution has some drawbacks—e.g., you can't read it at home in an easy chair—but the full-text searching has distinct advantages. It greatly increases the usefulness of the item for reference applications. The searching allows the user to look up specific facts in the article, not simply find the article through some rather limited cumulative index.

The capabilities and cost of the technology are now at the point of making electronic searching available to the general public. The next several years are going to be a period of change. Many new types of services will become available, but more importantly, there will be a dramatic change in users' information-seeking behavior. They will be exposed to these more powerful tools and will adopt them.

STEPHEN P. HARTER

Associate Professor
School of Library and Information Science
Indiana University
Bloomington, Indiana

Online Searching as a Problem-Solving Process

The broad subject of this article is how online searching (as a special form of information retrieval) can usefully be viewed as a problem-solving process. This is not an especially new idea. Several writers have taken this general position including Linda Smith (1976, 1980), Marcia Bates (1979a, 1979b), Don Swanson (1977, 1979, 1986), and the author (Harter 1984a, 1984b, 1986). However, this discussion will focus on a particular aspect of the identification of useful classes of *heuristics* for online searching. These ideas are not only interesting and significant from a theoretical point of view, but also because of their implications for education and training, for how librarians view end user searching of online catalogs and other in-house systems, and for the design of expert systems for online searching.

If online searching can be viewed as a problem-solving process, what is the problem that is being solved? An early modern description of the so-called "information retrieval problem" was published by Don Swanson (1963). However, as a source of intellectual concern, the problem must be nearly as old as the earliest libraries.

What is the information retrieval problem? Assume that a person is working on a scholarly, scientific, or practical project and has need for particular documents or pieces of data. That person decides to consult a library. How can the wanted information be found and retrieved from the library from among billions of pieces of recorded human knowledge that do not relate to the information need? How can one separate the wheat from the chaff without at the same time losing the greater portion of the wheat? A modern approach to this old problem is to use the tool of online information retrieval.

The discussion is arranged as follows. First, the components of a particular online search problem will be identified—i.e., the question, its context, and the goals the search is to achieve.

Second, a general problem-solving approach to information retrieval will be outlined, and a model for attacking information retrieval problems online will be reviewed. The model stresses the difference between rules and heuristics.

Third, the paper concentrates on classes of search heuristics—tactics that might be employed during a search. Two typologies for representing major classes of heuristics will be identified—first by the type of action taken, and second, by the search state that produced the action. A class of heuristics for a particular search state will be explored in detail.

Finally, implications for education and training, end user searching, and the design of expert systems for online searching will be briefly explored.

COMPONENTS OF THE SEARCH PROBLEM

What are the dimensions of a "problem" in online searching? One sometimes sees a problem described simply as a question: "I want survey results reporting attitudes of U.S. citizens toward Russia." Although every search problem certainly involves a question such as this, it can involve much more as well.

An online search problem has several components:

—the question: a verbal or written statement of a relationship between concepts;
—the context: the environment, background, or setting for the question;
—the retrieval goals: what the end user hopes to achieve in results and costs.

First consider the search question. Several levels of questions can be defined. Robert S. Taylor (1962, 1968) has described a model in which four stages or conceptual levels of a question are identified:

Q_1 the visceral need
Q_2 the conscious need
Q_3 the formalized need
Q_4 the compromised need

Taylor describes the visceral need as the underlying "information need of the end user" which may not be consciously recognized and is probably not expressible linguistically. The conscious need is fuzzy and ambiguous and is intimately connected with the context of the problem. Its linguistic expression may be rambling. At this stage the end user may talk about the problem (and its context) to his colleagues in the hope of understanding and clarifying these ambiguities.

According to Taylor's model, the formalized need is a precise, unambiguous expression of need. At this stage the question may be qualified by the end user and may not include a discussion of the problem context. Finally, the compromised need is a revised version of the formalized need restated in light of how the end user believes the information retrieval system (whether it be a librarian, a card catalog, a CD-ROM system, an OPAC, an expert system, or a commercial search service) can best address the question. At this stage the question may be a simple list of words or even a single subject heading.

Whether or not Taylor's model is accepted in its entirety, it makes important points regarding at least some search problems. First, it distinguishes between the concepts that make up the problem and the words used to represent them. As the end user (and searcher) moves from Q_1 to Q_4, the world of concepts is largely abandoned. Instead, one deals with terminology—i.e., words, phrases, and other symbols. If the search analyst is not careful, he or she will not accurately grasp the underlying concepts of the information problem. If the problem is presented at the level of Q_4, the search intermediary—human or machine—must presumably try to move to earlier levels. Ideally the intermediary will be able to understand the question at level Q_2 as a colleague of the end user. Note that this more extensive delving into a question is not always necessary; a discriminating searcher will know when it is and is not needed.

Taylor's model illustrates how compromises are made and constraints are set on the original information need. It especially stresses the importance of understanding the context of the problem. A search question is a product of an environment—the setting or background from which the question has emerged. An understanding of context will not only help the searcher understand the original problem (as opposed to how it was framed) but also will suggest ways of modifying the search as it progresses if necessary.

Consider the search question posed earlier: "I want survey data reporting attitudes of U.S. citizens toward Russia." The question seems straightforward. However, an interview designed to move beyond the words comprising the question might reveal that the end user is a university professor of political science, that this search problem is part of a larger research project on the evaluation of alternative methods of communicating political information about nondemocracies by the United States and other Western governments to their peoples, that the professor is only interested in research findings, that her actual interests extend beyond Russia to the Soviet Union, Eastern Bloc, and other communist countries as well as extreme right wing totalitarian regimes of which she names several.

Furthermore, the client is interested only in recent findings (the past few years). She can read only German and English and wants retrieval limited to findings presented in these languages. She is writing a grant proposal to explore these questions further and wants comprehensive results on the specific question (dealing with Russia and the United States). She would also like results to be as comprehensive as possible on the more general question. She thinks that there may be several dozen research articles on the former, and perhaps one or two hundred articles on the latter. She can afford to pay up to $50 on the search if necessary. Having gained this information regarding the problem context, the online searcher will be able to formulate alternative approaches to the problem consistent with the overall purpose of the search.

Besides the question and its context, the end user in the example has stated retrieval goals. They are of two types: goals identifying the comprehensiveness and/or purity of the retrieval results and goals stating cost constraints. Comprehensiveness and purity goals are often stated by desired levels of recall and precision:

—recall: the proportion of relevant documents retrieved (from a universe of documents) by the search
—precision: the proportion of retrieved documents that are relevant to the problem

Recall is a measure of the comprehensiveness of the search while precision is a measure of the purity of the output. Usually if a searcher is acting rationally, attempts to improve recall will degrade precision and vice versa. This point will be addressed more fully later.

In summary, an information retrieval problem is comprised of several parts: the question, its context, and the retrieval goals of the end user. The purpose of an online search of a bibliographic database is to solve the information retrieval problem: to identify documents that discuss the concepts of the question in the relationship indicated consistent with the problem context and the retrieval goals of the end user. Note that a given problem may be insoluble; negotiation and compromise may be necessary before a solution can be found.

PROBLEM-SOLVING AND INFORMATION RETRIEVAL

As was observed earlier, several writers have argued that information retrieval can be usefully regarded as a problem-solving process. Such a view takes online searching to be an iterative, trial and error process in which the searcher takes steps to move closer and closer to the retrieval goals of the end user.

Within the framework of an overall approach to a solution, the searcher prepares formulations to represent the major concepts and their interrelationships. These formulations can be regarded as hypotheses— statements that the searcher believes may succeed in satisfying retrieval goals. Normally, alternative formulations should be prepared as well since initial formulations (as uncertain hypotheses) may fail (for an elaboration see Harter, 1984).

When preparation has been completed, the searcher connects to the retrieval system and begins testing hypotheses. A formulation (a command or series of commands) is entered and the results are tested by printing a sample of retrieved records. The searcher evaluates these against the question, problem context, and retrieval goals. Based on the number of postings retrieved and on an estimate of recall and precision, the searcher tries to move closer to a solution of the problem by stating and testing a new hypothesis. A second formulation is prepared and put to the system. Again a sample of records is evaluated, and again the searcher considers what might be done to move closer to a solution. The process continues to cycle until, in the searcher's judgment, a solution to the problem has been reached (that is, the question, in its particular context, has been satisfied in terms of recall, precision, and cost goals).

How does the searcher know which hypotheses are viable? Of the infinity of possible ways of modifying a given search in progress, which should be selected? The searcher is guided by intuition and logical ability as well as by his/her knowledge of heuristics.

Heuristics (or tactics [Bates, 1979] or moves [Fidel, 1984]) are actions that are taken to approach a goal. By their nature, heuristics are not foolproof; they promise the possibility of success but offer no guarantee. Heuristics are perhaps best understood by contrasting them to rules. Rules are actions known to have a certain effect in all cases. Rules are not uncertain. Except for technical problems such as bugs in the retrieval system, line noise, or a scratched CD-ROM disc, rules in information retrieval always have the same effect.

In online searching, logon protocols are expressed as rules. Also, the effects produced by the various commands on the retrieval system files may usefully be regarded as rules. For example, the statement that the expression *A* AND *B* produces a new set *C* consisting of postings common to sets *A* AND *B* is a rule. Boolean AND always works this way. In addition to conceptual rules such as this, the searcher must adhere to the form in which commands are to be entered to the system. These are called syntax rules.

Obviously a searcher (or an intelligent front-end or expert system) must know certain rules to successfully solve a problem online. However, while knowledge of rules is necessary, it is not a sufficient condition for success in all cases. It is assumed here (an assumption supported by the professional literature) that online searching is not a deterministic activity governed solely by rules; at the heart of the matter are so-called "rules of thumb"—heuristics for successful searching. Experienced searchers tend to possess knowledge of such heuristics and novices tend not to possess them. A thesis of this article is that in the education and training process perhaps far too much attention is given to the acquisition of rules (which are, after all, the easy things to teach) and far too little attention is given to the acquisition of heuristics. The next section of this article describes major classes of heuristics.

A TYPOLOGY OF HEURISTICS

Numerous papers have been published that identify one or more heuristics (hints, tricks, strategies, approaches) for successful online searching. Library and information science has several professional journals devoted largely to these issues and numerous other journals that occasionally publish relevant pieces.

In a study published in *Online Review,* Harter and Peters (1986) proposed a typology based on heuristics identified in published studies. They located and read every published article in the professional literature that could be found discussing aspects of "how to do" an online search, in whole or in part, looking for suggestions made by the "experts" writing the articles. That the authors were indeed experts is one of the assumptions underlying this work.

These heuristics were then organized into classes. This proposed typology was largely built around the type of heuristic being considered rather than its function. The article identified six classes of heuristics. These were based on:

1. overall philosophy and approach of the searcher
2. language of problem description
3. record and file structures
4. concept formulation and reformulation (Boolean logic)
5. increasing or decreasing recall and precision
6. cost/effectiveness

While this organization is useful as a preliminary approach, it is perhaps not as helpful as it might be to a searcher looking for the correct approach at a given point in an ongoing search. For application to a search in progress, a typology is required that is based on the present state of the search—i.e., the situation in which the searcher currently finds himself.

Except for the item above on increasing or decreasing recall and precision, the searcher is given little guidance by this typology to which heuristic to pursue next at a given time. Thus this organization tends to be pedagogically oriented; it is better suited for classroom instruction than for guidance during an ongoing search.

This article proposes a typology of heuristics based on search states rather than form. The typology is based on the idea that there are several major states that characterize an ongoing solution to a search problem at least one of which is likely to be encountered in nearly every search.

Heuristics Based on Search States

What are the states in which a searcher might find himself? Ideally, the searcher would like to evaluate the search output against the problem statement and its context as well as recall, precision, and cost goals. Sometimes, however, one is unable to reach this point for technical or personal reasons. There are several preliminary states that one might encounter:

—inability to make connection with the host system;
—no response from system, no prompt, keyboard frozen;
—double characters or no characters are displayed when commands are typed;
—system error message is received;
—a command has been given that the searcher realizes is in error and wants to "take back";
—utter confusion, helplessness, panic

The first several of these states are technical in nature and the last is personal. In general, these states are properly addressed by rules rather than heuristics. These rules may be listed in search system documentation under the heading of "troubleshooting." For example, if no characters are displayed when commands are typed, the rule to be followed is to toggle the duplex switch to half duplex; and on some host systems the rule for stopping the execution of a command (taking it back) is to send a break or interrupt signal.

A good system error message will include an attempt at diagnosis and will state or imply a rule for solving the problem. Thus the error message "unmatched parentheses" implies that the searcher should review the formulation looking for an extra or missing parenthesis, and to reenter it with the correction made. The rule that might be suggested to beginners when they experience a state of confusion or panic is to disconnect from the system, take several deep breaths, review the output, and try to recover before continuing.

In conclusion, although the states listed earlier are legitimate states in which one might find oneself, they are handled with rules. They are also easily automated. Rule-based states are not considered further.

The remainder of this article concentrates on heuristics suggested for states that result from a comparison of system output with the components of the search problem—the question, its context, and the retrieval goals. The following states are among those that might be achieved as a result of this comparison:

1. *Records not related to the subject.* The search has resulted in the retrieval of documents that do not discuss the topic of the search problem; they are entirely off the subject. They bear no resemblance to either the specific question or its context. What is wrong and what should the searcher do?

2. *Unexpected null set.* The search has resulted in an unanticipated empty set. What are the possible explanations of this state, and what should be done?

3. *Need to increase recall.* The search has resulted in some documents relevant to the question but too few; the comprehensiveness of the search is inadequate when measured against the retrieval goals of the end user. What can the searcher do to increase recall?

4. *Need to increase precision.* The search has resulted in relevant documents, but the percentage of nonrelevant documents is unacceptably large. There are too many false drops when measured against the retrieval goals of the end user. What can the searcher do to increase precision?

5. *Need to limit search.* The search has resulted in the retrieval of an acceptable mixture of relevant and nonrelevant documents, but there are too many records to print; the desired recall and precision goals cannot be achieved for the stated cost goal. What can the searcher do to reduce the number of documents retrieved in a way that is consistent with the problem context and retrieval goals?

STUDY OF THE STATE
OF RETRIEVING NONRELATED RECORDS

Material in this section is drawn heavily from *Online Search Analyst,* a menu-driven diagnostic and tutorial program for IBM PCs and compatible microcomputers, written by and available from the author (Harter, 1987). The program is organized by the five states listed earlier. It provides a detailed discussion of each state, including the identification of several subclasses of heuristics that might be employed for each state. It includes numerous examples for each heuristic discussed and is presented in a tutorial fashion.

In the discussion that follows, a closer look is taken at the first of these states—a state that is perhaps rarely achieved by experienced searchers but is commonly found in searches conducted by beginners. The searcher has invented a hypothesis designed to retrieve records on the question. A formulation is prepared to test the hypothesis and is entered into the system. A solution set is created, and a sample of records from the set is printed. To the searcher's surprise, the records appear to have nothing whatever to do with either the question or its context; they are not at all on the subject. What are possible explanations of this state, and what are the heuristics for avoiding this problem in the future?

There are six major subclasses of useful heuristics for explaining the problem and for dealing with it or avoiding it in future searches. The problem may be: (1) poor choice of database, (2) misuse of Boolean logic, (3) semantic or language problems, (4) set number errors, (5) truncation errors, or (6) not enough search facets.

First, conceivably the searcher has obtained results not on the subject because he is searching in an inappropriate database. In particular, newspaper and magazine databases such as *National Newspaper Index* and *Magazine Index* are highly multidisciplinary. Not only are documents indexed that represent a wide variety of disciplines, but also such databases contain "popular" material—publications that are not technical in their information content.

Perhaps the searcher is looking for a technical subject in a "popular" database. What may be really needed is a technical, scholarly, or scientific database such as *MEDLINE, Chemical Abstracts,* or *Biological Abstracts*.

As a second possible explanation of retrieval results totally unrelated to the subject searched, an appropriate database may have been selected, but the command to the search system was put incorrectly. A DIALOG searcher may have forgotten to specify a file and is searching in the default database. Or possibly he made a simple typographical error with the file number.

In an organization that shares passwords, perhaps the searcher was connected to the database that his colleague had been using. In his hurry to get to the matter at hand, he may have failed to notice that he had been connected to the incorrect database.

Two heuristics are suggested:

—Has an appropriate database been selected? In particular, are you looking in a popular file when what is needed is a technical, scholarly, or scientific database?

—It pays to read the information carefully to verify that the correct file is being used.

Another possible explanation of the retrieval of records not on the subject is that the Boolean operators AND, OR, and NOT were used incorrectly. Misuse of Boolean logic is a common reason for retrieval sets that are completely off the subject.

In particular, mistakenly using OR when AND is the correct operator produces a relatively large set consisting almost entirely of nonrelevant records. Although it may seem obvious to many readers, in this author's experience with students, this is a common error.

A OR *B*	is the set of records that are either in set *A* or in set *B* or in both sets
A AND *B*	is the set of records that are present in set *A* and also in set *B*

Even if one assumes that a searcher knows which of these operators should be used in a given situation (a questionable assumption), there are still problems. Search systems typically have an implied order of operations to handle potentially confusing combinations of Boolean operators such as in the example: *A* OR *B* AND *C*. In the DIALOG system, for example, the order of operations is to first carry out all NOT operations then all AND operations, and finally all OR operations from left to right. Exceptions to this order are made possible through parentheses. Hence in the expression: (*A* OR *B*) AND *C*, the parentheses tell the system to do the OR operation first then to do the AND. If the parentheses had been absent as in *A* OR *B* AND *C*, then *B* AND *C* would be done first.

Suppose that one is interested in automation of either information centers or libraries. The expression *LIBRARIES* OR *INFORMATION CENTERS* AND *AUTOMATION* would produce a set of documents largely irrelevant to the search problem. The set would consist of records containing both of the terms *information centers* and *automation*. However, these records would be overwhelmed by a much greater number of records containing the word *libraries* in the fields searched. The correct formulation requires the use of parentheses: *(LIBRARIES* OR *INFORMATION CENTERS)* AND *AUTOMATION*. The following heuristics are suggested:

—Be sure that you know the order in which Boolean operators are executed in the search system you are using.
—Use parentheses to ensure that certain operations are carried out before others.

Semantic or language problems can also be the reason for retrieving records which are totally off the subject. There are two kinds of language problems that might result in this outcome: (1) the use of broad, general, or fuzzy terms representing a concept; and (2) the use of terms with multiple meanings to represent a concept. In both cases an unwanted meaning can overwhelm the concept of interest. For example, suppose that several terms are used to represent a concept, and that these terms are combined with Boolean OR as in: *RESEARCH* or *QUEUING THEORY* or *LINEAR PROGRAMMING*. If one term is broad or fuzzy and retrieves many postings (in this case *research*), then postings from this term will overwhelm postings from the other more specific terms. Although the final retrieval set will contain postings from both the specific descriptors *QUEUING THEORY* and *LINEAR PROGRAMMING*, there will be relatively many more postings from the broader term *research*. This problem can be solved by avoiding generic terms likely to retrieve many postings when it is really a more specific concept that is wanted.

—Use the most specific terms you can find to represent the concepts of a search.
—Avoid generic terms with many postings.

A second possible explanation of a retrieval set that contains records totally unrelated to the search problem is the occurrence of homographs in the database—e.g., words, acronyms, abbreviations—with multiple meanings. Such a term will retrieve records discussing all the concepts named by the term including many that are not on the subject wanted. For example, the term *salt* will retrieve records discussing various chemical compounds, Salt Lake City, as well as the Strategic Arms Limitation Talks.

The multiple meaning problem is most serious with multidisciplinary and popular databases. In *Magazine Index,* the term *mole* might refer to any of the following concepts: a spy, a congenital spot on the human body, an insectivore, or one gram molecule. *Mole* as spy is a popular term, but *mole* also has various technical or quasitechnical meanings in medicine, gardening and lawn care, biology, and chemistry. The searcher may have overwhelmed the "mole as one gram molecule" postings with postings to spies, congenital spots, gardening problems, or the biology of insectivores. The following heuristics are suggested:

—Watch out for homographs—words with more than one meaning.
—Use controlled vocabularies—thesauri, lists of subject headings, or classification codes—or specific search fields whenever possible to restrict a term to a particular meaning.

A careless set number error or command language error may also explain the lack of relevance of a retrieval set to the concepts of interest. In particular, the searcher may simply have typed records from an inappropriate retrieval set.

Often beginners follow their planning notes too unthinkingly. Their plans call for displaying records from set 7, so that is the command given even though for various reasons set 7 may not refer to the correct set in the search as it was actually conducted. A simple typo might also explain the result obtained.

—Watch for typos of set numbers.

—Don't follow your planning notes too slavishly; adjust set numbers in your notes to reflect what has actually taken place in the search.

A common error on DIALOG is to confuse the way in which set numbers are used with the *combine* and *select* commands. The command *combine 3* AND *7* creates the Boolean intersection of sets 3 and 7. However, the command *select 3* and *7* will create a set for the numeral *3*, another set for the numeral *7*, and combine these using Boolean AND. The result of the latter command will have nothing whatever to do with the previously created sets 3 and 7 or the underlying search problem.

To combine sets 3 and 7 using the *select* command on DIALOG, type: *select S3* AND *S7*.

—Be careful of confusing a numeral as a search term with a set number.

—Always precede a set number with the letter *S* when using the select command on DIALOG to perform Boolean operations.

Truncation is another possible explanation for retrieving records totally different from the subject. If a term is truncated too much, words representing different roots will be combined to form a retrieval set. Since many of these terms will not relate to the concept of interest, the result may be records totally off the subject wanted.

For example, searching on the truncated stem *LIB* will retrieve records containing the words *liberty, libation, libby,* and *libel,* as well as the library terms of *library, librarian,* and *librarianship.* The stem that one should search is *librar.*

Searching on the truncated stem *US* for the concept of "United States of America" will retrieve records containing the terms *use, ustinov,* and *usher,* as well as the wanted terms *US* and *USA.* Postings from these terms may greatly exceed the number of postings resulting from US and USA.

—Be careful where you truncate. A carelessly truncated stem may result in the retrieval of many records not on the concept wanted.

—Use Boolean *OR* to combine terms that are alphabetically related *rather than truncation* when truncation is likely to result in retrieval on unwanted terms.

Finally, it is possible, though not likely, that the reason the searcher has obtained records that seem to be totally unrelated to the subject is that he has not employed enough concepts (or facets) in his formulations.

Assume that the "subject" to be represented has three concepts to be intersected: *A* AND *B* AND *C*. If the original formulation is comprised of only two of these facets, then records will not be on the specific subject of the search. If this is the case, a possible solution is to create a search formulation for the third facet and intersect it with the previous two facets.

—Consider forming another facet to intersect with existing facets.

Note, however, that the tendency of most beginning searchers is to *overspecify* rather than underspecify problems. Underspecification is unlikely to be the source of difficulty, and other possibilities should be considered first.

MOST RATIONAL PATH

The previous section of this article proposed six subcategories of heuristics for a particular search state—i.e., that records retrieved in a search formulation are completely unrelated to the search problem. A total of fifteen heuristics, each representing a class of possible actions, were suggested as possible ways of addressing this retrieval state. Each of the fifteen, or a combination of several, are possible explanations (and solutions) of the state.

Which of these fifteen subclasses of heuristics should be employed in a given search in which this state is experienced? Should they all be considered, one by one, in checklist form? Or, more likely, is it possible that they will not work equally well in a given situation? In that case the searcher would need to carefully consider each heuristic in the context of the particular search being conducted to identify the one most likely to produce the desired retrieval results. It is the nature of heuristics, as compared to rules, that what works sometimes will not work at other times.

Moreover, given that a particular heuristic has been selected to pursue, many different formulations might be employed to operationalize it. Suppose that a searcher wants to increase precision and decides to implement the heuristic: Consider forming another facet to intersect with existing facets. Once the decision to implement this heuristic has been made, there are an infinity of ways to go about it involving choices of terms, proximity operators, fields, truncation, Boolean operators, etc. Thus the problem is not solved merely by selecting a heuristic to pursue; the searcher must then operationalize it by formulating system commands. In general, there are an infinity of possible formulations.

Each formulation would result in a different level of recall, precision, and cost if implemented. Imagine that the universe of possible formulations can be viewed as a three dimensional space where each point in the space is the retrieval result associated with a given formulation. As the searcher moves in this space, he attempts to approach as nearly as possible the recall, precision, and cost goals of the end user.

Some formulations are clearly better than others in the sense that better recall can be obtained for equivalent levels of precision and cost, or that higher precision can be achieved at an equivalent level of recall and cost.

One can hypothesize the existence of what might be called "the most rational path" (Harter, 1986, p. 199) through the infinity of search formulations derived from the various heuristics that might be employed. Visualize the searcher moving through this three-dimensional space. The most rational path is a three-dimensional surface which maximizes precision for given levels of recall and cost. Actions taken by an expert searcher will presumably approximate movements along this surface while actions taken by a novice may more closely resemble random movement through the space.

If cost is kept fixed or ignored, the three-dimensional surface becomes a two-dimensional plane, and the most rational path can be defined as the set of formulations that maximize recall for a given level of precision. The selection and operationalization of a heuristic is then simplified but potentially is still enormously complex.

It should be emphasized that these ideas are hypothetical and have not been subjected to empirical testing. They represent one view of the difference between an "expert" searcher and a nonexpert. However, little is known about how experts go about selecting which heuristics to pursue in a given search, or how to operationalize them when they have been selected. Indeed, little is known regarding which heuristics tend to be superior to others in general (that is, on the average), or even if such an idea makes sense. The idea of a "most rational path" must therefore be regarded as hypothetical.

Clearly many search problems are so simple that the ideas presented in this article are not applicable. A high school or college student who wants a dozen or two nontechnical references on AIDS for a three-page paper probably does not even need an online search. But if one is conducted, the searcher will need to employ few if any heuristics. A "fast batch" approach—an approach using few if any heuristics—will probably work quite well. It is not known what proportion of searches in the real world fall into this "simple" category, although it is obvious that a great many of them can be characterized in this way.

IMPLICATIONS

Training programs for online searching tend to stress learning the retrieval language—that is, to learn the syntax rules and other rules for logging on, inputting commands to the search system, and so on. But it could be argued that rules are relatively easy to teach and at the same time are less significant. (A significant difference between training and education may be that the former deals mainly with rules and the latter with heuristics.) Perhaps too much attention in online searching is paid to training concerns and too little is given to evaluative, conceptual, or artistic aspects of online information retrieval, especially the acquisition and effective use of heuristics. The diagnostic and tutorial software package *Online Search Analyst* was developed as an initial step in this direction.

End user search systems can be viewed in terms of the analysis just presented. Some end users search *Knowledge Index* and BRS After Dark systems that are now several years old. Others employ DIALOG, BRS, or other systems directly. Still others are beginning to search CD-ROM and videodisc systems physically located within the library.

By most accounts, end user searching is reported to be enormously successful in achieving user satisfaction. End users are reporting high levels of enthusiasm and success. How are these reports to be evaluated in light of the model of online searching as a problem-solving process, especially since end users typically are not only unfamiliar with search heuristics but also of the basic concepts and rules of online searching (syntax rules, Boolean logic, etc.). How is this possible if online searching is truly a problem-solving process as represented in this discussion?

One likely explanation of the reported successes of end user searching is that the recall goals of the individuals using these systems are not especially stringent—that goals of high precision are the norm. A second possibility is that the end user with comprehensive search goals lacks the knowledge to assess the extent to which recall goals are met. (Note that cost goals are typically not a consideration in end user searching supported by a library since connect time charges do not exist or are absorbed by the sponsoring library.)

If the end user only wants a few records, then good success can often be achieved by end users employing controlled vocabularies. In this case the end user could probably get by equally well with a print index. Alternatively, if a comprehensive search is wanted, then the end user is not likely to achieve success for a variety of reasons. This result should be distinguished from a result in which the end user thinks, erroneously, that he has achieved comprehensive retrieval results. An end user who is naïve about the extent of the literature on a subject may well conclude that he has found "everything" on a topic when in fact only a small portion of the available literature has been retrieved. The long-term effects of such cases are bound to be negative.

Obvious questions that are raised are:

1. Should libraries provide instruction in rules and heuristics for end users? If so, what should be the content of such instruction?
2. What are the implications of providing a complex and sophisticated search system and making it publicly available but *not* offering instruction in it? Is this ethically defensible?

Finally, some comments are in order regarding the development of expert systems to do information retrieval. Such systems must, presumably, be able to employ heuristics just as human experts do, at least for complex or comprehensive problems. However, systems do not yet exist that can make such independent decisions as:

—The present file is too "popular" for this particular search.
—Boolean operators were used improperly.
—This search term is too generic for the information need.
—This term is too common for use in representing the information needed.
—This term suffers from multiple meaning—steps must be taken to disambiguate it.
—A set number was used improperly.
—A term was truncated improperly.
—Another facet must be created and intersected to increase the precision of the search.

By and large, these decisions must still be made by human beings. Future expert systems in online information retrieval may make such decisions based on ongoing information provided by the end user in an interactive mode. But to do this effectively for complex and comprehensive searches, system designers will need to know much more about how experts search—the thought processes leading to the choice of one heuristic over another, and how particular heuristics are best operationalized. As noted, the current state of knowledge regarding these questions is extremely limited.

Some work in this area has been done. For example, Raya Fidel (1984) has studied how the expert searcher selects terms—e.g., free text vocabulary, controlled vocabulary elements, etc.—by analyzing the online searching behavior of several human intermediaries. Fidel identified several heuristics (she calls them "options") for selecting search terms, and reduced them to a set of rules formalized into a decision tree. She is optimistic about the design of expert systems for online searching through the study of the searching behavior of expert human intermediaries.

Although this author shares Fidel's view of the value that could result from a careful study of human experts, there is no optimism regarding the eventual design of an online searching machine that will do as well as or better than human expert intermediaries. Proponents of mechanical translation of languages in the 1950s and 1960s also felt that rules could be proposed that would eventually result in algorithms that would prepare expert translations of texts from one language—e.g., Russian—to another language—e.g., English. The goal of this research was to develop expert systems to do translation of languages. However, systems capable of producing expert translations of general texts without human intervention have never been developed.

Some of the problems inherent in doing online searching are the same problems that eventually caused extraordinary difficulties in creating computer programs to do mechanical translation of languages. These include: the importance of the problem context, the distinction between meaning and the representation of meaning in words and phrases as well as the computer's inability to recognize meaning as such, the existence of homographs in natural language, and the enormous complexity of language, especially at the semantic and pragmatic levels. These are extremely difficult problem areas. Only time will tell whether they are insurmountable.

In the meantime, educational and training programs for librarians as well as end users should be examined with the goal of evaluating the attention given to the study of online search heuristics. The study of heuristics rather than rules addresses the truly difficult and challenging aspects of online searching, and it is precisely here that training and educational programs for novice search specialists and end users, as well as commercial intermediary search systems, fall short.

REFERENCES

Bates, M. J. (1979a). Information search tactics. *Journal of the American Society for Information Science, 30*(July), 205-214.

Bates, M. J. (1979b). Idea tactics. *Journal of the American Society for Information Science, 30*(September), 280-289.

Fidel, R. (1984a). Online searching styles: A case-study-based model of searching behavior. *Journal of the American Society for Information Science, 35*(4), 211-221.

Fidel, R. (1984b). Toward expert systems for the selection of search keys. *Journal of the American Society for Information Science, 37*(1), 37-44.

Harter, S. P. (1987). *Online search analyst* [Computer program]. Bloomington, IN: Online Consultants of Indiana.

Harter, S. P. (1984a). Online searching styles: An exploratory study. *College & Research Libraries, 45*(4), 249-258.

Harter, S. P. (1984b). Scientific inquiry: A model for online searching. *Journal of the American Society for Information Science, 35*(March), 110-117.

Harter, S. P. (1986). *Online information retrieval: Concepts, principles, and techniques.* Orlando, FL: Academic Press.

Harter, S. P., & Peters, A. R. (1985). Heuristics for online information retrieval: A typology and preliminary listing. *Online Review, 9*(5), 407-424.

Smith, L. C. (1980). Implications of artificial intelligence for end user use of online systems. *Online Review, 4,* 383-391.

Smith, L. C. (1976). Artificial intelligence in information retrieval systems. *Information Processing and Management, 12,* 189-222.

Swanson, D. R. (1986). Undiscovered public knowledge. *Library Quarterly, 56*(2), 103-118.

Swanson, D. R. (1979). Libraries and the growth of knowledge. *Library Quarterly, 49*(1), 3-25.

Swanson, D. R. (1977). Information retrieval as a trial-and-error process. *Library Quarterly, 47*(April), 128-148.

Swanson, D. R. (1963). The formulation of the retrieval problem. In P. L. Garvin (Ed.), *Natural language and the computer* (pp. 255-67). New York: McGraw Hill.

Taylor, R. S. (1968). Question-negotiation and information seeking in libraries. *College & Research Libraries, 29*(3), 178-194.

Taylor, R. S. (1962). The process of asking questions. *American Documentation, 13*(October), 391-396.

CHARLES T. MEADOW

Professor
Library and Information Science
University of Toronto
Toronto, Ontario

Tailoring System Design to Users

We seem to have finally reached the point of almost general acceptance of the concept that computer software should be designed for ease of human use. There remain questions, however, of whose ease and of what is meant by tailoring design to users.

Design for Whom?—Some Fallacies

Thirty years ago software had to be designed first to accommodate hardware. Whether it was speed or reliability at issue, the foibles of the computers had to be catered to. They were expensive, more so than their programmers or operators, so operating speed was a critical factor. Software designed in this manner is mainly gone now.

The convenience of the programmer is another possible design goal. It is simply easier to write a parser of syntactic statements that says "syntax error" than to have that program explain what the error was, how it was detected, or what the user might do about it. A spreadsheet program does not have to wait until you have used up all available space and then announce a fatal memory overflow error. It could warn you ahead of time, but it is easier to wait.

Yet a third object of design may be an erroneous assumption about user characteristics. Program authors are not always thinking selfishly of their own interests. Sometimes they mean well but do not understand those who are not professional programmers or, horrors, those who do not have much interest in programming. This author began his career as a professional programmer, a profession to be respected. I understand and still share the fascination with computers and getting them to do one's bidding. But one of the aspects that was always the most fascinating was the

121

different levels at which one could deal with a computer. There was never much interest in the hardware. I was always content to view the machine as defined by its programming languages. But the programming languages do not normally include any way of dealing with intricate timing problems or unreliable discs. To some extent, a user has to know the hardware, but for me it is always the least that can be gotten away with and never the most that can be learned.

The point here is the belief that some programmers assume that all users are as interested in the detailed operation as they themselves are. They do not reply to an error with the message "syntax error" out of meanness, but because they truly believe that all users: (1) know the syntax or the general language structure thoroughly, and (2) will not rest until they have worked out the nature of the error. That, after all, is how the hypothetical program author would have behaved. This seems to be the basis upon which UNIX was designed—an operating system that generally assumes everything is being done correctly and either does not respond to errors or does so only minimally. (UNIX does not require that it be used in this way—organizations can build in their own user interfaces, but apparently not many do so.)

In fact, however, many simply lack the time and interest to pursue intricate details of program malfunctions. They may go to the extreme of abandoning use of the program rather than spending an entire evening reading the users' manual. It is a defensible point of view, but one that does not often enter the consciousness of software designers.

The so-called end user is more likely to have this last point of view than he or she is to share the programmer's point of view and fascination for computer details. The key is to design software for the user and take the trouble to find out who that user is.

Who are End Users?

Who then are end users and what do they want from their software? The very term is something of a negative descriptor. It is not truly a positive description of a person. It is merely an assertion that this is a person who is not a search intermediary, or, in programming terms, not a professional programmer. Whoever they are, the world is only now discovering them and making the usual noises of discoverers enchanted with their finds. But they have been around forever. An end user is simply a consumer rather than a provider of information service. We all play the role at some time, even if information service providers by profession. Hence, an end user is someone operating, at least temporarily, outside his or her own profession.

To design for end users, it must first be determined who they are, what their interests are, and what they do when they are using the particular type of software in question. In other words, tailoring design to users does not, and cannot, mean treating all users alike. We should try to negate the earlier statement that end users are temporarily operating outside their own professions and bring searching into their various professions.

Often software is described in such terms as natural language interface, menu-driven, or user friendly as if these words alone guaranteed proper user support. But the first two are technical terms descriptive of the means of representing information. They are not sufficient to describe a means of communication between user and system. It has to be known what is to be said in natural language, or what information is to be represented in a menu, how it is represented, and in what context it is presented. The term *user friendly* has no meaning at all to this author.

Why is it Important to Design for Users?

Learned language affects the understanding of the world around us. That is essentially the hypothesis of Benjamin Whorf (1956) the linguist. If that language is a computer programming language (which domain includes database command languages), then a user is going to understand computer functions in terms of the language learned. If the language is low level, difficult for the person to learn, and limited in functional capability, then the user's perception of what can be done in a database search is necessarily limited. If users are to treat database searching as a routine part of their own professions, they must be allowed to "see" database searching in their own professional terminology.

Some Cases

In-Search

Probably the best known intermediary software for online database searching, until about a year ago, was In-Search (Newlin, 1985). It originally appeared in 1983 and was intended as an end user intermediary for DIALOG, presumably for any user of any of DIALOG's then about 200 diverse databases. Its advertising stressed ease of use compared to use of the DIALOG language.

My personal assessment was that it would not work out. This, of course, is stated with the benefit of hindsight. But In-Search had a rather thick users' manual, came with six discs (including four holding the content of DIALOG's "blue sheets" or brief database descriptions), and many found that installation was relatively difficult. The original plan was for the database descriptions to be updated by direct downloading of the corrections to the user's computer. This plan was never realized.

It had basically only one way to search. True, there was no need to learn commands, but a user did have to use Boolean expressions, previous set numbers, truncation, proximity, etc. Hence, In-Search forgave only use of the name of a command for searching. It had no active help; it merely simplified the command language.

On the good side, the programming craftsmanship was superb. There was imaginative use of windows, and the method of searching one of In-Search's files, such as that of database descriptions, used simulated index cards. Everyone knows how to do that without any real instruction. Each card had a tab with a short title or code, and the current card popped up as the user riffled through the "deck." This is what happens when a manual file is searched. Truly, here was a form of searching that needed no instruction. But this was not how DIALOG was searched. It was only how the database descriptions were searched. The telecommunications were good. This part of In-Search later served as the basis for DIALOGLINK (Witiak, 1986).

The idea to convert In-Search to Pro-Search (Quint, 1986) was probably a good one. It reduced the market but ensured a better fit of product to users. When it was converted, a new accounting function was added which is of great use to institutional searchers who must charge services back to clients.

Info Globe

Info Globe is an online database containing the text of the Toronto *Globe and Mail* newspaper (Ross, 1981). Its basic search language is somewhat cumbersome. What is interesting is the array of front end techniques that Info Globe has developed to overcome this, tending to be fitted to the situation. An example is a method of scrolling of headlines based on selection of articles by use of menus and a few key words. The menu portion might get the user to the point of asking for a search based on company name. The user then enters the name and scrolling begins, showing date and headline.

The advantage is that if you know what you are looking for and approximately how to get it, it goes very fast and places little demand on the user. The versions this author tried were developed for securities analysts; people who probably can be relied upon to know how to spell the company name without much difficulty. In this sense, it is fitted to the user's knowledge of the field in which he will search and his assumed lack of interest in having to get too involved in a search.

A disadvantage for anyone who knows much about searching is that a complex search can be difficult to express. But choices must be made if products are to be designed for users, and no product is going to be well suited to all potential users.

Stock Quotation Systems

While having no personal experience with this class of system, they are intriguing because at least some of them operate on the basis of a single type of query—i.e., one may ask for current information on the shares of a given company, or not ask—the question is constant. The single variable is the name of the company entered as a stock market symbol. The output is fixed, consisting of latest price, recent high, low, sales volume, etc.

For persons not familiar with the market, this system can be useless because they may not know the ticker symbols and they might not know how to interpret the data. A highly specialized language is in use, but the people who work in this field or who trade in the market all know the language, so its use causes no trouble. It takes time to develop the skill, but this is not time taken out of the regular job—it is part of the job and the skill would have to be learned with or without the computer system.

Aspects of Systems to Consider

What aspects of a system can be tailored for the user? Realistically, expect that there are limits and that software people have always been able to conceive of and promise far more than could be produced.

Databases

In general, the search system is considered and not the database. If the database does not have the kind of informaiton the searcher wants, there is relatively little the search system can do about it, except to recommend or help find another database. This author has tried several times to find material in *MEDLINE* that can give information in layman's terms about some medical condition a personal physician has not fully explained. It does not work well; *MEDLINE* does not generally include such material, and the database cannot be faulted for not having what it was not intended to cover, nor can any intermediary find information that is not there. On the other hand, in the early days of the industry, ERIC on DIALOG did not permit limiting a search by publication year. Instead, the searcher had to use ERIC accession numbers. The real pros kept a table showing the first number occurring in each year. A search service or a search front end could easily have done the same and made the conversion for the less experienced searcher.

Display

Dealing with full text is another example of where the search service or mediator can overcome inherent database problems. The search software, whether centralized or front end, can divide the text into smaller segments and can use highlighting to help the user see the context that would lead to retrieval of any text segment. For example, the option to display only the individual paragraphs that contain search terms can be offered. Without this, if only the full item were retrieved, browsing would be more difficult.

Time and Cost

Fiscal and time controls can be built in which are often necessary especially when a library allows patron access to its accounts and must exercise some sort of control over use. A very simple example is the practice, now fairly popular, of allowing the user to prepare and store a query before automatic logon to the search service. A similar technique used by EasyNet and Search Helper is to run a search, download some records, then log off. While this detracts from the full interactive potential of most retrieval systems, it does accomplish the objective, important to some users, of tight cost control.

Types of Question

Most accommodations to user style, interest, and knowledge in use of software can be made in language and type of question asked. First, just as in the stock market systems, there are often quite standardized questions in any profession that require only the addition of one or more values at search time. Such questions are coming to be called scripts. Selective dissemination of information (SDI) is a form of this; the search is defined once and then run repeatedly, changing only the date or database update code each time. The same can be done for company information searches—for example, defining what kind of information is sought beforehand and filling in the name of the company at search time. It can be done in searches for articles about the toxic effects of a substance where the substance name is provided at search time and the toxic effects portion defined well beforehand.

As an extension of this concept, professional searchers might prepare for their company or laboratory an extensive library of search segments or scripts, carefully and completely defining key subjects of interest. These could then be assembled by the user who could add his/her own information—such as dates, corporate sources, or authors of interest—at the time of the search. The tailoring process comes with the design of a system that can store and assemble search fragments. The creation of the fragments is up to user organizations.

Vocabulary and Syntax

There are two sets of vocabulary and sometimes syntax to consider—e.g., that used to describe the content of records and that used to tell the retrieval system what to do. First consider the content descriptive language. There is no substitute for the searcher's understanding of the vocabulary of the field in which he or she is searching. There are ways to help find terms, but it is hard to imagine successful searching of, say, chemical or legal files not based on a good grasp of the vocabulary of the fields.

A number of computer assistance programs were developed to aid in selection of the vocabulary or its improvement based on preliminary trials (Marcus, 1983). But in general they depend on the user to be able to recognize which of the offered "associated" terms would be most helpful where there is a host of definitions of word association. This is quite reasonable: if the person does not know the vocabulary, there is hardly any way to judge the value of—hence to select—retrieved items.

When it comes to the language that is used to tell the computer what to do, rather than what the desired information looks like, it is important to avoid bringing in new vocabulary and usages. These can intrude on the search process or require the investment of significant amounts of time before the search process can begin. Longitudinal studies of how users have adapted over time to a new information system are rare to nonexistent. Lacking formal proof, one must make do with informal studies and intuition.

Experience and intuition indicate that users do not want to spend much time learning to use systems. They want to start right in using them. Then, as they become more experienced, they will gradually recognize what they cannot do and look either for improvement in the system or for greater knowledge of how to use it. To designers, this means making the system simple to learn but expandable. A requirement for learning is acceptable when users have a precise goal, know what they want to do, and seek instruction in how to accomplish their goals. In other words, when a user wants to be able to change the sequence of records in the output, he will be amenable to seeking instruction in use of the sort procedure. But seeking instruction in information before using the system will not meet with ready acceptance.

Of course people vary. The suggestions just stated apply to myself and to many others, but there are also those who want to start a new endeavor by reading all about it first.

The Expected Output

One of the great fallacies of online searching is that everyone wants high recall or even high precision. It is a fallacy to believe that the average searcher even thinks in these terms let alone uses them for setting a goal.

There are, however, recognizable classes of objectives which have system design implications. There are users who want "everything" on a subject, one implication of which is high volume output. Another possibility is that the results will be used as part of a document, hence the need for processing of the retrieved records in the correct format. Yet another common possibility is that the searcher wants only "a few good items," which implies no particular need for any further processing or storage beyond the ability to print or download a few records.

These goals can be designed for fairly easily. Downloading is now common and often the records can be in a format acceptable to word processing software. For those needing programmed reformatting there is such software as Pro-Cite (Hoyle & McNamara, 1987). For those needing no special handling, none need be provided thereby avoiding asking the user cumbersome questions about what is wanted and how to get it.

How to do This

In any activity, more options mean more decision-making; this, in turn, means that more information must go from the system to the decision-maker and from the decision-maker to the system. This is true when doing an online search, buying a computer, or buying a shirt. When buying a shirt, however, the task is usually simplified by such measures as adopting favorite brands, shops, or colors. Every type of fabric or style need not be investigated because we know about them or know as much as we want to know. There is a willingness to risk a mistake to avoid the time required to find out about possible new fabrics each time one shops.

In computer buying, the buyer is probably doing the corresponding thing—using brand preference or looking for a clone of a preferred brand and a fairly standard configuration. If an experienced buyer, one may well be fatalistic and take the attitude that any selection made may well be outdated by a new announcement next week—and not worry about it.

In online searching, we are to some extent still expecting customers to consider everything, to invest the time and energy required to make the most intelligent decision each time. This is just not realistic. Just as there is a limit on how much we care about an error in shirt buying, most users have a limit on how much they care about online search results.

Hence, a critical design feature of any search service should be that it not ask more of the user than the user wants to invest in it. Command language systems tend to ask too much of end users. There is too much to learn before effective use. This means that search systems should be designed to have a different appearance to different classes of users.

How can this be done? There is a need for more than merely the option to replace long computer messages with short ones. There should be systems that truly behave differently for different users. Someday there may be computer programs that are able to determine the level and intensity of use the user wants and to respond accordingly. This lies in the domain of artificial intelligence. Human beings are not universally adept at this. It may even be suggested that those with great depth of subject matter knowledge will be most reluctant to adapt themselves to the unknowing client, and that those with the greatest adaptation skills may lack depth of subject knowledge. It is not even clear, if this hypothesis is accepted, that there is a good model of human behavior to try to replicate in a computer program.

A personal preference for a short-term approach to this problem (the problem, remember, is designing a system that has the right appearance or makes the right demands on its user) is different programs for different situations. There is no universal reference book. It is accepted that different subjects and depths of presentation demand different typographic and contextual designs. Users do have to invest some effort in finding the appropriate book, but repeat users will return to the same sources again and again and not have to go through the selection process each time.

We can do this—continuing to borrow a design concept from the print world—by allowing individual authors who can visualize a problem situation to design for that situation. A "situation" is a combination of a set of available information and potential users. The physician interested in current information about drugs on the market has a different need than the research pharmacologist; the average undergraduate has a different need than the average professor and so on. In all these cases, the different groups may have not only different needs, but different searching or computer-using skills and available funds as well.

There are a number of search "front ends" or computer intermediaries available, and they do reflect different user needs and skills. Pro-Search has high expectations but allows the skilled user to exercise all the many logical search options DIALOG (and now BRS) can offer. EasyNet (O'Leary, 1985) requires no preparation before use but limits the precision with which the user can control a search. My own system, OAK (Meadow et al., 1989), which was developed for the Department of Energy, falls between these. The user is expected to be well educated but not necessarily in searching techniques. OAK, like EasyNet, requires no prior instruction, but it is offered and better results can be expected if it is used. The system is designed for bibliographic database searching. It would not serve well, in the same form, for numeric database searching, nor would the others mentioned. There are different relationships to be stated, hence different language requirements for doing so.

A program like DIALOGLINK is not a front end in the sense that this author means it. DIALOGLINK does not change the language of communication with DIALOG. It helps a great deal with telecommunications and allows for local storage of the search statements, but users still talk DIALOG's language.

To accommodate the diversity of front ends that are needed, the central services should be designed to expect their use and not merely tolerate them. No software change is required to do this. The central system does not know whether it is receiving its command language statements from a person or a computer since the normal means of operation has the front end translating the user's expressions—however they may be stated—into the target system's commands.

A central service could design a lower level command language, one requiring less effort on its own part to parse, and then require that all use be via a front end. One form of front end, of course, could deal in the traditional command language. But others need not use anything resembling the "native" languages. An incentive for the central services to do this is that the parsing function would be largely carried out at the user end in the user's computer. The user is connected for the same amount of time, but the work is done outside the central system thereby increasing its work capacity.

Another requirement of this mode of operation is that central services be prepared to warn independent front end designers of impending changes. This is not a characteristic of the industry now. Both search and communications services are willing to make changes without warning other software vendors who are dependent on them.

In this way, any central retrieval service could be accessed by any number of front ends, each designed to suit its users' needs and capabilities, likes, dislikes, and budget. This is fundamentally no different than a computer manufacturer planning for users to use a wide variety of software, not all produced by itself. In the long run, this would make the search services more attractive to more users.

Summary

What has been attempted to be covered in this discussion can be summed up briefly. Computer software, regardless of the application, is something worked with and not merely consulted. Some of it is very complex. Some of it is not well suited to the needs and skill levels of its intended users. There is no reason why this should continue, at least not in the database search field, because it is relatively easy to separate the user interface from the main system.

People will use systems that are easy to use. A professional goal should be to make systems easier to use without trivializing them. A major way to do this, at least in the short run, is to design systems around specific user groups who share common professional jargon and use of databases, and to arrange for standardized mechanical interfaces with the major retrieval services. This approach has the added advantage of allowing for totally different points of view on how to search databases to be available to users.

The point is to give the users the choice of method and not reserve it for the distributors.

REFERENCES

Hoyle, N., & McNamara, K. (1987). Biblio-Link and Pro-Cite: The searcher's workstation. *Database, 10*(February), 73-78.

Marcus, R. S. (1983). An experimental comparison of the effectiveness of computers and humans as search intermediaries. *Journal of the American Society for Information Science, 34*(6), 381-404.

Meadow, C. T.; Cerney, B.; Borgman, C. L.; & Case, D. O. (1989). Online access to knowledge: System design. *Journal of the American Society for Information Science, 40*(2), 86-98.

Newlin, B. B. (1985). In-Search: The design and evolution of an end user interface to DIALOG. In M. E. Willimas & T. H. Hogan (Eds.), *Proceedings of the 6th national online meeting* (pp. 313-19). Medford, NJ: Learned Information.

Niehoff, R.; Kwosny, S.; & Wessells, M. (1979). Overcoming the database vocabulary barrier— a solution. *Online, 3*(4), 43-54.

O'Leary, M. (1985). EasyNet: Doing it all for the end-user. *Online, 9*(4), 106-113.

Quint, B. (1986). Menlo Corporation's Pro-Search: Review of a software search aid. *Online, 10*(1), 17-25.

Ross, N. M. (1981). Newspaper databases. In M. E. Williams (Ed.), *Proceedings of the national online meeting* (pp. 415-20). Medford, NJ: Learned Information.

Whorf, B. J. (1956). In J. B. Carroll (Ed.), *Language, thought and reality: Selected writings* (p. iv). Cambridge, MA: MIT Press.

Witiak, J. (1986). Dialoglink: A review of DIALOG's search assistance software. *Online, 10*(6), 39-42.

BETH S. WOODARD

Central Information Services Librarian
Library General Services
Library
University of Illinois at Urbana-Champaign

Strategies for Providing Public Service with an Online Catalog

Dagmar Schmidmaier (1983) has written that:

> The online catalogue is not simply a new tool which performs the same functions, via the same access points as the card catalogue. The online catalogue provides the user with an expanded and more convenient access to bibliographic records and it provides functional capabilities which are much more varied and powerful than those of any other form of the catalogue. The online catalogue is an interactive information retrieval system and its significance lies in the way the user can be assisted.... (p. 2)

In light of this viewpoint that the online catalog is not simply a card catalog on wheels, but a significantly different tool utilizing alternative approaches to providing the patron with not only the traditional card catalog information but also additional information, what strategies can librarians take to enhance service to their patrons both in answering specific questions and in providing instruction in catalog use?

STRATEGIES FOR DIRECT SERVICE TO PATRONS

The online catalog at the University of Illinois at Urbana-Champaign (UIUC) consists of two separate systems—LCS, purchased from Ohio State University, is a short-record automated circulation system with limited access points by main name entry, title, and call number, and FBR, purchased from Western Library network, which provides full bibliographic records through multiple access points including Library of Congress Subject Headings. The two systems are linked so that those using the full record portion can enter a simple command to find the availability and location of a particular item. LCS, while limited in the number of access points, has some advantages over FBR in that it is excellent for known items particularly one word titles since it uses words in order in the title. It also has all the items cataloged at UIUC. FBR, with its much more sophisticated structure, has unique access points such as keyword in title which can be manipulated in various ways providing different advantages. However, it provides access to a small number of items—i.e., those cataloged using OCLC which the library started using in 1975.

IMPROVED USEFULNESS FOR VERIFICATION

The reference librarian or staff member attempting to find materials for patrons often notices that bibliographic citations for items may be totally correct and complete but incompatible with the form or choice of entry in the library's catalog. Examples of this type of citation would include items listed as monographs in a bibliography but which the library has cataloged as a series, or conference proceedings which may have either individual or series titles. The online catalog provides multiple access points to obtain the correct entry. For example, the patron looking for the First Congress of International Physicians for the Prevention of Nuclear War can simply type in Find Corporate Author (KAC—Keyword Author Corporate) Physicians Nuclear to find the papers which are cataloged under the title *Last Aid: The Medical Dimensions of Nuclear War.*

Librarians are also often challenged with incomplete or incorrect citations. Prior to the implementation of the online catalog, reference librarians expended a great deal of time and effort verifying an item with words out of order, extraneous words added, misspellings, or with the subtitle in place of the actual title, only to have to return to LCS or the card catalog when it was discovered in *Union List of Serials, NUC (National Union Catalog),* or OCLC, that the University of Illinois actually owned the item in question. With an online catalog, when patrons give incorrect information it is easy to use keywords in those titles to identify the true or proper title. For example, one patron requested a University of Illinois Press book called *Daughters of Misery; Sisters of Shame.* A keyword in the title search "Find Title Daughters Misery" retrieves nothing. A librarian can either eliminate words such as "Find" "Title" "Daughters" "Misery" or search the stem of the ISBN number to identify works by the University of Illinois Press and combine with a keyword in the title, "Find ISBN 025201# .and. title Daughters." Either search would bring up the correct title *Daughters of Joy, Sisters of Misery: Prostitutes in the American West, 1865-90.* While using a card catalog would have retrieved the correct title immediately because the first word is correct, this example illustrates the reliance of the card catalog on alphabetic cues. If the first word in the title is incorrect, it would not be retrievable in the card catalog. Similarly, verifying the item by checking *Books in Print* also relies only on alphabetic cues. A patron bringing a title *Economic Problem-Solving in Brazil, 1956-1969* would not be able to identify the title in the card catalog because the actual title is *Politics of Export Promotion,* and the title the patron brought is the subtitle. A keyword title search would have found the item easily.

Access to other materials through the online catalog has greatly expanded its usefulness to librarians. Reference librarians previously had to consult the card catalog, the serial record, the shelflist, the thesis file, individual department circulation files, as well as order files and check-in records in the acquisitions department to gain access to the information that is now available in the online catalog. While librarians in the reference department always had access to the thesis file, main catalog, and serial record, they were frequently asked by other libraries on campus to search these files. Now author and title from the main catalog, full record information for items cataloged from 1975, approval plan materials, orders, and serial check-in files are available to anyone who has access to a terminal. Not only are items not traditional to a card catalog added, but they are added at a much faster rate. While the card catalog filing backlog at one time was two years, the time lag for adding materials to the online catalog is now approximately two weeks.

As Leigh Estabrook (1983) has pointed out: "Potentially, the online catalog can provide access to more recent materials more quickly; and, when it is used for interlibrary loan, the online catalog can more easily provide access to a wider range of materials" (p. 73). The UIUC online catalog has extended its users' capabilities to find information outside the Urbana campus collection through the additional holdings available from the other twenty-eight schools in the LCS network which can be directly charged and borrowed from an online catalog terminal. William Potter's (1986) study shows that this statewide resource sharing via LCS using the interface "resulted in an increase in interlibrary borrowing at one library from 3 percent to 8 percent of the total circulation in just two years" (p. 244). To further service, the Illinois State Library supports an LCS terminal in all eighteen regional headquarters of ILLINET, the state network. As Betsy Wilson (1986) describes it, this access "expands exponentially the ramifications of known-item searching" (p. 6).

The relationship of the statewide LCS with direct patron borrowing also affects strategies patrons take when identifying a title they need in the local collection but to which they cannot gain access because the item is checked out. While some of the LCS direct borrowing use of other schools is for items not owned by this library, some are also for items owned but unavailable such as those which are checked out or on reserve. To most patrons this means only one thing—that they cannot take the book home.

The implication is that LCS direct borrowing may actually serve different needs than traditional interlibrary loan since those statistics are completely separate. In following ILL codes, items owned and checked out to another patron or on reserve are normally not requested from other libraries unless they are missing. Through LCS, patrons can go directly to another school for both unique items in other collections and duplicate items and obtain them in a more timely fashion.

The statewide LCS system also helps reference librarians make better referrals. Students going home on spring break often do research in their hometown college library or travel to nearby locations and wish to know if certain items are held there. This function of reference service will presumably be even better with statewide full bibliographic records.

READY REFERENCE QUESTIONS

The use of the catalog to answer questions was probably never better illustrated than by Isadore Mudge (1935), who cited the example of the student who used the catalog to study for an exam (p. 11). Winifred Ver Nooy (1940) illustrated the variety and breadth of biographical information available on R. R. Bowker in the card catalog (pp. 313-20). Similar kinds of information also exist in an online catalog, of course, although it may not be so readily apparent.

An example of a ready reference question which can be answered with the online catalog is "how is 'Demming' spelled?" In this case, the patron knew only that "demming" is a concept concerning quality control in factories, that it might be spelled with two *m*s, that it is probably named after someone, and that it is a recent concept. After cursory examination of some dictionaries of terms, a librarian could easily try the online catalog to see if a book was written about this topic. A keyword in title search of "demming" only reveals one title which is a children's book. A keyword in title search of an alternate spelling "deming" reveals eleven bibliographic items with "deming" in the title. A quick examination shows item nine as *The Keys to Excellence: The Story of the Deming Philosophy* to be a likely title. After viewing the full record, the librarian can see that the subject heading "Quality Control" is assigned and is also assured that this is the correct spelling. The online catalog, then, may be used to successfully answer ready reference questions as well as bibliographic or holdings questions.

This example also illustrates that reference librarians must be even more aware of variant spellings because the computer will retrieve only what is entered into it. A certain amount of inconsistency can be absorbed in a card catalog because of the "fumble factor" and because a human

being can examine each element of information and make allowances for
variation. Another example of the elimination of the "fumble factor"
would be hyphenated words such as test-tube babies or the title *Cultural-
Ecological Perspectives on Southeast Asia* in which the hyphenated word
must be entered as one word on LCS.

STRATEGIES FOR SEARCHING A SUBJECT

Douglas Ferguson (1982) notes that the online catalog "users report
subject search objectives in numbers almost as high as specific item search
objectives. The percent of subject searching is far higher than reported in
studies of manual catalogs" (p. v). Subject searching in any catalog is a
difficult proposition. In an online catalog, there has been much debate on
the extent to which the traditional subject headings are adequate.

In an online catalog such as UIUC's, there are many ways a librarian
can help a patron gain access to library materials by subject. The most
obvious one is through the use of Library of Congress Subject Headings
available online in an authority file. By accessing this authority file, all
instances of a subject heading, whether in the first subfield (which would
show up in an alphabetic LCSH or in a card catalog), or in subsequent
subfields (which would not show up in the regular alphabetic listing), are
brought together in one listing. This ability to see all subject headings at a
terminal is a very useful feature. For example, a "Term Subject Somalia"
or T S Somalia search brings together such alphabetically-dispersed headings as Explorers—Somalia—Biography and Somalia—Discovery and
Exploration or Herders—Somalia and Nomads—Somalia or Military
Bases, Russian—Somalia and Russian—Foreign Relations—Somalia and
Somalia—Foreign Relations—Russia.

The use of the Boolean operators AND, OR, and NOT combining
subject headings or subject headings with corporate authors or words in
the title is a potentially powerful tool. At present it is somewhat hampered
by the arbitrary limitation of the number of items searchable at one time in
an effort to keep computer search time from being too lengthy. This
"intermediate hit" problem, so called because of the message given by the
computer, keeps subjects with large numbers of items, such as Illinois or
United States, from being searched. When used appropriately, users can
combine such different headings as "Narcotics, Control of" and "Smuggling" in order to find books with both subject headings.

Implied Boolean searching is a very powerful strategy available to
online catalog users. This allows the user to find a subject term anywhere
in a subject heading in the bibliographic file and to combine it with
another subject term anywhere in a subject heading merely by connecting

the two terms with a double-dash. For example, instead of entering "Find Subject Narcotics, Control of .and. Subject Smuggling," all that is necessary is to type in " Find Subject Narcotics, Control of—Smuggling," as if smuggling was a subfield. This search will retrieve items that contain both terms wherever they appear in the subject tracings. They need not be part of the same tracing. While implied Boolean searching is very useful, the librarian must be careful to watch for false drops. For example, if "Find Subject United States—Defense" is entered, the patron and the librarian will be surprised to find a book by the title *Football's Fierce Defenses* retrieved. If one looks at the tracings or the access points for that record, it is obvious that all the subject headings are strung together making defense from "Football—Defense" and United States from "Football Players—United States—Biography" retrievable as if they were together in one subject heading. If the patron or librarian had gone into the authority file first, inputting "Term Subject United States—Defense" and finding the bibliographic records directly from that file, only five records would have been retrieved, all with the exact heading United States—Defense such as the record for *Defense Challenges of the 80s*. Implied Boolean searching allows manipulation of subject subfields, allows the user to narrow or broaden the number of items found, and sometimes eliminates the problem of intermediate hits.

Probably the most useful strategy for finding subjects in an online catalog is using the keyword in title approach. While librarians have always tried to teach their clientele the usefulness of tracings in subject searching, the prior necessity of a known title precluded all but a few users from taking advantage of this knowledge. Using keywords from probable titles helps identify both titles and subjects because nonfiction titles are often indicative of subject matter. For the patron looking for a few books on the Strategic Defense Initiative or drug use in sports, entering "Find Title Star Wars Defense" or "Find Title Drugs Sports" is a good way to get around LC's inevitable time-lag in keeping up with terminology. Using the ability to look at the full record to identify tracings or the headings or expand commands which list tracings and tracings along with *see* and *see also* references, respectively, allows the patron to identify relevant subject headings such as Ballistic Missile Defenses, Weapons Systems, Space Weapons, or Strategic Defense Initiative or Doping in Sports or Anabolic Steroids to use for a more comprehensive search.

Truncation is another strategy online catalog users, both librarians and patrons, can use to identify all items in the system on a particular subject. A person entering "Find Subject Smoking" retrieves 156 bibliographic items. Combining the search with a Boolean "OR" with cigarette# and smok# retrieves 171 items—15 more than the subject search alone.

PATRON USE AND INSTRUCTION
Physical Access

Patrons can physically access the UIUC online catalog in a number of ways. With a card catalog, patrons had to use the central card catalog to access the entire collection. Individual departmental libraries' card catalogs listed only what was in that individual library. It was especially difficult for people in interdisciplinary studies to access the library's holdings in several locations, and it also meant that undergraduates sometimes limited themselves just to what was located in the undergraduate library because the library system was too intimidating.

For the online catalog, 250 terminals, at least one in each of forty departmental libraries, are provided. Busier units, like the undergraduate library or the information desk in the main card catalog area, have multiple terminals—twelve and twenty-four respectively. Patrons can also dial up the system from campus offices, from dorm rooms using a local computer hookup called Localnet, or from across the state or the country through the use of a modem and a personal computer. Not only can patrons search the database from outside the library but also charge out the materials to themselves and have materials sent to their campus address. This remote access to the entire collection has affected not only how patrons access the collection but also the questions reference librarians receive over the phone. Librarians answer fewer holdings questions from other libraries within the campus but answer more procedural and instructional questions about the online catalog from patrons.

Modes of Access

Two searching modes are available for patron use. The first is the command mode in which the patron must know the command structure in order to access the online catalog. This mode is available on all terminals, but it is the only mode available on almost all staff terminals on over half of the patron terminals in the library and on all dial-up ports. While LCS has a fairly simple and easy to use command structure, FBR is a little more complex. This complexity often creates problems for users who are not familiar with the two systems and their separate command structures. For example, a patron wanting a book about Enuma Elish, the Babylonian creation myth, would normally just look in the card catalog under the title of the work not realizing what kind of entry it was. He or she would have no idea that to find this in the online catalog necessitates an author-uniform title search. A key search entering "Key Enuma Elish" would identify the number of times the term or phrase is used in FBR and the appropriate search keys such as "Term Author Uniform Title" or "Find Author" in the bibliographic file.

In an attempt to free the user from questioning the librarian as Dagmar Schmidmaier (1983) suggests, an interface program was written to allow the patron to use the system by answering simple questions without knowledge of system commands and protocols (pp. 3-4). The interface works on a personal computer rather than on the mainframe allowing customizing of individual terminals with specific locations or local idiosyncrasies and borrowing policies rather than reliance on a universal statewide system. This allows interaction to be at the local level within the personal computer rather than consuming time with long-distance telecommunications. Some of the advantages are that a personal computer cannot formulate a "wrong" search as in mixing LCS commands with FBR or in entering the wrong number of letters. It is especially good for first time users and for searching other LCS campuses. Normally, those commands would have to be reentered for each campus searched, but the interface strings the same command with different location codes very quickly. Terminals with the interface program can also access the system by commands so that both modes are available at one terminal. Unfortunately, the interface is not yet available for purchase by individuals so that all dial-up users must learn the commands.

An analysis of online catalog questions recorded by the information desk staff before and after the introduction of the interface program indicates that patrons asked fewer questions about the online catalog after it was implemented. Monthly LCS terminal statistics created from transaction logs indicate that for the month of December 1986, interface terminals averaged 11,000 LCS transactions per month while dumb terminals ranged from 326 to 5,400 depending on their location.

Administrative Structure

These divergent methods of physical access and searching modes have created demands for different services. The library has responded administratively to devise strategies to deal with these service demands.

Douglas Ferguson (1980) stresses "that public service librarians cannot sit on the sidelines while patron access systems are being discussed, planned, and built" (p. 9). The notion that reference librarians can make meaningful contributions in the planning stage is one that has been addressed substantially in the literature. "It is essential that the reference librarian, as a knowledgeable and frequent user of the catalogue, help to shape the product, particularly in terms of content, format and the man machine interface" (Schmidmaier, 1983, p. 6). Similarly, public service librarians should also be represented on committees involving maintenance of the online catalog to provide essential representation of the user's perceptions in the ongoing development of the system. At UIUC, the Online Catalog Advisory Committee is made up of both technical services and public services librarians who make recommendations about changes in the interface program, port assignments or allocations, etc. This way the people who observe the problems that patrons encounter with the system have input into potential solutions.

Telephone Center

Since library users no longer need to be physically in the library to utilize its collections or services, a large number of phone requests are received. The UIUC Library has set up a Telephone Center for phone queries dealing with routine online catalog procdures such as renewals, saves, charging, or simple known-item searches of both systems and state-wide LCS. As was the case at Ohio State University, UIUC library users have also found that the ability to renew books over the phone or to have books charged out and sent to their dorm or campus office "has funneled many of the questions formerly asked of the reference desk to the student workers in the Telephone Center, saving the professional staff for more involved information and reference needs" (Hodges, 1982, p. 329). The Telephone Center also doubles as a central reporting system for terminal problems from departmental libraries as well as for dial-up problems.

Information Desk

The Information Desk at UIUC was established in its present form and with its current mission in 1980, two years after the implementation of LCS. The reference staff experienced an increased workload in helping patrons learn the system finding that they not only needed to go through a careful problem analysis process, but also needed to share this process with their clientele so that patrons could do it on their own (Ferguson, 1986, p. 30). It was decided to use paraprofessional staff to ease the burden on the reference desk. Among other duties, information desk staff instruct patrons in the use of the card catalog, but particularly in the use of the online catalog in an informal impromptu manner. In addition, a great deal of time and effort is spent in troubleshooting and interpreting results and messages on the computer. Similar needs for user assistance were identified by Pauline Hodges at Ohio State University (Hodges, 1982, pp. 331-32).

Instruction

Strategies for instructing patrons to use the online catalog must have greater variety and depth than those used for the card catalog. Although patrons may not have really known how to use the card catalog, they could usually depend on the alphabetical arrangement and browsing to find what they wanted. This is not the case with an online catalog.

Betsy Baker (1986) has stressed the need to teach patrons concepts such as file structuring and indexing and not just procedures. She contends that teaching concepts makes what patrons learn transferable to other situations (pp. 39-40). Betsy Wilson (1986), in a presentation at the 1986 ALA Conference, also discussed the online catalog as a teaching tool to teach concepts of Boolean searching and keyword searching that patrons can use in other databases (p. 7). A recent article stresses that "attention to information-seeking strategies and judging relevancy should be the ultimate goals of most user training, not the mechanics of using a particular index or system (Marchionini & Nitecki, 1987, p. 105).

One of the major concerns of a public services librarian attempting "to help and train users to harvest the benefits the library catalogue can yield" (Satija, 1982, p. 218), is that people learn in different ways. Reference librarians are well aware that no one method of instruction can meet the needs of all users (Baker & Nielsen, 1983, p. 160; Baker 1986a, p. 91). Not only do people have different backgrounds, widely-varying experiences with libraries and computers, and various expectations, but also various learning styles which are best approached with the development of a variety of instructional methods.

Pat Swanson reported on a survey concerning reference staff involvement in planning and implementing online catalogs by the RASD Reference Services in Large Research Libraries Discussion group. She cited recognition of a need for several instructional formats including "signs, printed handouts suitable for wide distribution, printed instructions affixed near terminals, detailed user manuals, instructions on the CRT screens, audiovisual presentations and structured presentations to groups" (Swanson, 1983, p. 24). Kranich et al. (1986) have also reported that AV programs, training sessions, manuals at the terminals, manuals for purchase, and posting of command charts have been listed as desirable improvements to computer catalog service (p. 139). Research at Ohio State University reported that 34 percent of online users "learned from printed instruction materials at the terminals" and suggested that "it is important, in addition to offering formal and informal instruction, to concentrate efforts on providing simpler terminals and instruction sheets both of which are designed to prevent patron errors at the point of use" (Pease & Gouke, 1982, pp. 290-91).

Self-instruction materials for patrons at UIUC include a series of online help screens for both systems, eight handouts describing the content of the database and general search techniques, and four handouts describing special techniques such as Boolean and truncation searching and the separate system commands and codes. The FBR Starter Kit and Workbook, originally prepared by Gary Golden, is a good introduction to the system but is not available to the public. The reference library, in addition to creating terminal help sheet summaries, is preparing a more detailed manual for patrons to use beside the terminals. The Online Catalog User

Services Office is also developing a manual which would be sold to patrons wanting more detailed information about the system.

Sandra K. Ready (1983, p. 123), Donna Senzig (1983, p. 85), and Mary E. Caspers (1984, p. 201) have all written about the importance in all instruction of hands-on experience during training and the actual interaction with the system using a terminal. The Undergraduate Library sponsors a series of workshops each semester which involve first a demonstration of the features of the system using slides and then an opportunity for guided practice searching.

While these training sessions are "beneficial to those who attend them,... research suggests many users will not be reached through such instructional programs" (Caspers, 1984, p. 200). Noticeable throughout a great deal of literature about online catalogs is the emphasis that "self-paced and self-directed methods for learning OPAC are appreciated and will be used by patrons" (Ferguson et al., 1982, p. 67). One possibility that should be explored further is computer aided instruction (CAI) tutorials for both patron instruction and training of library staff members. CAI could encompass the desirable aspects of self-paced instruction with the interactive hands-on training at a terminal as well as its capacity to be moved out of the library to wherever the user needs it.

The expanding of the system to the rest of the state in the near future provides a unique opportunity for sharing public service strategies. Every library in the state can become a laboratory for testing methods of online catalog instruction, training staff members, and finding new strategies for providing public service. Librarians must stop thinking of online catalogs as computerized cards and remember that: "The card catalog, then, is not an end in itself, but a means to the end of more effectively serving the reader in his attempt to utilize the library's resources. The catalog should be a dynamic and flexible instrument, molded to its user and the collection which it records" (Kuhlman, 1951, p. 269).

REFERENCES

Baker, B., & Nielsen, B. (1983). Educating the online catalog user: Experiences and plans at Northwestern University Library. *Research Strategies, 1*(Fall), 155-166.

Baker, B. (1986a). A conceptual framework for teaching online catalog use. *Journal of Academic Librarianship, 12*(May), 90-96.

Baker, B. (1986b). A new direction for online catalog instruction. *Information Technology and Libraries, 5*(March), 35-41.

Caspers, M. E. (1984). Online public access catalogs: The user. In C. F. Grippo et al. (Eds.), *Festschrift in honor of Dr. Arnulfo D. Trejo* (pp. 197-204). Tucson, AZ: University of Arizona, Graduate Library School, College of Education.

Estabrook, L. (1983). The human dimension of the catalog: Concepts and constraints in information seeking. *Library Resources & Technical Services, 27*(January/March), 68-80.

Ferguson, D. (1980). Online catalogs at the reference desk and beyond (column). *RQ, 20*(Fall), 7-10.

Ferguson, D. K., et al. (1982). *Public online catalogs and research libraries.* Final report to the Council on Library Resources. Stanford, CA: Research Libraries Group (ED 229 084).

Ferguson, D. K. (1986). Reference and online catalogs: Reflections and possibilities. In J. R. Matthews (Ed.), *The impact of online catalogs* (pp. 25-33). New York: Neal-Schuman.

Hodges, P. R. (1982). Reference use of an online catalog at Ohio State University. *Journal of Educational Media Science, 19*(Summer), 327-335.

Kranich, N. C.; Spellman, C. M.; Hecht, D.; & Persky, G. (1986). Evaluating the online catalog from a public services perspective: A case study at the New York University libraries. In J. R. Matthews (Ed.), *Impact of online catalogs* (pp. 89-140). New York: Neal-Schuman.

Kuhlman, C. A. (1951). How catalogers can help the reference librarian. *Wilson Library Bulletin, 26*(November), 267-269.

Marchionini, G., & Nitecki, D. A. (1987). Managing change: Supporting users of automated systems. *College & Research Libraries, 48*(March), 104-109.

Mudge, I. M. (1935). Present day economies in cataloging as seen by the reference librarian of a large university library. In *Catalogers' and classifiers' yearbook* (No. 4), (pp. 9-23). Chicago: American Library Association.

Pease, S., & Gouke, M. N. (1982). Patterns of use in an online catalog and a card catalog. *College & Research Libraries, 43*(July), 279-291.

Potter, W. G. (1986). Creative automation boosts ILL rates. *American Libraries, 17*(April), 244-246.

Ready, S. K. (1984). Putting the online catalog in its place. *Research Strategies, 2*(Summer), 119-127.

Satija, M. P. (1982). Reference service and the catalogue: The story of changing relations. *Herald of Library Science, 21*(July/October), 215-222.

Schmidmaier, D. (1983). Can a reference librarian be friends with a computer produced catalogue? *LASIE, 14*(July/August), 2-8.

Senzig, D. (1983). Teaching the use of online catalogs. *Wisconsin Library Bulletin, 78*(Summer), 84-86.

Swanson, P. (1983). Reference librarians and online catalogs (column). *RQ, 23*(Fall), 23-26.

Ver Nooy, W. (1940). The consumer and the catalog. In W. M. Randall (Ed.), *The acquisition and cataloging of books* (papers presented before the Library Institute at the University of Chicago, July 29 to August 9, 1940), (pp. 310-30). Chicago: University of Chicago Press.

Wilson, B. (1986). *Changing what come out of the catalog.* Unpublished paper presented at the RASD Catalog Use Committee Program: The catalog on the microcomputer: Implications for service and use, American Library Association, 105th annual conference, June 30, 1986 (pp. 1-10).

SHARON CLARK

Automated Systems Librarian
Unversity of Illinois at Urbana-Champaign

The Online Catalog:
Beyond a Local Reference Tool

In 1980, the Illinois State Library sponsored a project to mount the software of the Western Library Network (WLN) to demonstrate how that software might be used as the basis of a statewide automated system for Illinois. The cooperative venture of the University of Illinois at Urbana-Champaign (UIUC) and the River Bend Library System resulted in a joint catalog of their holdings that became operational in summer 1984. The joint online catalog, which now contains over 1 million titles and supports approximately 250 terminals, has proven to be a cost-effective prototype for a statewide online catalog. At present, the database of this online catalog only contains records for these two institutions. However, the database can be searched from a dedicated terminal in each of the eighteen regional library systems headquarters in Illinois as well as in each of the twenty-eight LCS academic libraries.

The reasons for choosing the WLN software in the late 1970s were based on several important factors. There was a need for features and capabilities that would allow the user to transcend the limitations associated with a paper-based card catalog (i.e., at the UIUC, the card catalog became impossible to keep up to date and very difficult to use, as well as far too expensive to suggest that it be continued indefinitely). What the UIUC sought was access to full bibliographic information from multiple access points and effective authority control of the files. Most important from the perspective of the project was to find a system which could function in a cooperative environment. The advantages of networking were already evident in the success of OCLC for cataloging and interlibrary loan in Illinois, and in LCS, the automated circulation system in place at the University of Illinois which was already becoming successful among academic institutions in the state. Most desired was the implementation of a full bibliographic record system with authority control which would allow for the continued use of OCLC as the source of database records, but one that was not dependent on the use of LCS (for the benefit of libraries such as the River Bend Library System which do not use LCS). However, the system had to be adaptable to linking with LCS. WLN was already functioning well in a network environment. Therefore, in 1980 the WLN programs were purchased with Library Services and Construction Act (LSCA) funds administered through the Illinois State Library to create an online public access catalog.

ILLINET ONLINE

Since 1985, when more LSCA funds were received by the UIUC Library, work has proceeded to create a statewide online catalog. Called IO (ILLINET Online), the union catalog will provide:

—statewide subject access with Library of Congress name and subject authority files online;
—keyword title searching capability;
—Boolean searching;
—capability to search the collections of over 800 public, system, academic, and special libraries throughout Illinois; and
—opportunities for timely, inexpensive resource sharing.

As part of fulfilling the requirements of the grant, the WLN software was upgraded and now provides enhanced searching capabilities as well as the addition of the music scores and sound recordings formats. Disc storage has been increased to accommodate the projected growth of the database which will contain an estimated 3,200,000 full OCLC/MARC records representing over 10 million holdings.

The database is constructed as a series of files including the bibliographic, authority, holdings, and key files. The bibliographic file contains bibliographic descriptions, pointers to headings, and the Record IDentifier (RID) number which for local purposes is the OCLC number. Contained in the separate authority file are the headings from the Library of Congress names, series, and subject tapes. Since headings are stripped as a function of loading full bibliographic records into the database, the headings also form the authority file. The holdings file contains Library IDentification codes (LID) and location codes corresponding to geographic regions within Illinois. It is this file which will have dramatic implications for the online catalog in an expanded statewide environment. This file is discussed in more detail later in connection with a special searching feature under local development for the statewide online catalog. The key file has been especially beneficial for reference work as it contains keywords and subfields as access points to records in both the bibliographic and authority files. The key file lends itself to discovering how a particular word—often obscure—is used in context.

The special feature developed as a result of the two-year grant project is called *scoping*. In essence, this feature allows searching the catalog in various ways (e.g., by individual library or groups of libraries). As an aid to help users locate needed information, the state will be divided into geographical areas representing current library system boundaries. These areas will be accessible as individual entities. Utilizing "scoping" commands, a user will be able to search the database by: the entire state, individual LCS schools, all LCS schools as a group, individual ILLINET research and reference centers, all four research and reference centers as a group, and any selected geographical area. In addition, the Center for Research Libraries (CRL) has been approved as a separate scope. CRL's holdings, as on the ILLINET tapes, include extensive newspaper collections encompassing foreign, ethnic, and U.S. secondary, regional, and city newspapers. The exchange program between CRL and the Russian Academy of Science has resulted in CRL maintaining a premier and extensive Slavic collection, all of which will be included in the statewide catalog. Of interest to statewide users will be CRL's plan to convert retrospectively their serial catalog of over 45,000 records and one-third of their total monographic collection representing over 240,000 records. Circulation data for all LCS schools will also be accessible through a link which will be built from the union catalog to individual LCS databases.

Design and specifications for scoping and holdings were the result of cooperative efforts of UIUC librarians, University of Illinois computer services staff, and the Statewide Online Catalog Advisory Committee. After considering various options, the resulting configuration was based on several factors. Primary among them was the premise that effective use of this statewide online catalog is dependent on the user's capability to scope the database holdings geographically. While it was hoped that each library in the state (approximately 290 libraries) could be defined as institutions in the database and therefore would be scopable entities, such a decision would have necessitated the purchase of at least 20 percent more computer storage space. This expenditure was not feasible within the existing grant budget.

For interlibrary loan and delivery purposes, it was considered advantageous for numerous individual libraries to be first represented on a regional basis. With the present arrangement, a user can determine whether a non-LCS library in a geographic area owns an item by scoping on the geographic area, then reviewing the holdings in that area to determine if the item is held by the library in question.

Data Elements

Data elements include the institution, geographic area code (GAC), Library IDentifier, scoping symbol, and OCLC holdings symbols. An institution refers to the library or group of libraries used to limit the results of a search. For each full bibliographic record (FBR) in the database a set of flags are set on or off indicating which institutions hold the record. Allocation of space is required for the flags of each institution except for the global (the entire state as a group) one. Currently, space is used for fifty-three institutions. To provide for institutions which may be defined in the future, space has been allocated for a total of ninety-nine institutions or scopable entities.

The GAC is limited to thirty-five characters and may include upper and lowercase characters, digits, spaces, and punctuation. It is used primarily in the display following the hold command.

For each institution there is one or more Library IDentifiers which will appear on the display following a hold command. To conserve space in the database, it was determined to keep them short, typically under twelve characters. They may include upper and lowercase characters, spaces, and punctuation as desired. An institution having more than one member library will have a distinct LID for each member. Since LCS institutions do not have member libraries, each will have one LID represented by the two-character institution code used in LCS commands.

Each institution will have one scoping symbol. This symbol will be used to specify the institution when an FBR search command is scoped. Since these symbols will frequently be typed by patrons, they will be kept very short. The scoping symbol for the LCS schools will correspond to their two-character LCS campus codes. For the regional library systems, scoping symbols will be limited to three or four characters in length. Special scoping symbols such as ALL for the entire database, LCS for the LCS schools, RRC for the research and reference centers, and CRL for Center for Research Libraries will be three characters long.

For each institution the GAC and its scoping symbol were specified. For each library in the state, its LID, the institution(s) to which it belongs, and a list of OCLC holdings symbols corresponding to the library were defined. The holdings symbols were specified at the two-, three-, or four-character levels. While many libraries will belong to more than one institution, a library is limited to having only one LID.

Command Syntax

Four of the FBR commands, FIND, HOLD, LINK, and DISP, may be scoped. In each case, the user types the scoping symbol of the desired institution in the first options field at the end of the command. There are a total of three options fields. The command "F S BIRDS $LTLS,M,T" instructs the system to find all of the books about birds held by libraries in the Lincoln Trail Libraries System, sort them by title, and display them using the minimum level display. If a user attempts to scope a command for which scoping is not allowed, the system ignores the scope and continues processing as if there were no error. When a user specifies an invalid scope on a command which may be scoped, the system displays the error message, "Incorrect scoping symbol. Please try again."

The FIND command may be scoped for any author, subject, title, or series title searches. It may not be scoped for searches by control numbers such as the ISN, RID, ISBN, and ISSN because of space constraints in the database. In the event a patron enters a scope command on a search of control numbers, the following error message will be displayed: "Scoping is not possible with control numbers. Omit the scope, then do a HOLD." On the scopable searches, if no scope is provided in the options field, the default is assigned based on the terminal name.

No special restrictions exist for scoping the HOLD command used to identify libraries owning an item. The default scope is the same as the scope of the previous "FIND" command. Users will need to be made aware that a nondefault scope on a HOLD command will display different holding libraries for the same set of bibliographic records that would have been retrieved with the default scope. Therefore, a scope on a HOLD command merely shortens the holdings display rather than changing the selection of records that are displayed.

The default scope for a LINK command, used to link to LCS circulation records, is the scope of the previous FIND command. The LINK command may be scoped only for a single LCS institution. If a user tries to scope a LINK command for a non-LCS institution or for the all-LCS institution (L 1-5 $LCS), the system displays the error message: "The LINK works only for LCS schools. Try a 2-letter scoping code."

The DISP command, while rarely used by patrons, is an effective mechanism for diagnosing problems with links. It displays links from the link file, but does not actually cross the links to LCS. Because some FBR records will display more links than can appear on one screen, scoping the DISP command will help to alleviate this problem. The same error messages are used for the DISP command as are used for the LINK command.

Displays

The only display affected by scoping is the holdings display. Some of the changes include removing the "collection I.D." line from the top of the display and storing LIDS in FBR so that they appear in place of call numbers on the holdings display. The "NUC" symbols that had formerly been displayed were replaced by GACs. Although no changes occurred in how holdings records were sorted, the holdings lines within each record are sorted by GAC, making it easier to see the holdings of libraries that are in close proximity. Within each institution, holdings lines are sorted by LID.

The scoping feature has been developed from a prototype in use at the University of Missouri—the other WLN licensee using that software for a public access online catalog. The University of Missouri implemented scoping for FIND commands. While UIUC utilized their online programs for this feature, the batch programs to create and update the database were locally developed. Also locally developed was the LINK command which was designed to allow for scoping with minimal problems. The concept of scoping as it was developed and initiated at the University of Missouri represents another advantage in using the WLN software—the ability to participate in shared development efforts of other WLN licensees.

The final phase of this project, to load all of the ILLINET OCLC tapes into the database (800 tapes), was completed March 1989. Completion of tape loading will occur by the end of the 1987 calendar year.

ISSUES IN STATEWIDE ONLINE CATALOG DEVELOPMENT

To ensure that the diverse user needs are met in creating an online catalog of this type, the Illinois State Library appointed a committee to advise in the construction of the database. The Statewide Online Catalog Advisory Committee is comprised of twelve librarians representing the State Library, public, college, community college, special, and system libraries. In conjunction with input from a special subcommittee created to address specific needs of LCS users, committee members from both groups have been invaluable in reviewing and approving technical specifications such as scoping, authority control measures, as well as addressing ongoing issues such as funding, maintenance concerns, and retention of local information.

Quality Control

Issues being faced as a result of extending the online catalog are many. Of major concern has been the ability to ensure quality control and provide ongoing maintenance of this vast database in a statewide environment. Provisions for quality control were addressed prior to the online catalog's original implementation three years ago and directly involve the authority file.

The online catalog, operational since 1984, had the overall objective of testing the feasibility of being utilized throughout Illinois. Several decisions made were designed to create an online catalog which would reflect up-to-date and complete cataloging based on national standards and an authority control module necessary for ease of access for users. In order to create a database reflecting as much as possible AACR2 cataloging, UIUC and River Bend Library System contracted with the AMIGOS Bibliographic Council, Inc. to have headings from all records (since 1975) converted to AACR2 form and to merge duplicate records.

The decision was made that forms of headings in the authority file should reflect national standards. Authority control is achieved by adding names, series, and subjects from the initial loading of the 1981 LC Name Authority tapes and tapes for the ninth edition of the *Library of Congress Subject Headings*. The LC Name Authority and LCSH tapes were loaded into the online catalog prior to loading the full bibliographic record file. The decision to purchase the LC Name and Subject Authority Tapes and the strategy of loading the authority file first accomplished two purposes. The first of these involved UIUC providing a cross reference structure in the authority file. The WLN programs only provide for authority control by creating a file of authority headings as a result of loading bibliographic records. Cross references among headings are not automatically created and must be added manually. Therefore, by loading the LC Name and Subject Tapes, the LC references were also loaded in the process. The second objective achieved by loading the LC tapes was the ability to take advantage of the system's "mapping" feature (i.e., when an exact match occurs between a heading from a bibliographic record and the heading of a "see" reference, the bibliographic record links to the authorized heading to which the "see" reference leads). In affect, the heading is converted to the correct AACR2 form (Clark & Chan, 1985).

A sequence of events similar to that which occurred in the initial load of the online catalog from 1983 to 1984 will occur with the statewide expansion of the online catalog. For example, UIUC staff have been adding the cross-references from UIUC's manual authority file, and the LC update tapes are being loaded prior to loading the ILLINET tapes (Romero & Wajenberg, 1985).

At the UIUC Library, card production was stopped in October 1984 and FBR was accepted as the permanent access tool to the collection. In September 1985, the manual processes of authority control, in place to service the card catalog, were transferrred to the Automated Systems Maintenance Unit and were developed to service the online catalog. Online authority control at Urbana presently consists of two major processes carried out through the FBR authority file. The first involves updating access points and the second involves adding appropriate cross-references to already correct access points. These two processes help ensure more accurate access to the database and represent the same type of authority control processes that occur with a traditional card catalog.

Updating access points usually involves validating the form of the heading through the LC Name-Authority file and correcting any headings in FBR which do not conform to LC standards. Spelling errors and MARC coding errors are also corrected as part of this process. Cross-references are added manually to headings which enter the FBR authority file through the weekly loading of bibliographic records from OCLC/ILLINET tapes. Once a cross-reference is in place, FBR will prevent nonstandard forms of the heading from entering the authority file, as well as provide a means of directing the user to the correct form of the heading.

System maintenance at UIUC has drawn its staff resources through redeploying professional as well as paraprofessional staff from the original and copy cataloging units and from the LCS maintenance unit. The staff in the OCLC searching and inputting units have been relieved of such tasks as typing and filing of authority cards. The quality of online authority control is steadily improving with the increase of AACR2 headings and appropriate cross-references in the database. The current loading of new LC Name-Authority update tapes will greatly reduce the number of obsolete headings which may enter the authority file when the ILLINET tapes are loaded to create the statewide database.

Libraries with card catalogs already expend effort to maintain and ensure integrity of those catalogs through authority control. It is assumed that any library which adopts FBR as their online catalog will recognize the necessity to ensure the integrity of the online catalog through supporting authority control. At present in this country there is a tendency to distribute cataloging and authority work. The precedent was set by the Library of Congress, whereby their cooperative arrangements with other libraries are in place to contribute authority records to LC's own authority file (i.e., the NACO project). These records are then included in LC's MARC distribution service. Plans under discussion for the statewide online catalog include provisions for distributed maintenance, perhaps involving four of the larger LCS institutions initially.

Another area of concern relates to the desire on the part of an institution to include local data such as notes (especially donor information) and local subject headings in the database. As a result, a questionnaire was distributed to all OCLC/ILLINET members designed to elicit information on how local data are currently used. Specifications have been developed based on that data so that following the statewide database load, a system called "record enrichment" can be implemented to allow for loading relevant local data.

Funding and Governance

Of continuing concern is the issue of funding. Therefore a lengthy proposal has been issued which seeks support of the online catalog through a combination of sources including the Illinois State Library, Illinois Board of Higher Education, and participating libraries. The purpose of the proposal is to expand access to the online catalog as well as to enhance LCS, the older circulation module. The last issue involves how the statewide catalog will be administered. Ironically, governance was at the onset perceived as possibly the most difficult issue to resolve. In reality, it is turning out to be one of the easier resolutions.

Almost a decade of experience in cooperatively administering LCS is providing the framework for the organization of IO/ILLINET online. The Illinois LCS Organization (ILCSO) is comprised of a policy council and an operations committee. The policy council includes six elected LCS directors and the operations committee chair, as well as representatives from the University of Illinois computing services and financial planning office. The name reflects its charge—to establish directives and policy involving the use and future of LCS. At the operational level, one representative from each LCS institution is appointed to the operations committee. Various subcommittees handle the wide range of activities associated with a large automated database and make recommendations to the policy council. Both groups will undergo some change involving expanding the representation to reflect expansion of access to the online catalog across the state. Although the organizational structure may be modified to better meet the needs of diverse participants, the goals should remain intact. It will be critical that it remain a library service organization, and as Bernard Sloan, who has worked with LCS users for years, emphasizes, "not a data processing management organization" (B. Sloan, personal communication, March 1987). In a paper presented at the "California Conference on Networking," Hugh Atkinson (1985) expressed the need for "keeping a sustained effort and commitment to the ideal of networking," noting that technology allows us to "make a new beginning in library service,...concentrate on the improvement of library service," and that "accesses, services and new procedures developed at the network level will spill over to our own (local) processes," with very real potential to cause "changes in our libraries themselves." Our own library at the UIUC has changed as a result of the online catalog, and clearly service to users has been enhanced.

REFERENCES

Atkinson, H. (1985). *California conference on networking.* Unpublished paper, December.
Clark, S. E., & Chan, W. (1985). Maintenance of an online catalogue. *Information Technology and Libraries, 4*(December), 324-338.
Romero, N., & Wajenberg, A. Authority records and authority work in the online catalogue. *Information Technology and Libraries, 4*(December), 318-323.

PAULA D. WATSON

Assistant Director of General Services
University of Illinois Library
Urbana-Champaign

University of Illinois Library Catalog on CD-ROM: Impact on Resource Sharing and Reference Work

In spring 1985, the University of Illinois Library at Urbana-Champaign received a grant of more than $83,000 in Library Services and Construction Act (LSCA) funds through the Illinois State Library to create and distribute its online catalog on optical disc. The grant had several objectives. The first was to determine whether optical disc technology and industry production capabilities had advanced sufficiently to make it feasible to produce a database of more than 900,000 bibliographic records on laserdisc which could be searched by microcomputer.

The database used in the demonstration was the university's online catalog database created in 1980 as the result of an earlier LSCA grant. The objective of the earlier grant had been to mount the software of the Western Library Network (WLN) to demonstrate how that software could be used as the basis for a statewide online union catalog for Illinois libraries. The result was the creation of a joint online catalog of the holdings of the University of Illinois Library and those of the River Bend Library System (one of the state's eighteen regional library systems). This joint catalog, which became operational in summer 1984, serves as the prototype for a statewide online union catalog. Additional funding has since been obtained to expand this catalog into a union catalog by including the holdings of all libraries participating in ILLINET, the state's library resource sharing network. The projected statewide database, to be called IO (ILLINET Online), will contain, at the outset, 3 million to 4 million titles reflecting over 10 million holdings and will be accessible at locations throughout the state and through dial-up access. Like the existing joint UIUC/River Bend online catalog, the ILLINET Online will provide sophisticated access to bibliographic information, including subject, key-word, and Boolean searching as well as the ability to limit searches, for example, by library or by geographic region.

The optical disc project described in this article had the second objective of evaluating the feasibility of distributing the statewide union catalog database on optical disc and testing the expectation that distribution in this format to certain libraries would enhance resource sharing. Ultimate distribution would be to libraries which did not want or could not afford online access through the mainframe system or which would not be satisfied with dial-up access. Small libraries in the state were viewed as the most likely potential beneficiaries of the proposed optical catalog. As matters developed, technical considerations made it simpler to place only the University of Illinois portion of the joint catalog on optical disc. According to the terms of the grant, data retrieval from the laserdisc version of the catalog was to be at least as effective as in the online mode. Therefore, the optical database was to be searchable by keyword anywhere in the bibliographic record or at least where keyword searching is now possible online. This requirement necessitated high capacity storage to accommodate indexes and bibliographic data and the use of full-text search software. An additional aim of the grant project was to familiarize staff at the University of Illinois Library with emerging information technology. In the end, this educational role became quite important since the evolution of the technology and other factors necessitated several significant changes to the original grant plan (for additional information on the project *see* Watson [1982, 1987a, 1987b] and Watson & Golden [1987]).

The original proposal was written just as optical disc products were beginning to appear in the library marketplace. Discs were still mastered abroad and turnaround time was uncertain. It was unclear whether updates could be issued in a timely fashion to satisfy the demands of public catalog use. The capacities of digital optical media were still being tested. The original proposal therefore stressed the realism of a one-year time frame to create the desired product. It also called for the use of a 12-inch videodisc as the storage medium. By the end of the experiment, it was clear that the issue was no longer whether a 900,000 record database could be put on optical disc, but rather how useful it was to do so in light of the retrieval capabilities of available software and the response time possible with optical drives searched by means of a microcomputer. The other more or less unanticipated issue raised by the demonstration was the determination of the precise value of optical catalogs as resource sharing devices in a highly articulated library network environment such as that which exists in Illinois.

THE ORIGINAL TECHNICAL PLAN

As indicated earlier, the LSCA grant was obtained in spring 1985 when promotion of optical disc products for libraries had only just begun.

A few systems made their debut at the American Library Association meeting in January 1985. Carrollton Press demonstrated three 12-inch videodisc systems: DISCON (a retrospective conversion aid), DISCAT (a cataloging product), and MARVLS (part of the Library of Congress shelf-list which was searchable in limited ways for reference purposes). None of these products ever reached the market. InfoTrac, an index to 1,000 general interest and business periodicals on 12-inch disc, was also on display in January 1985. This product was the most successful optical disc reference system available for some time, and it is only recently that it has competitors in CD-ROM products which have been developed in the last two years.

At the time the Illinois grant was written, however, there was no public access catalog product on the market either on 12-inch disc or on CD-ROM which satisfied grant specifications for search capabilities. There was a company, however, which had worked successfully on two library projects and had developed a workable configuration employing a 12-inch videodisc, a system which might be used for a catalog. The company was LaserData of Cambridge, Massachusetts. They had collaborated with the Information Access Company to create InfoTrac and had also worked with the National Agricultural Library (NAL) on an agricultural information system mounted on a 12-inch disc. The goal of the NAL project was to test the feasibility of using laserdiscs in conjunction with microcomputers for storage and retrieval of agriculture related full-text databases, including graphics.

The initial NAL database was the *Pork Industry Handbook,* a text containing illustrations. To fill up the disc, a selection from the AGRIC-OLA database was also converted to optical format. The search software is BRS/SEARCH modified by LaserData to retrieve graphics. NAL set out to test full-text retrieval from a print source with illustrations as well as from a set of bibliographic citations. The hardware for the NAL system consisted of an IBM XT with a memory of 512K, a Pioneer LD-V1000 videodisc player, a LaserData TRI0 110 controller with an interface card, and a Panasonic TR 124 monochrome video display monitor for graphics. LaserData played a key role in developing the NAL system by providing the interface controller that connects a standard videodisc player to the personal computer allowing the retrieval of the multimedia information stored on the videodisc. The unit controls the videodisc player, retrieves the analog information from the disc, and recreates the digitally encoded material. LaserData also used proprietary encoding techniques to premaster the NAL database and the company took essential responsibility for integrating the system. (For a complete description of the project, *see* Andre, 1985.)

According to the original plan, Illinois was to work with LaserData in exactly the same manner as NAL had done, relying on the company for premastering, for system hardware and software, and for final integration of the system. There was one major reservation concerning the NAL system, however, which was reinforced by conversations with NAL staff. BRS/SEARCH is powerful and flexible software but, at that time, it could be run on only the PCIX operating system. We wanted BRS/SEARCH search capabilities but were uncertain about PCIX as an operating system, particularly for a public access catalog which was ultimately to be used in small public libraries by presumably fairly unsophisticated end users. NAL staff reported that they were not comfortable with PCIX. It was difficult to learn, the documentation was unclear, and they experienced frequent system crashes due to improper shutdown procedures, power irregularities, too rapid advancement of the video screens, and for other reasons. An ordinary user could normally not rebuild the system without the help of an expert librarian. Another quite important objection NAL staff brought out was that searching was surprisingly slow on the bibliographic portion of the database (J. Zidar, personal communication, Fall 1986).

The PCIX problem was raised during initial contacts with LaserData. The project technical consultant seemed to recognize that an MS DOS-based system would be an improvement and reported that attempts were being made to identify or design DOS compatible software. LaserData never made good on assurances on this point and the project could therefore not proceed. Three months into the grant year found the library without a systems integrator. (For details of the breakdown of Illinois' relationship with LaserData *see* Watson & Golden [1987].)

NEW VENDOR: NEW PLAN

Conversations with cooperative individuals in the industry (J. Schwerin and D. Corney, personal communications, 1986) led us to Brodart. Brodart is a well established and broadly-based library company with experience in the online public access and COM catalog markets. They had experimented for some time with a CD-ROM-based public access catalog product to market to larger libraries and library systems which were already customers for their COM catalog. They called the new product LePac. (For a complete description *see* Schaub, 1985.) In its earliest stage of development, LePac functioned mainly as a browsing search system. This capability still exists in the novice mode in which the user may search by either author, title, or subject using a specially designed ten-key pad and proceeding through a simple menu. Segments of the menu appear on each screen to help the user narrow the search to progressively smaller sections in the alphabetic hierarchy and finally to the desired individual item or items. The total number of phrases viewed by the user in each pass is dependent on the total number of titles in the catalog. The lists of phrases run continuously through the alphabet and are selected so that they are spaced evenly throughout the title, author, or subject parts of the database. With authors and subjects, authority control can be provided. Were LePac to have remained with only these capabilities, we would have been unable to meet grant specifications for retrieval by relying on it as our system. Brodart's development of the product was continuous, however, and by the time the database was ready to be mastered there was a somewhat more sophisticated system to work with. Version 4.0 of the software allows for search in an "expert" mode which employs a full keyboard and permits keyword searching of authors, titles, and subjects out of context along with Boolean combinations. It also provides a search field called "Anyword" which allows searching for a known term anywhere in the record and also permits a search by Library of Congress card number and International Standard Book Number. The expert system is not menu driven and relies only on the natural prompt provided by the screen format to indicate to the user what an initial search strategy should be.

Because of Brodart's experience in the library marketplace, the infrastructure for marketing, pricing, and technical support of a CD-ROM product was already in place within the company. One of the conclusions reached by Watson and Golden (1987) is that libraries experimenting with technological development will find it easier and more productive, for a variety of reasons, to deal with a company whose business is libraries (p. 70). The University of Guelph—the only university library known to the author to be relying on a CD-ROM catalog for local public access—was successful in working from first principles with Reteaco, a company which had no previous experience with bibliographic records. To avoid embarking on an entrepreneurial technological development project independently with neither adequate skills nor time and because LePac seemed a reasonably sound product, the decision was made to continue the project by signing a contract with Brodart in January 1986.

Development of the American optical information industry had progressed sufficiently by early 1986 so that it was at last possible to master optical discs in this country and thus substantially reduce production time. Since Brodart already had an integrated system and since delays due to mastering abroad were about to be eliminated, creation of the Illinois catalog within the timeframe of the grant ceased to be very much in doubt.

During the first week in April 1986, a LePac unit and sample discs were delivered to test. Changes to the screen could be suggested so that the menu would make more sense to Illinois users and clear answers could be obtained to the questions about the system. In late spring the UIUC online catalog database was loaded from the mainframe onto eight 6250 bpi tapes. The tapes were shipped to Brodart in late June. In mid-July a set of formal specifications for the content of the database, indexing, and display of records was received. The completed optical database was received from Brodart in September 1986. The disc held 700,000 of the 900,000 records to be mastered and the indexes to the database: mid-1986 state-of-the-art storage capacity for a single side of a CD-ROM.

The first industry connections were made with LaserData, a company on the leading edge of development in selected aspects of videodisc technology. Seemingly, the library's interests were not a good match with the long term business interests of that company. Good advice from concerned experts led to a company whose experience and goals gave them a natural reason to work on the project even though it might well turn out to be a pilot which would never be implemented on a large scale. The lesson to be learned from this appears to be that best results with application of a volatile technology in a library setting are likely to be gained by collaboration with a company which is in the business of serving libraries. There are exceptions, of course, to every apparent rule. NAL found LaserData cooperative and supportive. They have gone on to a second project with the company to mount thirteen full-text sources on 12-inch discs. Also, Reteaco, the company with which the University of Guelph Library worked to develop its CD-ROM local public access catalog, specializes in business applications such as the storage and retrieval of catalog and inventory data.

IMPLEMENTATION

The system was tested at four Illinois sites: Champaign Public Library and Information Center (280,000 volumes), Decatur Public Library (220,000 volumes), Lincoln Public Library in Springfield, Illinois (40,000 volumes), and Parkland College Library in Champaign, Illinois (80,000 volumes). The regional public library system headquarters for two of the public libraries (the Rolling Prairies Library System for Springfield and Decatur) and the University of Illinois at Urbana-Champaign also participated in the test.

The two test sites originally named in the grant—the UIUC Library and the Rolling Prairies Library System headquarters—used off-the-shelf equipment specifically purchased for the project. Brodart agreed to lend preconfigured equipment to the additional test sites. Duplicate discs were also made for all participating libraries and each received a copy of the LePac system software. Initial contact with the cooperating libraries was made in early October 1986 at a general planning meeting. Contact librarians named by each institution received a brief overview of the project and its relationship to state online union catalog development. Equipment, security, and maintenance issues were addressed as well as plans to involve other members of each library's staff in the evaluation. Realistic means for obtaining feedback from users were assessed and the preconditions for making the systems available for public use were discussed. In all but one of the libraries it would be necessary to distinguish this computer-based system from an online system already available in house. Signs and handouts would be required. A general evaluation plan and timetable were agreed to. Contact librarians were to orient staff at their library to the use of LePac, to motivate them concerning the project as they saw fit, and to choose a site for the equipment.

Owing to the newness of the product, Brodart's technical documentation for LePac was informal and really quite inadequate. Librarians practicing on the system discovered features of the software and peculiarities of the database which had to be verified with the company. Brodart made revisions to the existing users' manual at the suggestion of the principal investigator which were passed on to the project participants. Before public testing, it was necessary to develop concise user aids addressing system features which were not explained in Brodart's documentation.

EVALUATION METHODOLOGY

A consultant assisted in the development of the evaluation plan and took the lead role in evaluation activities. (The consultant on the evaluation phase of the project was Dale Brandenburg, associate head, Division of Measurement and Evaluation, Office of Instructional Management Services, University of Illinois at Urbana-Champaign. He was assisted by Ping Der Wang, a graduate student at the university.) In his view, the issues to be examined in the evaluation included: ease of use or improvements needed to the technology, utility of the technology in relation to present methods of access, and, in general, its perceived value. The data collection instruments were designed expressly for this project, although concepts and questions employed in the National Online Catalog Use study formed the development of some of the tools used. Librarians at the various sites were the primary target of the evaluation since it would be their opinion which would be most important in determining the usefulness of the system (see Appendix A). The views of users were also obtained by means of a concise reaction card concentrating on a few central questions. Also, a class in the UIUC Graduate School of Library and Information Science (GSLIS) was asked to evaluate the system by means of a detailed questionnaire focusing on software and retrieval capabilities (see Appendix B). An expert was called upon (F. Wilfrid Lancaster of the GSLIS) to assist in defining indexes of perceived value. Because the original duration of the grant was to be only one year and an extension was required due to the problems encountered in the initial identification of a vendor, only three months were available for evaluation and testing. Methods used reflect this shortness of time and also what could reasonably be expected of librarians volunteering to evaluate a new product not likely to have an immediate impact on their work and of users interacting with a test system which was available in their libraries for only a few weeks.

Librarian reaction was captured during site visits by the evaluation team. After staff members had sufficient time to become acquainted with LePac, a group interview was scheduled at each library. These interviews centered around the use of three checklists—two pertaining to the operation of the system and one pertaining to its use. Librarians were asked to respond quickly either positively or negatively to features listed on the checklists. Each checklist was tallied immediately and any areas of disagreement were explored. A set of predetermined questions were also asked of all site librarians. The checklists and the prearranged questions appear in Appendix A. During the site visits, the evaluation team was also able to observe the placement of the terminal. This choice of location was crucial to the acceptance of the system by users. Three test libraries placed it in highly visible, high traffic locations close to library staff who could explain its capabilities. One located the system in a carrel behind the reference desk where it remained largely invisible to users unless they were specifically referred to it. Enthusiasm for the project and the system were lowest among librarians at this site and this was quite naturally reflected in user response.

Members of the GSLIS class answered a thirty-seven item questionnaire (see Appendix B) which addressed system effectiveness, overall value, documentation, display design, system feedback to the user, search records, and cost of the user's time. There were also two open-ended questions.

RESULTS

Operation of the System

General Assessment

The following discussion of the effectiveness of LePac as a system should of course be understood in terms of the hardware and software which were standard at the time of the study. Brodart is continually refining the system, hardware improvements have occurred and continue to occur, and optical technology is being driven continually forward by the desire to develop better products. As is indicated, several of the problems mentioned in this section have already been addressed by Brodart or are likely to be dealt with soon. For the test, an IBM or IBM-compatible PC with 512K RAM was used along with a Hitachi 1502s CD-ROM drive. The software employed at most of the sites was version 4.0.

Most librarians were quite positive about the general operation of the LePac system. They stressed its user friendliness and simplicity in particular. The overall reaction to the technology on the part of patrons was definitely skewed to the positive side at four out of the five sites. Despite the fact that the database is limited to UIUC holdings since 1976, 73 percent of patrons who filled out the reaction card said they found what they were looking for.

The "expert" and "novice" search modes for LePac were described earlier. Librarians' response to the novice mode was less positive than to the expert mode. Significant criticisms included the time required to arrive at a match and the tedium of searching through long alphabetic displays. Of the users surveyed, 63 percent went beyond the novice mode to the expert mode. Librarians generally thought the term *expert* was misleading and acted as a barrier to the use of what is a quite straightforward search system. The novice mode was the first stage of development of the product and grew out of Brodart's original idea for replacing the COM catalog with a faster and more efficient product. Feedback regarding the novice mode has caused Brodart to consider an enhancement which would include the ability to block its use.

Improvements Needed

There was consensus on certain necessary improvements. One change noted as critical by librarians was the addition of a mechanism for exiting long searches which were in fact quite common on the system. A search interruption feature was incorporated by Brodart into version 5.0 of the software. Librarians did not see it as critical, but they did suggest the need for a mechanism for predicting search results. LaserGuide, a competing product on the market, for example, had this feature as long ago as July 1986. Brodart's recently released version 5.0 of the LePac software produces a display for the number of matches obtained in author and subject searches and also provides continuous reporting of the percentage of the database searched as the search progresses.

On the test disc, there was a particular problem with foreign words containing diacritic marks. Most were essentially irretrievable due to programming and processing problems which had not been resolved when the disc was mastered. These difficulties were not unique to the Illinois project, and Brodart expected a solution in future releases. It has been reported that the retrieval problem was solved, but diacritic marks still do not appear in the display.

As mentioned earlier, the user aid available at the time of the project was seen by librarians as completely inadequate both as a tool for the public and as an explanation of the system for professionals. Since the system is under continuous development, Brodart's reluctance to invest a great deal of time and money in documentation is understandable. On the other hand, at the time of the study, there was a strong inclination on the part of company representatives to avoid excessively complicated explanations, seemingly without the realization that librarians need a complete understanding of system operation in order to facilitate its use by the public. For example, a user who has been unable to bring up anything on the system on Apple II computers should be able to find out from a librarian that the software will not search a term with three characters or less and to receive advice on alternate search techniques. Brodart had developed a new LePac Reference Manual package as of fall 1987 which includes a tutorial database with software that coordinates with sample searches. (Information on recent LePac enhancements in the foregoing paragraphs is based either on a telephone conversation with Russ Thompson, senior technical specialist, Brodart Automation, Williamsport, Pennsylvania on January 28, 1988 or on reporting in the company newsletter, *Interaction.*)

Response Time

The issue of response time on a CD-ROM public access catalog assumes particular importance when the catalog database to be searched contains more than 100,000 to 300,000 records. The views on LePac response time collected as part of this study were quite dependent on the expectations and previous experience with online systems of both users and librarians. There were certainly some users who were quite dissatisfied with LePac response time, but most did not find this a significant problem. Most librarians tended to use the online system currently available in their institutions as a point of reference and found LePac performance acceptable in this context. On the other hand, UIUC users who tested the system were comparing it with a highly sophisticated and responsive mainframe system, and their reaction was, predictably, markedly different from that of other users.

To provide some objective data on speed of response, we timed eighty-seven sample searches at the UIUC Library. The searches were based on actual questions collected at the UIUC Information Desk, a general service point which handles numerous catalog inquiries. The first aim was to explore the amount of time needed for LePac to provide its first response to a query, whether this response was a complete answer, a positive indication leading onward toward a complete answer, or a negative answer ending the search without result. The time needed for initial response ranged from one second or less to several minutes if very common terms were necessarily part of the search. The average for all types of searches was twenty-nine seconds. It is, incidentally, interesting that far more informal experimentation at the community college test site produced a similar result. For the sake of comparison, three to four seconds is considered an acceptable initial response time on a mainframe online catalog system. One of the sample searches turned out to be for a common one-word title and was abandoned by the searcher after nineteen minutes. Such a search would cause problems on any system, but there were other queries involving common subject or title terms which required unacceptable intervals for an initial response. The absence of an escape mechanism and the persistence of the message "Please Wait" on the screen may have caused high frustration levels for some test site users. As a means for comparison and to test the state of the art, the same searches were run on WLN's LaserCat. Evidently owing to major differences in software capability and to the layout of data on the discs, by and large the searches ran significantly faster on LaserCat than on LePac. (Copies of the search forms were sent to Jerry Maioli of WLN who arranged to have them replicated on LaserCat.) Again, a caveat must be introduced in relation to interpretation of the time test results especially with regard to those which made a fairly casual comparison between the two CD-ROM systems. There are obviously factors which may have influenced the results including the exact hardware and software in use on the system at the moment, the search strategy employed, the skill of the searcher, and the searcher's experience on the system.

Brodart was clearly aware that searching could be painfully slow under certain circumstances with the then-standard hardware configuration and version 4.0 of the LePac software. With the implementation of version 4.9 and its optimization of search logic, company representatives expect that search will be five times faster. However, speed of response is a well-known limitation of CD-ROM technology due to the high seek time required by the drive to locate data on discs as they were normally arrayed at the time of this project. In an early study of the technology written for the Council on Library Resources, McQueen and Boss (1986) observe that: "Advocates of the technologies suggest that these speeds can be significantly improved by attention to the layout of the data on the disks and by development of specialized software" (p. 64). Brodart representatives predict further improvement in response time beyond the 500 percent they have already achieved. They expect these advances to be accomplished largely through software enhancements since the hardware still places inescapable limits on response time.

CD-ROM CATALOGS & RESOURCE SHARING IN ILLINOIS

One of the conclusions drawn from this study was that CD-ROM technology had not advanced quite to the point that it was entirely feasible to mount a database as large as the Illinois Statewide Union Catalog on CD-ROM. When the study was completed in February 1987 it was certainly possible from a purely technical standpoint to store bibliographic data for 3 to 4 million items on CD-ROM. However, with data storage techniques in use at that time, four separate discs would have been required. The Western Library Network had developed software to search 2.1 million records on three discs in two separate drives, and such software was also under development at Brodart. A four-disc configuration had not yet been attempted, however, and, besides, the Illinois database was expected to grow at the rate of 15 percent each year. Furthermore, firsthand searching experience, together with the time tests done on LePac as part of the project, suggested that response time on a 3 to 4 million-record database might be problematic.

During the year since the Illinois project was completed, developers have pushed back the earlier limitations of the technology, and prospects for further progress seem bright. As of January 1988 Brodart had succeeded in mastering a database of 3.2 million records reflecting 17 million holdings on two discs and a small part of a third to be used by Wisconsin as a statewide union catalog. As of August 1989 this database was under distribution to 150 of the 700 libraries whose holdings it represents.

Greater storage has been achieved through triple density data compression in which full MARC records can be reduced for storage purposes to less than 180 characters per record. With standard indexes, 3 million records may now be put on one disc when it was only possible previously to store 1 million. Additional space was required on the Wisconsin disc for the large number of holdings records in a statewide system and because detailed indexing (of notes fields, for example) was thought to be desirable. To increase disc storage, proprietary methods are used to encode and decode bibliographic records at the field and subfield level. Data density is further increased through word, character, and bit level techniques. Decompression is performed by the LePac display software and this reformatting of the data retrieved adds slightly to the response time. Brodart technical experts expect a degradation in response time due to decompression of no more than one second (information on data compression was provided by L. Anderson, marketing manager, Brodart, personal communication, February 1988). Wisconsin libraries will use the system first at the reference desk for answering queries and for interlibrary loan. No assessment of the system's success seems likely before spring 1988. Given these advances, the purely technical feasibility of creating an optical disc version of the Illinois Statewide Union Catalog is less in doubt than it was at the close of the study. Since the technical obstacles are rapidly being overcome—with the possibly very important exception of response time— other issues assume a more important place in considering the usefulness of a CD-ROM version of the Illinois statewide union catalog. The most important of these is an understanding of where such a service would fit in to the already highly developed state network for resource sharing.

Potential Applications of CD-ROM Catalogs

Resource sharing and library cooperation have historically had a high priority in Illinois. The Illinois Library and Information Network (ILLINET) has been in existence in some form since 1965. It consists of about 2,900 academic, public, special, and school libraries whose cooperative efforts are coordinated by the Illinois State Library through eighteen regional library systems, four research and reference centers, and two special information centers. Automation plays a key role in enabling libraries of all sizes and types to share their resources and to make materials at all libraries available to all citizens.

Experimentation with the distribution of the projected online union catalog database in optical disc format was wholly in keeping with the direction of library development and cooperation in Illinois. The long-range plan calls for the expanded use of technology in Illinois libraries and for development of appropriate linkages between the system, network, and local libraries. Specific goals in the long-range plan to which the Illinois optical disc catalog project was related include: expanding interlibrary cooperation, assessing means for making data communications between libraries more cost effective, expanding the use of the statewide database, and promoting personal computer access by citizens to library bibliographic databases. In funding projects for the increased use of technology, state granting agencies also take into account the recommendations of a May 1983 conference of Illinois public library leadership. Recommendations from this conference relevant to the funding of the optical disc catalog project include: providing direct off-site access using appropriate technology to the information resources of the public library and coordinating collection development between all libraries to ensure that user needs are met.

To make an assessment regarding the second goal of the project, that is, to assert that the availability of a CD-ROM version of the statewide union catalog would enhance resource sharing, requires an examination of exactly where and how such a system would fit into the array of cooperative mechanisms, and correct access to the bibliographic utilities available in a state in which networking has received priority attention for decades. The ILLINET system is a highly developed and efficient network relied upon by libraries of all sizes for interlibrary loan and reference service.

The LCS system, which links more than twenty academic and special libraries in the state and which can be accessed by the system libraries, already provides direct user access to a very large number of holdings. Some non-LCS libraries can easily dial up LCS and use it fairly routinely to identify loan material.

The statewide network itself, to be implemented in fall 1987, will provide an additional 300 libraries with bibliographic access to each other's holdings. Even with this giant step forward, however, close to 90 percent of the state's libraries will still lack this access.

Since the database made available to test libraries was not the union catalog but rather the catalog of one of the largest research libraries in the country, only suggestive inferences may be drawn from the results of this study as to whether or not the availability of the statewide union catalog in optical format would significantly enhance resource sharing in the state. The reaction of the participants in the study was of course conditioned by the current means available to them to satisfy their interlibrary loan needs. As was mentioned earlier, more than twenty-five libraries and the regional system network nodes in the state have direct access to LCS, the state online circulation system. Many non-LCS libraries (three of the sites where the CD-ROM catalog was tested, for example) can easily search LCS through dial up and routinely use it to identify material for loan. Larger libraries in the state may also have direct access to OCLC and may use it for verification purposes, even if they rely on the regional system library to obtain the item for them.

Smaller libraries in each region are under no obligation to fully identify or locate items their patrons wish to borrow. Responsibility for this may be borne entirely by the regional system library. The system director who participated in the grant project estimated that approximately 80 percent of the interlibrary loan requests received by system headquarters are from public and school libraries, many of which are without even the most basic bibliographic tools. About 40 percent of loan requests come without any verification whatever. Although the test librarians implied that they do not view the need as compelling, they did generally agree that the smaller libraries, though least able to pay for it, had the most to gain from access to a stand-alone system on CD-ROM which could be used to identify materials of interest to their users beyond their own collections. Librarians from small public and school libraries who saw a demonstration of LePac were clearly concerned about costs, but they were also highly enthusiastic about the possibilities of radically expanded access for their users. Although the broad array of options for cooperation that already exists in Illinois for the larger libraries dampened enthusiasm for the creation of a CD-ROM-based union catalog among the test librarians, they did identify various potential benefits. For example, rising telecommunications costs might make it more appealing in the future to resort to a stand-alone system than to dial up what may be a distant node in the LCS network or a bibliographic utility. Difficulty of access and slow response time were cited as frequent problems with OCLC.

In order to provide an index of the perceived potential value of a CD-ROM union catalog, librarians were asked to estimate how much use would justify purchase and also what cost they thought would be reasonable. Purchase was judged to be worthwhile if patron/staff use was to be five searches each day (at three sites) or fifteen to twenty searches each day (at one site). The site at which librarians were least enthusiastic about the project, surprisingly enough, were willing to pay $2,000 annually. The other test libraries were willing to pay $500 per year for the service.

In terms of workload, the test libraries saw little gain to themselves. All felt, because of the large number of unverified requests received by the systems libraries, that real work savings could be effected at that particular point in the interlibrary loan process.

A slightly surprising result of the study was the observation that even in Illinois, where resource sharing has been emphasized for a quarter of a century, not all librarians in the test were entirely positive about the potential of LePac for increasing direct user access to information about library materials. Two sites placed little value on and did little to promote the system as a means for users to identify items of interest completely on their own in a very comprehensive collection. Librarians at one site could see the CD-ROM catalog as valuable only to a small class of users—i.e., researchers and business people. At a second site, the staff saw the work of interlibrary loan being passed back to the patron. The staff also displayed a definite resistance to direct charging out of books by users were this to be a future possibility.

On the other hand, at a third public library site, librarians encouraged individual public use by strategic and highly visible placement and by frequent referrals of users to the system with an explanation of its capabilities. This promotional effort resulted in a measurable increase in interlibrary loans during the test period: a 15 percent increase over the normal lending rate for a like time period. At the community college library, librarians also viewed the system as a significant way to broaden the information horizons of their users.

The lack of appreciation for direct user access to information about distant library materials is reminiscent of the consistent views expressed by Thomas Ballard on the value of networks to public libraries. According to Ballard (1985), "patrons are unwilling to accept a definition of access to books that requires them to go somewhere else or await future delivery" (p. 257). He argues that browsing is the most desirable or at least the most pleasurable means to identify needed materials and that users will not be prompted by a mere bibliographic citation to want something they have not laid hands on. Networks are expensive luxuries because they "tantalize patrons with bibliographic records instead of books" (Ballard, 1985, p. 258). What is more, patrons do not want everything on a subject and librarians are foolish, he asserts, if they tie their professional status to their ability to provide information. William Gray Potter, writing from his experience in resource sharing in Illinois, turns aside Ballard's arguments with some telling statistics and an eloquent statement of the philosophy that has informed recent library development in the state. He points out that at the University of Illinois interlibrary borrowing as a percentage of circulation rose from approximately 3 percent to approximately 8 percent in just two years largely due to direct patron charges on the LCS network. The lesson to be learned from the UIUC experience, Potter (1986) believes, is that librarians "must find ways to make access to library networks as easy, direct, and painless as possible," meeting the untapped demand for resource sharing "graciously and with devices that emphasize our willingness to serve" (p. 246).

Potter's view, obviously, is that the possibilities for sharing are endless and are unrelated to the size of the library. While librarians in the test libraries recognized the value of a CD-ROM union catalog to small libraries as borrowers, they failed to recognize the potential of such libraries as lenders. As was indicated earlier, even though ILLINET Online, the Illinois statewide online union catalog, is quite an extensive database, it nevertheless falls far short of providing direct access to all the library holdings in the state. There are more than 2,000 libraries of various types and sizes whose holdings are not included. The eighteen regional systems serve many of these libraries, and these services might be improved by the availability of union catalogs of regional holdings. CD-ROM cataloging systems (offered by Brodart and a number of other vendors) might be a cost effective way of converting the records of these libraries to machine-readable form, and CD-ROM public access catalogs might be an economical way of distributing these union catalogs around the region and the state. Were their holdings known, the smaller libraries in the state might be changed from only borrowers to lenders. It is well known that even the smallest rural library may hold something unique and, taken as a group, these libraries contain a sizable and perhaps seriously underrutilized share of the state's library resources. For example, Illinois school libraries are frequently not served by the regional systems. Other states are moving to bring school libraries into the resource sharing network, both to allow cooperation among the schools and to make more comprehensive holdings available to students. It is interesting to note in this context that a study done in 1985 to lay the groundwork for the Access Pennsylvania program described later found that the average high school library in Pennsylvania contains 20,000 items including materials of all types. The investigators estimated that the total number of items in all high schools, public and nonpublic, if placed in a union catalog, could be as many as 17 million and that 50 to 60 percent of these items are probably unique. This information was contained in processed material obtained by the author from Richard Cassell, consultant on the Access Pennsylvania project.

A good example of this kind of development is the Access Pennsylvania project which has used LePac in the establishment of a resource sharing network. The ultimate goal of this project, which is part of the Governor's Agenda for Knowledge and Information Through Libraries and has been funded by the legislature, is to ensure that all citizens of Pennsylvania have access to the holdings of the 4,000 publicly supported school, academic, public, and special libraries in the commonwealth. Initially, Pennsylvania used LSCA funds and state funds to convert 700,000 records in thirty public and school library catalogs into machine-readable format. The databases thus created are being used for resource sharing purposes on a local basis through CD-ROM, microform, and online catalogs. Ultimately, development will continue through the creation of both regional and statewide databases.

Brodart has shown that a CD-ROM catalog can be made to interact efficiently with existing systems and can be an effective tool for resource sharing. The company has developed interface capabilities for LePac with several standard circulation systems making it possible for the system to provide status as well as location and holdings information. A communications package now allows LePac terminals to dial other terminals in a given network. Interlibrary loan requests may be transmitted in this manner. Brodart has also developed an interlibrary loan "director" for more complex networks. The director is a message-switching system that functions automatically to gather and route interlibrary loan requests, acknowledgments, and related messages throughout the network.

In Illinois, another potential use for CD-ROM catalogs is in individual libraries which want their own local public access catalog. These libraries may not be satisfied for one reason or another with the alternatives provided in the region or they may not want or be able to avail themselves of the existing alternatives. They may regard available systems as too expensive or too limiting in terms of local control. Staff of the community college library which tested LePac, for example, became highly interested in a CD-ROM catalog as an alternative to the online system currently available to them. The use of that system results from their participation in the regional network, but they do not find it satisfactory for their needs, do not use it even for circulation, and do not encourage its use by patrons as a partial substitute for an online public access catalog. There are many benefits to a CD-ROM catalog for a community college library. Total local control is possible, the system is cost effective, and elaborate technical expertise is not required to maintain it. Quite sophisticated search capabilities may be presented to users in an understandable way. In addition, for a smaller library (the community college has 80,000 volumes), reasonable response time is possible.

CONCLUSION

This summary has presented the results of a pilot project to assess the effectiveness of distributing catalog records on CD-ROM to facilitate resource sharing and reference work. In addition, it has attempted to provide an analysis of the capabilities of optical technology for use in libraries at an early stage of the development of that technology. Where possible, the findings of the study were reviewed in light of the current state of the art. Much progress has been made in the year since the study was completed. Although its permanent viability has not yet been entirely established, the infant optical information industry has begun to gain a firmer foothold in the marketplace. While libraries represent only a small piece of the market base for the industry, the number of players in the library field has increased, competition has brought product improvement, and vendors are solidifying their positions. The disc mastered by Brodart for the Illinois project was only the third the company had ever produced. Now, within a year, Brodart has installed 400 workstations at more than 200 sites and is expectd to ship 1,000 more for installation by the end of 1987 (Brodart, 1987). Several states, including Washington, Maine, Pennsylvania, Wisconsin, and Louisiana, have already created, or are in the process of creating, union catalogs on CD-ROM. This proliferation has even begun to be regarded as a threat to existing bibliographic networks by proponents of large scale interlibrary cooperation. An article in *American Libraries* (1987) "20 Years of Networking: New Life—or Dead Dinosaurs" for example, reported the observations of speakers at the Public Library Association, Technology in Public Libraries Committee meeting at the ALA annual conference in July 1987. In it Henriette Avram of the Library of Congress is quoted as urging that libraries look beyond the shortsighted goals of self-sufficiency toward the longer term benefits of networking. The article "Will Optical Discs be the End of Online Networks?" (1987) asks experts to comment on the impact of the technology on various types of online services. Most who commented shared the view that there is a place for optical tools in certain circumstances and that libraries must understand the tradeoffs in using one technology or another for internal library functions or for the provision of services.

The study has been in no way definitive concerning the future place, if any, for CD-ROM catalogs in Illinois. Their potential for bringing a larger number of libraries in the state into active cooperation is certainly in line with the traditions of library development in Illinois. Still, further investigation is required before the state can commit to any broad-based employment of CD-ROM catalogs to provide access to holdings which are not recorded in currently available online systems. It would be useful to create a CD-ROM union catalog containing the holdings of all libraries within one of the regional systems and to evaluate the reciprocal borrowing which takes place among member libraries of different sizes. A plan for increasing system resource sharing in an Illinois region was written by McMorran (1987). His idea was to use one of three available CD-ROM based cataloging systems (most probably General Research Corporation's Laser Quest) to add full MARC records to the system's existing catalog database. The headquarters library and the nine out of one hundred member libraries whose holdings were in the database already were to participate directly. Smaller libraries were to submit holdings for addition to the database and have cards produced for them. Only the ten direct participants would have online access to the regional union catalog. The catalog would contain only current holdings since retrospective conversion was viewed as being prohibitively expensive. If the database created was large enough to make storage in optical format appropriate, such a plan could be carried one step further by distributing CD-ROM versions of the database to libraries other than the ten online participants. Users in the smaller libraries, as well as the larger libraries, could then have direct access to the information on the holdings in the regional database. Such an experiment should be designed to measure the extent to which smaller libraries can assume some of the interlibrary lending burden from larger libraries. It should also address the true magnitude of the unmet need for library materials among the populations served by smaller libraries. Cost benefit issues would certainly have to be addressed. It would of course be difficult to place a quantitative value on the benefit to users of direct access to remote library materials. The idea that such access does have significant value, however, is central to the philosophy which has informed library development in Illinois for at least the last ten years.

APPENDIX A

Checklists and Questions Used at Sites During Group Interviews

Operation

Please check one response per mode for each of the following features of this information retrieval system.

	NOVICE MODE		EXPERT MODE	
	Positive	*Negative*	*Positive*	*Negative*
1. Subject searching	____	____	____	____
2. Boolean searching capability	____	____	____	____
3. "Anyword" searching	____	____	____	____
4. Response time	____	____	____	____
5. Searching through alphabetical lists	____	____	____	____
6. General ease of search	____	____	____	____
7. Following directions on screen	____	____	____	____
8. Use of keyboard	____	____	____	____
9. Amount of training needed to operate well	____	____	____	____
10. System reliability	____	____	____	____

Purpose/Use/Application

How is this system useful or potentially useful to you?

	YES	NO	DON'T KNOW
1. Verification of information	____	____	____
2. Reference	____	____	____
3. Identify location for interlibrary loans	____	____	____
4. Stimulate demand for follow-up services	____	____	____
5. Efficiency over any present method	____	____	____
6. Would some patrons prefer this over any present method?	____	____	____

7. How much time have you spent using the system?
   _____ minutes (estimate)

Improvements/Limitations

If this system was improved, which of the following elements are important?

	CRITICAL	NICE TO HAVE	NOT IMPORT- ANT
1. Printer access	____	____	____
2. Clear, more concise user manual	____	____	____
3. Single-sheet user search aid	____	____	____
4. Add user-truncation feature	____	____	____
5. Delete automatic truncation	____	____	____
6. Improve response time	____	____	____
7. Add escape mechanism for long searches	____	____	____
8. Provide estimate of size of search results	____	____	____
9. Present more than one match at a time	____	____	____
10. Charge-out feature	____	____	____
11. Larger or more targeted database	____	____	____
12. Need for more than one terminal	____	____	____
13. Call number availability	____	____	____
14. Call number searching	____	____	____

Interview Questions

1. Did you find the 'NOVICE' mode useful?

2. Did you find the 'EXPERT' mode useful?

3. What would be the ideal database to use this system on in your library (discuss various databases)?

4. How much of your present workload would be eliminated if the system was permanently installed in your library?

5. Discuss results from checklists. Arrive at consensus.

APPENDIX B

Questionnaire Used with University of Illinois Graduate School
of Library and Information Science Class

LePac Software Evaluation

I. In answering the questions below, make reference to your experience using the Expert mode.

EASE OF USE   EASY   DIFFICULT

1   2   3   4   5

A search by (1-4)

1. title

2. author

3. subject

4. combining authors or titles or subjects

5. Finding the correct subject term

6. Scanning through a long display (forward or backward)

7. Increasing the result when too little is retrieved

8. Reducing the result when too much is retrieved

9. Using "or" logic

10. Use of the "anyword" search

SATISFACTION

EFFECTIVENESS   LOW   HIGH

11. Taking into account the dates of coverage of the database, I found what I wanted

12. Sequence or order of search steps

OVERALL SATISFACTION

13. Most of my trial searches

DOCUMENTATION

14. LePac user manual

AIDS (Signs and Search Guides)

15. Accuracy

16. Sufficiency

17. Usefulness

DISPLAY DESIGN

18. Capability of interrupting or stopping the display of information

19. The order in which items are displayed

20. The rate at which items are displayed

21. Understanding the display for a single book, journal, or magazine

22. Understanding the display that shows more than a single book, journal, or magazine

SYSTEM FEEDBACK TO THE USER

23. Usefulness of the screen format as a prompt

24. Adequacy of on-screen instruction explanations

25. Conciseness of the wording of the screen instructions

RECORDS OF SEARCH

26. Cumulative records of searches being informative to the user

TECHNICAL DESIGN

27. Length of response time

28. Clarity of keyboard design

29. Ease of identification of function keys

USER'S TIME COST

30. Selecting from a list of choices

31. Learning to use the Expert mode

32. Searching by author on the Expert mode

33. Searching by title on the Expert mode

34. Searching by subject on the Expert mode

35. Searching combined authors and titles

36. Combinations which include subjects or terms entered in Anyword

37. Searching using the "OR" operator

REFERENCES

Andre, P. Q. J. (1985). Evaluating laser videodisk technology for the dissemination of agricultural information. *Information Technology & Libraries, 4*(June), 139-149.

Ballard, T. H. (1985). Dogma clouds the facts. *American Libraries, 16*(April), 257-259.

Brodart. (1987). *Interaction*, (Vol. 1, No. 3). Williamsport, PA: Brodart.

McMorran, C. E. (1987). Optical disks for union catalog creation: A proposal for the Northern Illinois Library System. *Optical Information Systems Update/Library and Information Center Applications, 2*(January/February), 6-11.

McQueen, J., & Boss, R. (1986). *Videodisc and optical technologies and the applications in libraries. 1986 update.* Chicago, IL: American Library Association.

Potter, W. G. (1986). Creative automation boosts interlibrary loan rates. *American Libraries, 17*(April), 244-246.

Schaub, J. A. (1985). CD-ROM for public access catalogs. *Library Hi Tech, 2,* 7-13.

20 years worth of networking: New life—or dead dinosaurs. *American Libraries,* 18(July/August), 612-614.

Watson, P. D. (1987a). *Creation and demonstration of optical disk version of the University of Illinois/River Bend library system online catalog.* Final report of the LSCA Project III-86-0485-30, February 16, 1987.

Watson, P. D. (1987b). CD-ROM catalogs—Evaluating LePac and looking ahead. *Online, 11*(September), 74-80.

Watson, P. D., & Golden, G. A. (1987). Distributing an online catalog on CD-ROM: The University of Illinois experience. *Online, 11*(March), 65-73.

Will optical discs be the end of online networks? (1987). *American Libraries, 18*(April), 253-256.

BARTON M. CLARK

Director of Departmental
Library Services Library
University of Illinois at Urbana-Champaign

KAREN HAVILL BINGHAM

Assistant to the Director
University Libraries
Case Western Reserve University

The New CD-ROM Technology: Shaping the Future of Reference and Information Research

It has been said more than once that students will do online searching as long as it does not cost more than a pizza. That premise is probably true. Several years ago when the University of Illinois at Urbana-Champaign (UIUC) had to almost double the cost of ERIC searches, the number of student searches dropped dramatically. These increased costs and the introduction of laser technology were major factors in the university library's examination of electronic reference tools which could be run by in-house microcomputers rather than vendor-operated mainframes. UIUC, like many other libraries, entered this new world of technology through Information Access Company's InfoTrac. This article describes UIUC's experiences with InfoTrac and the manner in which those experiences contributed to the library's analysis of in-house microcomputer-based electronic reference tools.

InfoTrac indexes approximately 900 journals from *Magazine Index* and *Business Index*, plus the last sixty days of the *New York Times* and the current year of the *Wall Street Journal*. Full citations are given for all entries. The alphabetic index includes subject headings, personal and corporate name headings, authors, and titles. The subject index uses Library of Congress subject headings which have been enhanced by Information Access Company (IAC). Searching is done on single entries with no capabilities to perform Boolean searching.

InfoTrac is marketed as a 12-inch laser disc containing four years of data. The disc is updated and cumulated monthly. Also available is an InfoTrac backfile database containing four years of retrospective data. Title coverage in the retrospective file is the same as in the current database, except that the *New York Times* and *Wall Street Journal* are not indexed. The backfile is updated and cumulated annually. The InfoTrac system hardware allows four microcomputer workstations to be used with a single disc player. Several hardware configurations, software packages, and databases are available from Information Access Company. An annual subscription to the InfoTrac database is $4,500 plus $8,500 for a subscription plan which includes the annual license fee, software package, control unit, all hardware, and hardware maintenance for one access station. The price increases $1,000 with each additional access station up to a maximum of four. After five years on this purchase plan, the hardware becomes the property of the subscriber. Alternative plans allowing subscribers to purchase their own hardware and/or control unit are available. Discounts are available for multiple system and database subscriptions.

UIUC's experiences with InfoTrac began in mid-1985 through a generous grant from the Illinois State Library which allowed for the acquisition of three one-year InfoTrac subscriptions and the attendant hardware. The goal of the project was to demonstrate the value of optical disc databases for storage and retrieval of bibliographic citations to journal articles. The intent was to determine the usefulness and user acceptance of such a system within divergent environments. Three different sites were selected for the project: the University of Illinois Undergraduate library, the Champaign Public Library and Information Center, and the Lincoln Trail Libraries System headquarters. Because of the immense popularity of the system in the UIUC Undergraduate Library, the UIUC Library later acquired an additional subscription for a fourth site in the UIUC Commerce Library.

AVAILABILITY

InfoTrac was available to users in each library during all open hours. Champaign Public Library is open 73 hours per week, Lincoln Trail Libraries System 70, the Undergraduate Library 112, and the Commerce Library 102.

In each setting, with the exception of Lincoln Trail, InfoTrac was located in a highly visible area near the library's reference desk where it was easily accessible to both patrons and staff. At the Lincoln Trail Libraries System headquarters, access was limited to professional and paraprofessional library staff who provide support services to Lincoln Trail's member libraries.

TYPES OF USERS

Champaign Public reported that InfoTrac was used predominantly by high school and college students. Adults from the community also used it, but in most cases they had to be directed to the resource and encouraged to use it. Use by young adults was much more frequent than by older adults. Reference librarians as well as librarians from other departments within the library used InfoTrac heavily.

In the UIUC Undergraduate Library, InfoTrac is used almost exclusively by undergraduate students, although a few graduate students also use it. Use of the system by faculty is rare. Undergraduate librarians use InfoTrac when assisting patrons with difficult information searches and for demonstration purposes. User surveys at Colorado State University (Ernest & Monath, 1986) and Indiana University (Beltran, 1987) corroborate that undergraduate students are the heaviest users of InfoTrac.

The number of graduate students using InfoTrac appears to be relatively small and is confined primarily to the UIUC Commerce Library. Use of InfoTrac by upperclassmen, particularly by students searching for corporate information to prepare for job interviews, is higher, as might be expected, in the Commerce Library than in the Undergraduate Library.

Use of InfoTrac at Lincoln Trail was confined primarily to the system reference librarian who was responsible for answering queries from member libraries. While other Lincoln Trail professionals and paraprofessional reference support staff used it occasionally, they usually referred questions to the reference librarian.

USER RESPONSE

Champaign Public Library and UIUC reported frequent, heavy use of InfoTrac by patrons and library staff. During the school year, queuing of students at the InfoTrac station was constant at UIUC and frequent at Champaign Public Library and Information Center. Librarians at Champaign Public used InfoTrac at least once during every two hour shift. Lincoln Trail's library staff used the system about once a day or once every other day.

According to library staff in the UIUC undergraduate and commerce libraries, each with two InfoTrac workstations, user response to InfoTrac is uniformly and enthusiastically favorable. Both staff and patrons use superlatives when describing their experience with the database. This is especially true in the case of undergraduate students who are described as being "wild" about InfoTrac. Undergraduate students stand in queues at InfoTrac stations rather than use an available paper index located ten yards away. Students prefer using the laser disc product to all other availa-ble indexes such as the *Readers' Guide* or the *Business Periodicals Index*.

After a year, the Undergraduate Library still has long lines at its InfoTrac terminals during peak periods of the semester. Regardless of the time during the semester, at least two or three people can be found waiting at one of the Undergraduate Library's two workstations. Staff maintain that the library could keep an additional two stations busy throughout the semester. The two workstations in the Commerce Library are also in constant use, although that library does not experience the long lines that are typical in the Undergraduate Library. The enthusiastic response by students has been echoed in reports from California State University (Stephens, 1986), Colorado State University (Ernest & Monath, 1986), Indiana University (Beltran, 1986), the University of Colorado (Krismann, 1986), the University of Dayton (Walker & Westneat, 1985), and many other institutions (Tenopir, 1986).

UIUC undergraduate users are enthusiastic about InfoTrac because: (1) it is easy to use, (2) it provides up-to-date information on current topics, (3) it produces instant results, and (4) it eliminates writing down citations. It is the tool preferred by undergraduates for finding the five to ten citations they often need for term papers or speeches. In the UIUC Undergraduate Library, InfoTrac is used primarily for these purposes. In the Commerce Library its main use is in securing information about companies, particu-larly for job interviews, although it is used often for undergraduate papers.

The ease of use factor is important for users and library staff. The database is publicized as requiring no special training. It is, in fact, largely self-explanatory. UIUC librarians have found it unnecessary to prepare special instructions for using InfoTrac. The instructional card which accompanies the system, the function buttons on the keyboard, and the help screens provide adequate instruction for most patrons to easily access the system.

InfoTrac creates few, if any, demands for additional library staff time to instruct and interpret the system for users. UIUC librarians report that InfoTrac makes life at the reference desk easier because the database and search techniques are so user friendly. Only on rare occasions do staff need to assist users. The experience of UIUC librarians with user education demands is confirmed by other use studies reported in the literature (Tenopir, 1986, p. 19). Beltran (1986) suggests that students require less assistance with InfoTrac than with print indexes covering the popular literature (p. 64).

At Champaign Public Library and Information Center, students doing research papers and adult patrons appreciated the speed of searching and printing, the presence of multiyear references, and the clarity and ease of manipulation among subject headings. Orientation to the computer and InfoTrac was accomplished easily even by those who had no prior experience with computers. Champaign Public Library and Information Center reference librarians frequently used InfoTrac during information searches. Response speed, ease of searching various subject headings, cross-references, and the print feature made it an especially useful and labor-saving reference source. InfoTrac became a first-used source in the public library.

STRENGTHS

Librarians and users agree that InfoTrac's major strengths are that it is current, fast to use, and very user friendly. Indexing terms relate to the Library of Congress subject headings used in *Magazine Index*. Adequate cross references are used. Other features appreciated by patrons and librarians are availability of printed copy and no telecommunication costs.

In the public library setting, InfoTrac was most helpful and was used most frequently to find information on current topics such as AIDS, child abuse, Alzheimer's disease, drugs, urban gangs, etc. It was heavily used by students as a quick source of reference for reports and research papers. Champaign Public Library and Information Center and Lincoln Trail librarians said that InfoTrac also was used regularly to locate information on corporations and companies, computers and software, consumer product evaluations, and book and movie reviews. Lincoln Trail used it as a supplement to other tools, while the other two libraries' patrons used it as an independent source of information.

WEAKNESSES

The only complaints registered by library patrons are that the database only goes back to 1982 and that just two newspapers are included. Librarians complain that the cooling fan of the microcomputer is too noisy and that abstracts are not available.

Champaign Public librarians noted that an additional source of frustration is that InfoTrac gives incomplete access to the magazine collection film cassettes. Only part of the *Magazine Index* citations are on InfoTrac. Some citations on InfoTrac have no code letters leading to an article which is indeed present in the magazine collection. Other InfoTrac citations give only business collection code letters when the article can also be found in the magazine collection. In addition, codes are sometimes incorrect.

The most serious problem, however, is database errors. Librarians are critical of errors and searching problems in the database. Unfortunately, spelling errors are common. The precision of subheadings needs to be improved. For example, an article may be indexed under "United States—Economic Policy—Soviet Union" but not under the reverse heading "Soviet Union—Economic Policy—United States."

Another serious complaint is that users cannot enter the database at a subheading under a broad subject heading such as "Agriculture—United States." Rather, users must start with "Agriculture" and page through to "Agriculture—United States." Hall, Talan, and Pease (1987) document similar problems with the use of InfoTrac at California State University and discuss their reservations about the use of InfoTrac as a research tool in academic libraries. Other institutions such as the University of Wyoming have chosen to forego purchase of InfoTrac due to limitations such as these and the lack of software and hardware standardization among vendors (Van Arsdale & Ostrye, 1986).

Despite such criticisms of the database, many librarians believe that adding complex search features to InfoTrac might deter students who now require little help in using the system. It is interesting to note that users do not complain about the errors and indexing problems reported by most librarians who use the database. One can only surmise that despite these limitations InfoTrac adequately meets the needs of most high school and undergraduate students who are using it to find a limited number of citations on a current or popular topic or to obtain company research information.

IMPACT ON THE LIBRARY

The availability of InfoTrac has led to three indirect demands on the UIUC Library system: (1) a demand for more InfoTrac workstations to meet user needs, (2) a demand for more convenient access to journals indexed by InfoTrac, and (3) the desire to link InfoTrac to the UIUC Library's online catalog.

Providing InfoTrac in one departmental library, the Undergraduate Library, created a demand for it in another location on campus, the Commerce Library. As was mentioned earlier, both libraries indicate that their clientele would utilize additional workstations if available. There is no doubt that other departmental units in the UIUC library system would benefit from having InfoTrac stations as well. In addition, if sufficient InfoTrac workstations were available to meet user demands, it is possible that subscriptions to selected print indexes might be cancelled by the library.

Central Reference Services in the UIUC Library has responded with an InfoTrac II test site in the Reference Library of the main library building. The InfoTrac II database includes those titles in *Magazine Index* plus two months of the *New York Times*. It indexes fewer titles and more popular magazines than InfoTrac.

User response to InfoTrac II and preliminary observations of staff are similar to the reaction toward its predecessor. Patrons are enthusiastic, if indiscriminate, in their praise of the resource. Librarians routinely utilize InfoTrac II in answering reference queries. As with InfoTrac, lack of quality control in the database subject headings and errors in citations are reported. Staff note that the database is almost too easy to use and that patrons overlook nuances in searching that might uncover additional citations. The results of a recent user survey conducted by staff of the Reference Library promise to yield further analysis of InfoTrac II.

It is difficult to gauge whether use of journals indexed by InfoTrac has increased. While UIUC has not conducted a formal, full-scale study to analyze journal usage since the advent of InfoTrac, it generally is believed that use of titles covered by InfoTrac has increased. UIUC library staff are aware of the appearance of more and more students with InfoTrac print-outs and are questioned often about the library's holdings of these titles.

Librarians in the Undergraduate Library, and especially in the Commerce Library, find that students are most frustrated because the two libraries do not have all the journals indexed in InfoTrac. (Commerce owns 100 of the 900 journal titles covered by InfoTrac.) Although approximately 85 percent of the journals indexed in InfoTrac are available on the UIUC campus, undergraduate students prefer to consult journals available in the departmental library they are using rather than go to another location to get cited materials.

A recent informal study to evaluate the quality of service to undergraduate students in the Central Bookstacks, which houses over 4 million volumes, confirms this. Users were asked whether they identified needed stacks material through InfoTrac, the library computer system (LCS), a librarian's assistance, or all three. Of 225 responses to the question, only fifteen students said they identified material via InfoTrac, while another sixteen said they used all three sources mentioned. Library staff are convinced that users restrict journal usage to those titles owned by the libraries in which InfoTrac is located.

The Undergraduate Library has generated a UIUC holdings list of all journal titles indexed by InfoTrac to encourage users to pursue available copies elsewhere on campus. The holdings list is posted near each Info-Trac terminal. Despite its availability, there is a definite demand for a computerized link between InfoTrac and the library's online catalog. Students expect to be able to shift from one database to the other at the same terminal and are disappointed that such a feature is unavailable.

USER EDUCATION

As was stated earlier, students find that InfoTrac is extremely easy to use. Consequently, library staff have found that relatively little time is required in instructing patrons about how to use the database or search techniques. Librarians find that InfoTrac is self-explanatory and requires very little interpretation to users. In all three libraries user education is user-initiated; that is, library staff answer questions and provide assistance to patrons when asked. None of the libraries developed literature describing how to use the system, but all posted the "How to Use InfoTrac" card supplied with the system.

Some disagreement exists between those librarians who think that undergraduate students are well-served and satisfied with the InfoTrac search result and those who believe that unsophisticated users are unaware of the faults of the database and therefore are not locating all available information in searching the database. Tenopir (1986) reports that most librarians agree that InfoTrac should be used as a supplemental tool rather than as a primary research tool. Apparently staff in some libraries, such as the University of Hawaii's, have posted signs warning patrons that Info-Trac does not provide a comprehensive subject search (p. 168).

There is general consensus among librarians that subject headings in the database need improvement and that instruction to users in how to select the appropriate subject heading is desirable although not always possible. When using a system that is otherwise user friendly, students expect to find natural language headings. Since InfoTrac now uses LC subject headings exclusively, the student may fail to discover the relevant subject heading(s) when searching the database.

PROMOTIONAL EFFORTS

Promotional efforts in the UIUC Undergraduate Library include development of a short brochure to announce the availability of InfoTrac and describe its capabilities. The brochure was distributed to all classes in the Undergraduate Library's bibliographic instruction program and made available at all InfoTrac workstations. Undergraduate librarians also mention InfoTrac as a major reference tool in all bibliographic instruction classes. In the Commerce Library, librarians publicize InfoTrac during class presentations and provide demonstrations to interested faculty in the library.

Use of InfoTrac has spread largely by word of mouth among students. Major promotional efforts by the UIUC Library have been unnecessary. Additional publicity would create an overload on the workstations currently available.

OUTCOMES

Despite the success of InfoTrac, both Lincoln Trail Libraries System and Champaign Public Library and Information Center chose not to renew their subscriptions to the service. Because only librarians were able to access InfoTrac in the Lincoln Trail headquarters setting, the unique advantages which InfoTrac offers to patrons in public settings were reduced significantly in an environment restricted to librarians. Champaign Public Library's decision to cancel InfoTrac was tied directly to cost. While popular with users, it was felt that the $8,000 price tag for InfoTrac did not warrant the cancellation of other resources to continue it. However, the Champaign Public Library subsequently subscribed to InfoTrac II.

At the University of Illinois at Urbana-Champaign the experience with InfoTrac has resulted in an examination of the potential of electronic information systems in general and, in particular, those systems that can be run from a microcomputer. SilverPlatter's ERIC, AGRICOLA, and PsycLIT databases recently have been added to two departmental libraries, and WilsonDisc databases are now available in the Undergraduate and Library Science libraries.

SilverPlatter markets a range of CD-ROM information products whose retrieval software enables users to perform search functions equivalent to those now available from online systems. Key features include Boolean searching, right-hand truncation, searches in specific fields of a record, proximity searching, numeric range and limit searching, help screens, and display and print capabilities. The search techniques and strategies employed are inherently more sophisticated than in InfoTrac and therefore require more elaborate user instruction. Allen (1985) provides a useful system overview and search features of SilverPlatter's CD-ROM products.

While SilverPlatter's products do not compete with InfoTrac, the Wilson products do. The UIUC's first test of Wilson's CD-ROM product was in the Undergraduate Library where it is in direct competition with InfoTrac. Whereas in the last year undergraduate students often have ignored the paper versions of *Readers' Guide* and *Business Periodicals Index* in favor of InfoTrac, it is quite possible that this will not be the case with the new CD-ROM versions of these indexes. Since it will be possible to acquire *Biography Index, Business Periodicals Index, General Science Index, Humanities Index, Readers' Guide to Periodical Literature,* and *Social Science Index* for less than a single subscription to InfoTrac, it is possible that the UIUC Undergraduate Library may cancel its subscription to InfoTrac should a thorough review of the Wilson products indicate that they are as popular as InfoTrac. The UIUC Commerce Library will continue its InfoTrac subscription with additional workstations if queuing becomes a problem.

COSTS

It is important to note the inflated prices of optical disc products. One example is the pricing of SilverPlatter's ERIC database. The annual subscription to the current database with quarterly updates initially was

$1,750; the annual update was $950; and the archival discs were $2,000. When OCLC entered the market with a CD-ROM ERIC database at $600 for OCLC members and $675 for nonmembers, SilverPlatter's price immediately dropped to $650 for the current disc with quarterly updates, $390 for the annually updated current disc, and $900 for the archival discs. Similarly, the price of SilverPlatter's PsycLIT database has dropped recently from $4,995 to $3,995.

In addition, it must be realized that the cost of running the new optical disc products is far greater than the advertized annual subscription price. As Alberico (1987) points out, many hidden costs accompany the use of CD-ROMs. Equipping a single workstation with the necessary hardware—including a PC, printer, and CD-ROM disc drive—requires an initial outlay of between $2,000 and $3,000. Thereafter, equipment will incur maintenance costs.

Printing costs can be significant also, especially to operate quiet printers such as the Hewlett-Packard Thinkjet which are essential for use in public areas. Information Access Company estimated that supplies for one workstation cost from $500 to $750 a year (Pease & Post, 1985). Experience at the University of Illinois indicates that paper, ink, and/or cartridge costs can range much higher per year, from $1,000 to $1,500 per station when heavily used.

Based on usage during the first semester (Fall 1986) of operation in UIUC's Undergraduate Library, printing costs for two InfoTrac workstations with a Thinkjet and an Epson printer were estimated at $2,500 per year. During the next semester (Spring 1987) this amount decreased significantly to approximately $600 per year. These costs include paper as well as cartridges or ribbon cassettes for the printers. Library staff credit the precipitous decline in amount of printing not to a decrease in the use of InfoTrac but to the fact that students with more searching experience are much more selective in what they print. It is expected that a surge in printing activity may occur during the next fall semester when a new class of freshmen begin to use InfoTrac.

An additional hidden cost of workstations located in public areas is the cost of securing equipment. Anchor pads and lock down devices are often a necessary cost of business. The cost to lock down the equipment for a single workstation may run as high as $500.

CONCLUSION

InfoTrac has been phenomenally popular with patrons at UIUC. Its ability to provide bibliographic citations quickly with a minimum knowledge of system structure has overridden any shortcomings InfoTrac has, including failure to perform Boolean searches. This enthusiastic response indicates that optical disc databases will take their place alongside vendor-based online systems and locally produced electronic databases as an essential component of reference service in the years ahead.

This brings us back to the beginning point of this article and the price of a pizza. CD-ROM products are providing an alternative for students to the rising prices of vendor-based online databases. While the shift in charges from the user to the library places electronic reference products in the same category as paper sources which are free to the user, it presents serious questions concerning library cost and database quality. As more CD-ROM products become available commercially, librarians will be faced with difficult and perplexing questions about pricing, hardware and software, standards, compatibility, and search capabilities. Very few product reviews and use studies of specific databases are available now. Careful planning and evaluation will be essential in considering purchase of these high-priced resources (Herther, 1986). Product quality, comparable resources, and use or need assessments are factors which should be considered. Criteria will be needed to provide a framework for evaluating the burgeoning number of CD-ROM products (Miller, 1987). Many questions remain. It is clear that while InfoTrac marks the beginning of microcomputer-based electronic reference technology, it is definitely not the end.

REFERENCES

Alberico, R. (1987). Justifying CD-ROM. *Small Computers in Libraries*, 7(February), 18-20.

Allen, R. J. (1985). The CD-ROM services of SilverPlatter Information, Inc. *Library Hi Tech*, 3(12), 49-60.

Beltran, A. B. (1987). InfoTrac at Indiana University: A second look. *Database*, 10(February), 48-50.

Beltran, A. B. (1986). Use of InfoTrac in a university library. *Database*, 9(June), 63-66.

Ernest, D. J., & Monath, J. (1986). User reaction to a computerized periodical index. *College & Research Libraries News*, 47(May), 315-318.

Hall, C.; Talan, H.; & Pease, B. (1987). InfoTrac in academic libraries: What's missing in the new technology? *Database*, 10(February), 52-56.

Herther, N. (1986). A planning model for optical product evaluation. *Online*, 10(September), 128-130.

Krismann, C. (1986). Byte line. *Colorado Libraries*, 12(March), 32.

Miller, D. C. (1987). Evaluating CD-ROMS: To buy or what to buy? *Database*, 10(June), 36-42.

Pease, B., & Post, W. (1985). InfoTrac: A review of an optical disc based public index. *Serials Review*, 11(Winter), 57-61.

Stephens, K. (1986). Laserdisc technology enters mainstream. *American Libraries*, 17(April), 252.

Tenopir, C. (1986). InfoTrac: A laser disc system. *Library Journal*, 111(September 1), 168-169.

Van Arsdale, W. O., & Ostrye, A. T. (1986). InfoTrac: A second opinion. *American Libraries*, 17(July/August), 514-515.

Walker, M. A., & Westneat, H. (1985). Using InfoTrac in an academic library. *Reference Services Review*, 13(Winter), 17-22.

WILLIAM H. MISCHO
Engineering Librarian
Beckman Institute Librarian
University of Illinois at Urbana-Champaign

MELVIN G. DeSART
Assistant Engineering Librarian
Assistant Professor of Library Administration
University of Illinois at Urbana-Champaign

An End User Search Service with Customized Interface Software

Libraries have provided online access to bibliographic databases via commercial vendors since the late 1960s. Until recently, the direct interaction with these systems has been almost the exclusive province of trained intermediaries. However, in the past several years library services offering end user or direct searching by patrons of bibliographic databases have grown dramatically. To a large extent, this increased activity has been technology-driven caused by the introduction and rapid growth of online catalogs, the continuing proliferation of online databases, the introduction of new online services, the increased availability of microcomputer workstations, and the development of optical information technologies. These rapidly evolving technologies have combined to make end user searching an attractive and viable service option for libraries.

One highly visible end user searching tool is the online catalog. Online catalog user studies have revealed, among other findings, that catalog users have the most difficulty with subject searching and place the highest priority for improvements on various subject search enhancements. In addition, users approach online catalogs expecting to find enhanced access to a broader range of materials—in particular periodicals—than the coverage provided in the traditional card catalog (Markey, 1983; Hildreth, 1985). While the online catalog use studies indicate an overwhelming acceptance by users and high user satisfaction, they have also been interpreted as a mandate for enhanced subject access (Markey, 1984).

The provision of enhanced online access to periodical information has received a great deal of attention. Brett Butler (1984) has noted: "We face a seamless, or undifferentiated, demand from our library patrons. That is, our users are likely to be indifferent to the form—book or periodical—in which the information they desire is packaged" (p. 1). The card catalogs of the late nineteenth century provided access to periodical articles via 3 inch by 5 inch cards supplied by vendors or prepared in-house. There is a renewed interest in shaping the modern online catalog into an "analytic" catalog capable of providing the same function (Potter, 1987).

Libraries are presently investigating three methods of providing enhanced online access to periodical information. These are: (1) mounting commercially produced bibliographic databases in local online systems, often using the same software employed in the online catalog; (2) making available fixed-cost searching utilizing optical disc (CD-ROM) databases; and (3) providing an end user searching service utilizing front-end search software and/or the less expensive after-hours commercial vendor systems. Many academic libraries are exploring all three options. There are economic, service, and retrieval advantages associated with each approach. Clearly, the most comprehensive access to the periodical and report literature is through the commercial database vendors with their broad "information supermarkets" and sophisticated retrieval software. This continues to be particularly true in the sciences which possess numerous large and complex databases which have not readily lent themselves to optical storage and retrieval technologies.

This article describes a project at the University of Illinois at Urbana-Champaign Library that has focused on the third option described earlier—i.e., providing enhanced access to the periodical literature through an end user searching service which utilizes the commercial database vendors. This demonstration project employs customized microcomputer interface software designed to facilitate the search process for end users. The service offers controlled end user searching as an option within an online catalog interface.

End User Searching Studies

A comprehensive review of studies and trends connected with end user searching of bibliographic databases can be found in the 1987 *Annual Review of Information Science and Technology* (Mischo & Lee, 1987). It is clear that a number of factors have contributed to the increased interest in end user searching services. These include:

—the continued exponential growth of information and the increasingly obvious value of online retrieval skills;

—the wide availability of online full-text databases (such as LEXIS) directed at professional users;

—heightened awareness by end users of database services because of articles in the popular and professional literature and promotional activities by vendors at professional conferences touting the value of online searching;

—the development of research and commercial front-end and gateway software packages to facilitate online searching by untrained users;

—the inauguration of nonpeak-time, less expensive, more user-friendly search systems by BRS, DIALOG, and STN;

—the proliferation of microcomputer workstations with telecommunication capabilities in the workplace and home settings;

—the emphasis on computer literacy in education, office automation, professional occupations, and recreational activities;

—the growing familiarity of library users with online catalogs and, by extension, with online bibliographic retrieval in general.

Experience with establishing search centers, training end users, and providing follow-up assistance to users has given the library community some insights into the process of end user searching. In summary, an analysis of end user searching activities and services reveals:

—Users are very enthusiastic about performing searches in easy-to-use, inexpensive systems but have difficulty in performing effective searches.

—Users have serious problems with Boolean logic and search strategy formulation.

—Users resist formal training sessions and printed instructions, preferring computer-assisted instruction (CAI) and direct one-to-one instruction from library staff and peers.

—The services are very staff-intensive for libraries and require additional library (reference) personnel to assist users with logon and machine procedures, database selection, and search strategy formulation and modification.

—Users have difficulty with the simpler interfaces provided for after-hours services.

—Searches performed with intermediaries still yield better retrieval results.

—Most end users of online bibliographic systems search infrequently and never progress beyond the naïve user stage.

These results appear to hold for online catalogs, remote database searching, and optical disc systems.

Library end user searching services have used two approaches in offering access to remote search services: (1) training users in command mode searching, and (2) making available software search aids as interfaces to commercial systems. In this project, customized microcomputer interface software was developed to provide end user access to periodical citation databases.

Project Description

This project focused on the design and development of a microcomputer interface for searching remote bibliographic databases. The interface addresses the identified problems of end user searching in command mode and facilitates direct patron searching of periodical citation databases. The customized interface software permits searches of commercial vendor databases to be performed as a search option within the University of Illinois Online Catalog. From a public online catalog terminal (microcomputer), library users are provided with effective access to the periodical literature and a mechanism to link their search results with local holdings and availability information.

The University of Illinois at Urbana-Champaign Online Catalog is comprised of the LCS (developed at Ohio State University) short-record circulation system and a full bibliographic record search capability using the WLN (Western Library Network) search software. The online catalog is accessed via a microcomputer interface. Because the online catalog uses microcomputers as terminals, the capability exists to develop front-end and gateway software to access other off-site bibliographic data, including periodical citations available on the commercial database vendors. This project has been supported by an IBM equipment grant to the University of Illinois and a complementary grant from the Council on Library Resources.

This project was designed to investigate four areas of development: (1) interface design features that will expedite subject retrieval in bibliographic database systems; (2) enhanced subject access to periodical literature within an online catalog environment; (3) the automatic linking of retrieved database search references with online catalog holdings and availability information; and (4) the policy and service issues associated with enhanced subject access techniques. These remain important issues in bibliographic control.

This interface to remote bibliographic databases is designed to support fairly straightforward searches. More complex searches requiring the use of the full set of vendor software features or comprehensive searches still must depend on the assistance of a human intermediary. The system is designed to address the identified problems end users experience with database search strategy formulation and Boolean operators and to provide more effective searches within the constraints of online costs and staffing demands. The software utilized here controls the search process, minimizing connect time and controlling printing, resulting in essentially fixed-cost or upper-limit costing on the searching service.

While this project focuses primarily on an interface design for a commercial vendor system, the techniques identified and tested in this project are applicable to other online bibliographic searching environments, including online catalogs and optical disc systems. As Borgman (1986) has pointed out, users of both bibliographic retrieval systems and online catalogs exhibit similar behavior patterns and have the same types of mechanical and conceptual difficulties. In a situation where the two types of systems are linked, and, indeed, as the two types of systems evolve and become more similar, it is incumbent on the interface to assist nonlibrarian searchers in learning both the structure of the database organizaion and the mechanics of the systems.

Description of the Interface

There is evidence that software interfaces built around expert system techniques can facilitate database searching by untrained users (Marcus & Reintjes, 1981; Belkin et al., 1987). The interface design utilized in this project is based on an approach suggested by Marcus (1982). It also incorporates elements of other front-end packages.

The present demonstration system was tested in spring 1987 and has been offered to library users at selected departmental library sites under the rubric of the Self-Service Database Service (SSDS) since June 1987. The service utilizes the BRS/After Dark and regular BRS systems. An evaluation is ongoing.

The initial design criteria for the project interface called for a simplified menu-driven interface utilizing off line storage of search strategy, automatic logon procedures, and software-controlled navigated searching techniques. Following the practice of some other gateway or front-end software (e.g., OASIS, EasyNet, Search Helper), this interface is designed to minimize online connect time and printing options. After reviewing other end user projects, it was determined that the interface needed to address identified areas of user difficulty, particularly in the construction of search strategy.

Early tests of the initial software design verified the problems identified in previous end user searching studies and challenged the implicit assumption that the after-hours database services were sufficiently simplified to allow end users to perform effective searches. It was clear that the interface must assist users in search strategy formulation and manipulation of search results while not requiring any direct user knowledge of Boolean logic.

The project has developed and tested methods of dynamically linking retrieved periodical citations with local holdings and availability information in the online catalog. The interface presently allows users, after completing a database search, to "switch" over to the online catalog to retrieve call numbers and holdings information. Software has been developed to modify and link the already existing online catalog interface with the end user database search interface at both the initial menu and at the conclusion of an online database search.

The present configuration allows the user the menu option of searching either the online catalog for known-item and monographic subject information or external databases for articles within periodicals (see options 1 and 2 of Figure 1). After completion of a database search, users are offered the option of modifying the strategy and repeating the search and/or accessing the online catalog for availability and holdings information.

After the selection of the database search option, the ensuing search session follows a series of steps. First, the user chooses the subject field of interest from a customized menu. Next, multiple-term facets or concept groups representing the user's search topic are constructed. The interface assists the user in this search strategy formulation through the use of online tutorials and suggestive prompts. The search strategy construction requires no knowledge of Boolean operators and no operators are explicitly presented. The search strategy is formulated offline with the user given opportunities to modify the strategy as it is constructed. Stopwords are screened and a table of "go-words" (allowing substitution of preferred terms or added terms for one already) entered can be constructed.

The software then automatically logs on to the system, accesses the database, and executes the prestored search strategy to determine citation postings for each concept group. The resultant concept postings sets are manipulated by the software using a combinatorial algorithm which broadens or narrows the search in an effort to obtain the optimum search results. Finally, a selected number of retrieved citations are downloaded, capture of the search history and automatic logoff takes place, and the downloaded citations undergo postprocessing and printing.

Sample Search for Periodical Citations

A series of screen displays are presented to illustrate a sample search session. While these static screen "snapshots" are unable to capture the interactive nature of a search session, they serve to illustrate the process carried on in a search. These figures do not convey the use of highlighting and screen contrast visible to the user.

UNIVERSITY OF ILLINOIS ENHANCED ONLINE CATALOG
SEARCH OPTIONS:
1. SEARCH ONLINE CATALOG FOR ITEMS IN THE LIBRARY
   SYSTEM:
   Look for books, journals, theses, etc. by author, title, author/title, subject,
   call number.
2. SEARCH FOR CURRENT ARTICLES IN JOURNALS AND
   MAGAZINES:
   Self-service database search of an index (e.g. Engineering Index) to
   retrieve references to articles on a topic.
CHOOSE 1 or 2: 2

Figure 1

CHOOSE THE SUBJECT AREA YOU WISH TO FIND INFORMATION
IN:

1. Electrical and Computer Engineering
2. Physics
3. Computer Science (research journals)
4. Computer Science (microcomputer and data processing journals)
5. Materials Science (Physics/EE)
6. Materials Science (Engineering)
7. Civil Engineering
8. Mechanical Engineering and Engineering Mechanics
9. Aerospace Engineering
10. Nuclear Engineering
11. Bioengineering (consider also Elec. Engr. for Bioacoustics)
12. Chemical Engineering (see also Chemistry for Chem Abstracts)
13. General Engineering
14. Chemistry (Chem Abstracts
15. Popular Magazines--Time, Newsweek, Aviation Week, Science, etc.

 TYPE A NUMBER, THEN PRESS ENTER: 15

Figure 2

PLEASE READ THE NEXT TWO INSTRUCTION SCREENS CAREFULLY

The most important part of a database search is putting together the search strategy. The search strategy consists of a series of words or phrases entered by the searcher to describe the search topic.

The search system used here will retrieve references using the terms in the search strategy. These terms will appear in article titles, descriptors or keywords, or abstracts (summarizes).

TYPICAL SEARCH TOPICS:
    1. Numerical techniques in fluid dynamics on supercomputers.
    2. Microcomputers used in CAD/CAM.

**Note that these search topics are phrased like an article title.

**The terms in the search can be grouped into separate concepts.
    In the first example above the 3 concept groups are:
1) numerical techniques; 2) fluid dynamics; 3) supercomputers.
    In the second example, there are 2 concept groups:
1) microcomputers; 2) CAD/CAM.

**A search will typically have from 1 to 3 separate concept groups.
    PRESS ANY KEY TO CONTINUE

Figure 3

Figure 1 shows the initial menu used in the interface. After selection of option 2 from the initial menu, the user is asked to select the subject area of interest from a menu such as the one shown in Figure 2. This menu is customized for each departmental library site. One advantage in utilizing the large commercial vendors is that over 200 databases in all subject areas are readily available and accessible via a single search language. The database is software selected from the user's choice.

Figures 3 and 4 constitute the basic instructional phase of the program. Here, users are asked to read information screens that are designed to assist them in search strategy formulation. The model strategies presented are tailored to each departmental library site.

In Figure 5 the user is asked to enter a title-like description of the search topic to help identify the search concept terms (in this example, end-user searching with microcomputers). The use of natural language topic descriptions can be found in other expert-based interfaces, including the OAK front-end software package (Meadow, 1986).

The next screen (see Figure 6) repeats the previously entered title and prompts the user for a term to describe the first or primary concept of the

In the first example search on the previous screen, there are three concept groups;
     1) Numerical techniques;
     2) Fluid dynamics;
     3) Supercomputers.
    Other words or phrases may be synonyms or alternative phrases for each of the concepts. For example, for "numerical techniques", the terms "numerical methods" or "finite difference" could be added. For the concept "fluid dynamics", the searcher might also be interested in articles with the terms "fluid flow" or "supersonic flow".
    Using additional terms within each concept, the search strategy can be expressed in the form:

CONCEPT 1	CONCEPT 2	CONCEPT 3
Numerical Techniques	Fluid Dynamics	Supercomputers
Numerical Methods	Fluid Flow	Cray
Finite Difference	Supersonic Flow	Cyber 205
Finite Element		
Numerical Solutions		

***The search will retrieve references that contain at least one term from EACH COLUMN or concept.
       PRESS ANY KEY TO CONTINUE

Figure 4

YOU WILL NOW BE ASKED TO ENTER THE CONCEPT TERMS FOR YOUR SEARCH.

    The terms making up the separate concept groups will be used to find references to journal articles and reports.

**To help identify your concept terms, please begin by typing a one-sentence title of an imaginary (or real) article that would best meet your information needs.

This title will not be directly searched. Rather, it should help focus on a specific topic and help to identify concept terms.

    (TYPE ARTICLE TITLE BELOW, FOLLOWED BY ENTER KEY)
End-user searching with microcomputers

Figure 5

Your search title:
End-user searching with microcomputers.

You will be asked to enter the words in this title as separate search concepts.

You will be able to enter up to three concept groups.

Type below a term (word or phrase) describing concept 1 of your search request.

Type the word or phrase followed by the ENTER key.

Concept 1 should be the central or most important topic of your search. For a search title like 'Microcomputers used in CAD/CAM', concept 1 would be entered as: CAD/CAM

If you need to use chemical formulas, check with a site attendant.
Concept 1 (word or phrase): end-users

Figure 6

search. Note that all of the data entry and search argument formulation is done offline. Because of the assumed primacy of the first concept group, the postings set from this concept will be included in all set combinations done later online. The software allows the substitution of preferred terms for user-entered terms. These "go-words" with the preferred forms are stored in a table. Vendor system stopwords are removed and the software contains an additional mechanism to add nonsystem stopwords to the list.

In Figure 7 the user is asked to enter any additional terms to express the concept. Note that the user is instructed to look at a specific thesaurus or subject heading list to provide additional controlled vocabulary terms.

Figure 8 summarizes the search strategy up to that point and allows the user to go back and re-enter the concept terms if they are deemed inappropriate or inaccurate. The software employs a truncation algorithm patterned after Porter's (1980). At this point, earlier versions of the interface presented the user with the entered concept terms in native command mode in the form they were to be sent to the vendor system. It was determined that the native mode commands and operators are not understood and very few users were modifying their searches in response. However, this element does prove useful to site attendants in judging the efficacy of the truncation routine.

At this point, the search history is displayed and the user is prompted for terms making up concept 2. In the same manner as mentioned earlier, users are then asked to enter additional terms for the concept group. After completing the entering of the final search concept group (maximum of

You should now enter any:
    --synonyms (dual phase steel, two phase steel),
    --alternate spellings (sulphur, sulfur),
    --abbreviations or full spellings (NMR, TEM),
    --related or alternative terms (titanium, aluminum, niobium)
  for concept 1: end-users.

You may wish to consult the red Subject Headings in Engineering or the green INSPEC Thesaurus of terms on the table next to you.

Enter both general terms ('heavy metals') and specific terms ('cadmium'). The program will supply both singular and plural forms of words.

To exit, edit, or go on to the next concept, press the ENTER key only.

Type below any additional terms for concept 1: end-users.
Enter one term (word or phrase) at each prompt--one per line.
Additional term for concept 1: patron searching
Additional term for concept 1:

Figure 7

For your title:
End-user searching with microcomputers
The terms making up concept 1 are:
end-users; patron searching

Look at the terms in this concept group. Check the spellings.
  You do not need to enter plurals.
These terms should relate to the same topic. Different topics need to be put in separate concept groups.
If you need to re-enter this concept group, type NO and press ENTER.

Press only the ENTER key to go on with the search.

Figure 8

The search strategy is displayed below.

Concept 1	Concept 2	Concept 3
end-users	online searching	microcomputers
patron searching	database searching	personal computers
	searching	IBM PC
		Macintosh
		PS/2

***This search will retrieve reference that contain at least one term from each concept group.

Please examine these search terms.
   If you wish to stop the search and begin entering the strategy again type NO and press ENTER.

   Press only the ENTER key to continue the search.

Figure 9

three), the user is presented with the screen shown in Figure 9. The strategy is displayed in tabular form and the user is given a final chance to modify the search before going online.

After making the telecommunications connection and logging on, the software presents some database information to the user and begins uploading the search strategy which was formulated offline (see Figure 10). As can be seen in the example presented, for a search of the National Agricultural Library database on "aflatoxin in corn storage" the terms comprising each concept group (combined in an OR relationship) are searched over all database records online and document postings are obtained. The next screen (Figure 11) repeats the concept group postings and begins combining the postings sets in an algorithmic manner to obtain the optimum search result. In this example, the three sets are combined in an AND operation, and, because the resulting postings (numbering 20) are below a threshold value, no more combinations are made. The final set is limited to English language items.

After downloading of the designated references and logging off, a printout (see Figures 12 and 13) is generated. The user-entered search title and concept terms are printed along with a sample record and the retrieved citations. The actual search arguments and command history from the session are also printed. The user is given information needed for modifying and repeating the search and is asked if local call number and location information is desired. If this is so indicated, the online catalog interface is

You will now be connected to the National Agricultural Library database. This database contains primarily references to journal articles, but may also include conference papers and reports.
The database covers 1980 to the present.
You will not need to type until the search results have been printed.
Each concept group will first be entered separately, then combined in different ways in order to yield the best search results.

Now searching search concept 1:
corn; wheat; rye

  The terms in concept 1 appear in 38849 references.

Now searching search concept 2:
aflatoxins; molds

  The terms in concept 2 appear in 3908 references.

Now searching search concept 3:
storage; silos

  The terms in concept 3 appear in 11996 references.

Figure 10

The terms in concept 1 appear in 38849 references.
The terms in concept 2 appear in 3908 references.
The terms in concept 3 appear in 11996 references.
  Now determining the number of English language articles.

The retrieved references from each concept group will now be compared to determine which of the references have terms from all concept groups.

Now searching for articles that have at least one term from each concept appearing somewhere in the title, descriptors, or abstract.

There are 20 references that contain terms common to all concepts.

The most recent (up to 20) of these references will be first transferred to floppy disk and then printed.

Figure 11

loaded which contains the option of escaping to perform a search for journal articles.

Preliminary Evaluation

The evaluation component of this project utilizes a site monitor form and a user questionnaire. In addition, transaction logs are obtained of the user input strings, the manipulated search command arguments (with truncation and operations), the search history including the navigated search protocols, and the resulting downloaded citations.

A preliminary analysis of the data gathered from nearly 400 patron searches reveals: (1) the system is regarded very favorably by users and rated as easy to use; (2) the system is regarded as better than (or complementary to) searching printed indexes for information; (3) over 50 percent of the retrieved citations are, in the majority of cases, rated as relevant; (4) users have trouble locating call number information and want call numbers and holdings included with periodical citations; and (5) users have overwhelmingly indicated a desire to see the self-service system continued as a regular library service, but at a minimal cost to users. The early results of the study indicate a very positive user response and validate the approach taken by the interface. Several minor software changes have been instituted in response to the test questionnaires, while other changes will wait for later implementations.

Several insights have been gleaned from an analysis of the site monitor forms and transaction logs. These include: (1) users are often modifying their search strategies and repeating searches after examining the results of a previous search (an average of 1.8 searches are being performed at each session); (2) users do not understand set theoretic concepts and some fundamental principles of natural language information retrieval; (3) a fairly large percentage of users enter very specific search terms, requiring the system to do searches utilizing free-text searching capabilities over titles, descriptors, and abstracts; (4) terminology selection plays an important role in search success; and (5) students with specific and well-defined search topics tend to perform the most effective searches.

Analysis of the transaction logs has indicated that the use of several vendor software features in the construction of search strategies can optimize retrieval performance. For example, there is evidence to indicate that the use of a less restrictive WITH operator (to retrieve terms appearing in the same sentence regardless of word order) is preferred to the ADJ operator (which compels words to appear immediately adjacent to each other in the specified order). This allows retrieval, for example, of both "TCP/IP" and "IP/TCP" and also the phrase "construction industry accidents" when the

This is the printout from your online search of the National Agricultural Library database.

The title used to describe your search topic:
Problems of Aflatoxin in corn storage

Your search concepts and terms were:
Concept 1:
 corn; wheat; rye
Concept 2:
 aflatoxins; molds
Concept 3:
 storage; silos

Below is a sample printed reference to illustrate the format. Note the paragraph tags (AN, AU, TI, DE, ID, etc.) in the sample reference.

This database search will retrieve references (citations) to articles in periodicals (journals and magazines), conference papers and reports.

Below is a sample of a retrieved reference from the March 1987 IEEE Computer Journal.

AN (Accession number) From the printed index, used to find abstract.

AU (Author(s) names) Smith, John A.

TI (Article title) Finite Difference Techniques for Supercomputers.

SO (Source Journal) IEEE Computer Journal; volume 9, #, pp. 43-65, March, 1987.

YR (Year) 1987.

CT (Conference Title) International Conference on Numerical Analysis.

DE (Descriptors; Subject Headings) Finite-Difference-Methods. Software. Numerical-Techniques. Supercomputers.

ID (Identifiers or Keywords) Cray X-MP. Astrophysics Software. Fluid Dynamics. Finite Element Methods. Cedar Project.

AB (Abstract) Most citations include a short abstract or summary.

THIS SEARCH HAS RETRIEVED THE MOST RECENT REFERENCES ON YOUR SEARCH TOPIC.
A MAXIMUM OF THIRTY REFERENCES CAN BE PRINTED.
CONSULT THE LIBRARY STAFF FOR A MORE COMPREHENSIVE SEARCH.

***LOOK VERY CAREFULLY AT THE TERMS IN THE 'DE' AND 'ID' PARAGRAPHS.
THESE TERMS CAN BE USED TO MAKE THE SEARCH MORE SPECIFIC OR MORE GENERAL.

***THIS SEARCH CAN BE DONE AGAIN WITH ADDED TERMS IN A CONCEPT GROUP OR WITH SOME TERMS OR EVEN ENTIRE CONCEPT GROUPS ELIMINATED.
***IF YOU HAVE ANY QUESTIONS ABOUT THE SEARCH RESULTS, PLEASE CONTACT A SITE ATTENDANT OR LIBRARY STAFF MEMBER.

Figure 12

```
        1
AN ACCESSION NUMBER: ADL87040053. 8707.
AU AUTHORS: Blaney-B-J.
TI TITLE: Mycotoxins in water-damaged and mouldy *wheat* from
   temporary bulk stores in Queensland.
SO SOURCE: Aust J Agric Res, Melbourne: Commonwealth Scientific and
   Industrial Research Organization, 1986. volume 37 issue 6, pages 561-565.
DE DESCRIPTORS: queensland. *wheat.* *bulk-storage.*
   temporary-buildings. aspergillus-flavus. *aflatoxins.* ochratoxin.
   sterigmatocystin. *molds.* damage.
-END OF DISPLAY REQUEST-

RETURNING TO SEARCH
ENTER SEARCH TERMS, COMMAND, OR H FOR HELP
SEARCH 7-->


Strategy used in online search.
                                                          *

           CAIN          SCREEN        1 OF        1*

CAIN 1980 - JUL 1987
     1 (CORN OR MAIZE OR ZEA) OR WHEAT$1 OR RYE$1
       RESULT                            38849
     2 AFLATOXIN$1 OR MOLD$1
       RESULT                            3908
     3 STORAGE$1 OR SILO$1
       RESULT                            11996
     4 EN.LG.
       RESULT                            731814
     5 1 AND 2 AND 3
       RESULT                            20
     6 5 AND 4
       RESULT                            16
            **** END OF DISPLAY ****
PRESS ENTER TO CONTINUE OR ENTER COMMAND-->
```

Figure 13

user-entered search term is "construction accidents." It is quite clear that
the suffix stripping algorithm and truncation routine play an important
role in the retrieval process. The truncation algorithm employed in the
project appears to perform adequately. In addition, the software manipulation techniques performed on concept postings sets (such as the elimination of a concept group in response to a null combination) are invoked
quite frequently.

Future Enhancements

Several needed modifications in the interface software have been suggested by the evaluation process. The capability of interactively modifying the search online using a user feedback mechanism is being developed. While this will result in increased online time and costs, it will save in print costs and reduce the number of search sessions in which multiple discrete searches are performed by a single user.

The adoption of a fixed cost pricing relationship with database vendors and producers needs to be investigated. Clearly, if this type of service could be budgeted on a reasonable fixed cost searching basis, it would remove some of the advantages associated with CD-ROM products.

The capability of performing author searches, in addition to subject searching, will be added. Also being explored is the implementation of several methods of automatically linking the citations from a database search with online catalog holdings and availability information.

REFERENCES

Belkin, N. J., et al. (1987). Distributed expert-based information systems: An interdisciplinary approach. *Information Processing and Management, 23*(5), 395-409.

Borgman, C. L. (1986). Why are online catalogs hard to use? Lessons learned from information-retrieval studies. *Journal of the American Society for Information Science, 37*(November), 387-400.

Butler, B. (1984). Online catalogs, online reference: An overview. In B. Aveny & B. Butler (Eds.), *Online catalogs, online reference: Converging trends* (pp. 1-19). Chicago, IL: American Library Association.

Hildreth, C. R. (1985). Online public access catalogs. *Annual Review of Information Science and Technology, 20*, 233-285.

Marcus, R. S. (1982). An automated expert assistant for information retrieval. *Proceedings of the American Society for Information Science Annual Meeting, 19*, 270-273.

Marcus, R. S., & Reintjes, J. F. (1981). A translating computer interface for end-user operation of heterogeneous retrieval systems. I. Design. *Journal of the American Society for Information Science, 32*(July), 287-303.

Markey, K. (1984). *Subject searching in library catalogs: Before and after the introduction of online catalogs.* Dublin, OH: OCLC.

Markey, K. (1983). Thus spake the OPAC user. *Information Technology and Libraries, 2*(December), 381-387.

Meadows, C. T. (1986). OAK—A new approach to user search assistance. In C. E. Jacobson & S. A. Witges (Comps.), *Proceedings of the second conference on computer interfaces and intermediaries for information retrieval* (pp. 215-24). Alexandria, VA: Defense Technical Information Center.

Mischo, W. H., & Lee, J. (1987). End-user searching of bibliographic databases. *Annual Review of Information Science and Technology, 27*, 227-263.

Porter, M. F. (1980). An algorithm for suffix stripping. *Program, 14*(July), 130-137.

Potter, W. G. (1987). Expanding the online catalog. *LITA Newsletter, 9*(1), 5-6.

INDEX

AACR, 35, 150
Academic American Encyclopedia, 96, 99
Academic libraries, 2, 55-58, 69
Advances in Physical Organic Chemistry, 35
AGRICOLA, 65, 185
Agricultural Computer Network, 60
AIDS KNOWLEDGE BASE, 91
Alienation in an automated environment, 12
AMERICAN BANKER NEWS, 91
American Library Directory, 57-59
Anderson, Charles, R., 2, 71
Annual Reports on the Progress of Chemistry, 34
Annual Review of Information Science and Technology, 189
ART BIBLIOGRAPHIES MODERN, 80
ART LITERATURE INTERNATIONAL, 80
Association of Research Libraries (ARL), 43
Automated ready reference. *See* ready reference, online
AVERY index, 41

Baker, Betsy, 2, 38
Bibliographic Center for Research, 76
Bingham, Karen, 3, 177
Biography Index, 185
Biological Abstracts, 111
Boolean searching, 15, 20, 107, 111-18, 136-37, 185, 187, 190-93
Bowker Annual of Library and Book Trade Information, 57
British Library, 29
Brown, Rowland, 41
Browsing, 18, 20, 22
BRS, 20, 27, 41, 45, 58, 60, 65, 76, 117
BRS Bulletin, 60
Budgeting, 2; online searching, 72-73, 77-78
Business Index, 177
Business Periodical Index, 180, 184

California Institute of Technology Libraries, 34

Catalogs: analytic, 34, 37; card, 1; form, 16; online, 1, 14, 16-17, 144-52, 165
CD-ROM (Compact Disc-Read Only Memory), 2, 21, 41, 52, 83, 89, 92, 94-102, 117, 153-75
Center for Research Libraries, 146
Central Serials Service (CSS), 76
Champaign Public Library, 178-87
Chemical Abstracts, 48, 65, 101, 111
Chemical Abstracts Service, 60
CINEMA, 91
CITE, 28, 29
Clark, Barton, 3, 177
Clark, Sharon, 3, 144
Classification and Search Support Information System, 60
COLLEAGUE, 91
Communication Patterns, 1, 5-7, 8
Compact disc systems, 56, 58
Comprehensive Core Medical Library (CCML), 87
CompuServe, 88, 90
Computer Aided Instruction (CAI), 142
Computing centers. *See* Libraries: Computing centers
Controlled Vocabularies, 22, 113, 117-18
Correlation between database usage and periodical requests, 76-77
Creth, Sheila, 1, 4
CROS, 83
Cutter, Charles A., 15-16, 20

D & B's MARKET IDENTIFIERS, 73-74, 78
Database: access, 2; design, 30, 191-204; effectiveness, 2, 46; evaluation, 2, 46; full-text, 2, 85; vendor, 36, 59-60, 62, 64-66, 68, 74-76, 82-83, 89-90
Database Catalog: 1987, 85
Database policy. *See* online policies
Datalines, 60
DATASTAR, 20
DDC, 22
DELPHI, 90
Departmental libraries, 59
DeSart, Melvin, 3, 188
Dial access, 43-44, 51
DIALINDEX, 83

DIALOG, 20, 27, 30, 41, 45, 55, 58, 60, 65, 68, 73, 76, 82-83, 85, 88, 90-91, 111, 114, 117, 123-25, 129
DIALOG LINK, 80, 124, 129
Diodato, Virgil, 2, 55
DIOGENES, 88
Display design, 29
Document representations, 26-27
Doszkocs, Tamas., 27
Dow Jones News/Retrieval, 60
Downloading, 75, 126, 128, 193, 199
DUN'S MARKET IDENTIFIERS, 65

EasyNet, 60, 126, 129
ED-LINE, 88, 90
Electronic: in-house sources, 3; reference collection, 2; reference service, 1, 177
Electronic: Legislative Search System, 60
ELHILL, 27, 30
End Users: 2, 3, 15, 17, 20, 89-91, 94, 99, 101, 103-07, 110, 117-19, 121-31; search services, 188-204
EP-X, 29
ERIC, 31, 45, 60, 65, 78, 92, 125, 177, 185
ERLI, 29
ESTC, 41
Evaluation and selection, 18, 39, 42, 46, 159-60
Expert systems, 29-30

Famous First Facts, 83
Fee-based information service, 74
Free searching, 72
Full Bibliographic Record (FBR), 132-33, 138-39, 147-48
Full-text databases, 85-93, 99, 102, 125

Gatekeepers, 7
General Science Index, 185
Globe and Mail, 124
GPO MONTHLY CATALOG, 65
Guide to Reference Books, 50

Handbuch der Organischen Chemie, 48
Harter, Stephen P., 2, 103
HAZARDLINE, 87
Hildreth, Charles, 1, 14
Homographs, 113
Humanities Index, 185

ILLINET, 134, 165-66
ILLINET Online, 3, 145-53
Illinois Public Library Statistics, 72
Illinois Statewide Union Catalog, 164-65
Illinois, University of, 28, 133; Interlibrary Loan Department, 48-49
Impact of Automation: 1, 4, 9-13; communication patterns, 5-8; libraries, 5-6; library organizations, 4-5, 7
Indexing databases, 20, 47-48
Index-mediated retrieval, 36
In-house magazine collections, use of, 76
In-Search, 123-24
Info Globe, 124
INFOLINE, 88
Information retrieval systems, 14-15, 20, 24
Information-seeking needs, 53
InfoTrac: 3, 83, 155, 177-87; impact on library 182-83
Integration, 38-54
Intelligent systems. *See* expert systems
Intermediaries. *See* search intermediaries
ITEM-MARC, 37

Katz, W., 56, 73
Keyword searching, 137, 154
Kiesler, S., 7, 13
KING JAMES BIBLE, 90-91
Knowledge Index, 91, 117

LCC, 22
LePac search system, 156-66
LIBERTAS, 28
Libraries: Computing Centers, 5
Library Computer System (LCS), 28, 132-33, 138-40, 144-52, 166, 191
Library of Congress Subject Headings, 20, 22, 150
Library organization. *See* Organizational Structure
Lincoln Public Library, Springfield, 158
Lincoln Trail Library Systems, 178-79, 184
Local Area Networks, (LANs), 100-02

Machine-Readable Cataloging (MARC), 15, 23, 31, 34, 37, 164

Magazine Index, 78, 83, 111, 113, 177, 181, 183
Malinconico, S., 17-18
MARC. *See* Machine-Readable Cataloging
Marketing Analysis and Information Database (MAID), 88
Massachusetts, University of, 30
Matching and retrieval, 25-26
Meadow, Charles, 2, 121
MEDLINE, 20, 36, 101, 111, 125
Micrographic Catalog Retrieval System (MCRS), 46
Mischo, William, 3, 188

NASA RECON, 36, 60
National Agricultural Library, 155
National Library of Medicine, 59-60
National Newspaper Index, 111
National Union Catalog, 47, 133
The Nationwide Network: A Vision and a Role, 41
Natural language processing, 27-30
Networks, 6, 8, 40-42, 45, 50-53, 152
NEWS/RETRIEVAL, 90
New York Times, 177-78, 183
Northbrook Public Library (Illinois), 71-73, 75-76, 78, 81
North Suburban Library Systems (NSLS), 71, 76
Noreault, Terry, 2, 94
NTIS, 36, 65

OCLC, 2, 15, 34, 37-38, 40-41, 43, 45-50, 52, 55, 58-60, 68, 100, 133, 144-45, 147, 151, 166
Ohio State University, 29
OKAPI, 28
Online Catalogs, 1, 14, 16-17, 34-37; evaluation, 18, 67; first generation, 18; joint, 144-45; second generation, 18-20; statewide, 145-152, 165
Online conference. *See* Communication patterns
Online policies, 72, 81-83
Online Public Access Catalogs (OPACs), 14-33, 142
Online Reviews, 108
Online Search Analyst, 110, 117
Online searching, 2, 20, 36, 72-73, 99, 107-12, 115-19

Online systems, 2-3, 103, 121-31
Online Union catalog. *See* ILLINET Online
ONTAP, 82
OPACs. *See* Online Public Access Catalogs
Optical Publishing, 94-102
Optical Technologies, 2, 94-95, 153-54
Organizational Structure, 7-9

Parkland College Library, Champaign, 159
Patrons. *See* users
PCIX, 156
Pergamon Infoline, 60
Planning of Online Service, 2, 55-56, 68-69
PLEXUS, 29
Poole's Index to Periodical Literature, 83
PRECIS, 29
Precision, 106-07, 110, 115-17, 127
Pro-Cite, 128
Problem areas, 80-81
ProSearch, 80, 124
PsychLIT, 185
Public Libraries Online Databases, 71-84
Public Services, 1, 8, 132-43

Quality control, 149-51
Query-matching, 28
Questel, 60
Question analysis: 78; types, 126

RAMEAU, 29
Reader's Guide to Periodical Literature, 83, 180, 185
Ready reference, online: 2, 55-70; definition of, 73; parameters, 74
Recall, 106-07, 110, 116-17, 127
Reference librarian, 1, 38-39, 41-42, 44-45, 47, 51, 53, 67-68, 72, 82, 134-35
Reference services, 1, 3, 5, 38-42, 47, 49-50, 153-71
Reference staff. *See* Reference librarian
Reference tool, 47-48, 50, 53
Register of Corporations, 74
Relevance, 26-27
Relevance feedback, 28-29
Research Libraries Group (RLG), 15, 41

Resource sharing, 164-70
RLG Operations Update, 40
RLIN, 15, 38, 40-41, 44-45, 47, 50, 52, 55, 58, 60
Robbins-Carter, J., 8-9
Roth, Dana, 1-2, 34
Rothenberg, Dianne, 2, 85

Science Citation Index, 35
SCIPIO, 41
SEARCH HELPER, 60, 126
Search intermediaries, 14-15, 105, 118-19; experienced searchers *v.* inexperienced searchers, 75
Search problem, 104-06
Search strategies: 22, 28, 30; keyword, 137, 154; postcoordinated, 20, 22; precoordinated phrase searching, 20, 22; scoping, 146; truncation, 114-15, 118, 137, 185, 197
Security, 68
Shared cataloging, 40
SIBIL, 29
Skills, 9-10, 13
Smith, Linda, 3
Social Science Citation Index, 45, 185
Software, 66, 91, 121-23, 129-30, 144, 191-93, 195
The Source, 88, 90
SPECIALNET, 88
Spencer, Mima, 2, 85
SPORT, 91
Staff and Staffing, 2, 9-11, 67, 72, 89, 117, 119
The Statistical Abstract of the U.S., 44
STN International, 60
Subject headings, 48
Subject indexing, 20-21, 26
Subject retrieval, 28
Subject searching, 136-37, 154, 182, 188
System Development Corporation, 60

Technical Services, 2, 8
Thesauri, 29-30, 67
Time and Cost, 126
TINlib, 29
TINMAN, 29
TRADE AND INDUSTRY INDEX, 78
Treatise on Analytical Chemistry, 34-35

UK MARC, 29
Union List of Serials, 133

University librarians, 9
UNIX, 122
User interface program: 138-39, 191-93, 195, 197; evaluation, 201-04
User satisfaction, 188
User studies, 188-92
User: 14, 21-22, 26-27, 29, 34-36, 40, 45, 47, 52, 77, 88, 121-31, 157-61, 180-84, 188-204; access, 15, 137-39, 178; education, 2, 8, 11, 52, 183-84; instruction, 140-42, 190; interaction, 29; interface, 21, 138-39, 191-93, 195, 197; needs, 18, 30; online assistance, 18, 20, 190

Vendor manuals, 67
Vendors. *See* databases
Verification, 133-35
Vocabulary and Syntax, 126-27
VU TEXT, 60

Wall Street Journal, 78, 93, 177-78
Watson, Paula, 3, 153
The Way Things Work, 73
Western Library Network (WLN), 28, 38, 47-49, 60, 132, 144-45, 149-50, 153, 163-64, 191
WESTLAW, 60
WILSONLINE, 55, 58-60, 65
Windows, Icons, Menus, Pointers (WIMPS), 21
Woodard, Beth S., 3, 132
Work flow, 11-12
Work relationships, 12-13
WORK-MARC, 37
World Almanac, 74
Worlds of Reference, 3
Write Once Read Many (WORM), 95-98